Information
for the
Community

Information for the Community

Manfred Kochen

and

Joseph C. Donohue,

editors

American Library Association
Chicago 1976

Library of Congress Cataloging in Publication Data
Main entry under title:
Information for the community.
    Includes bibliographies.
1. Information Services—Addresses, essays, lectures.
I. Kochen, Manfred. II. Donohue, Joseph C.
Z674.4.I54   026'.361   75-40168
ISBN 0-8389-0208-1

Printed in the United States of America

Contents

Contents

Preface

This book is concerned with an individual's need for everyday information, especially information that will help him solve pressing problems related to his health and welfare. It is also about the agencies that make it their primary business to provide that information. The term most frequently used to refer to the services of these agencies is "Information and Referral," often abbreviated as "I&R."

The editors intend to present some background and conceptualization for the planning of such services, and methods for making them work. The primary aim is first to show how to characterize and measure needs, and then to develop the methods for designing the services that meet them.

The editors believe that people from many occupations and with many different concerns will find the book useful and enlightening. Anyone seriously concerned with the human struggle to survive amid the complexities of contemporary society will recognize that the information needed to both survive and live a rewarding life is not always readily obtained; it often demands the use of special services. Professionals in the healing and helping arts have already shown a remarkable degree of interest in the problems of providing such information services, and will find here, collected for the first time, discussions of virtually every aspect of these problems, as well as descriptions of different approaches toward their solution in various environments.

There is a growing cadre of people whose work is primarily informational in nature. In addition to the press and other media, this group includes librarians, computer specialists, system designers and operators, and researchers from many disciplines, all converging on the study of human information and communication processes. There is here a challenge, to discover ways of apply their knowledge, experience, and ingenuity to the solution of the massive problems that weigh upon the individual and his society.

This book is neither a directory nor an exhaustive description of types of I&R services. It is not a handbook, a "how to" manual, or a "whole earth catalog" of resources. It is also not exclusively or primarily directed to the public library's participation in the I&R movement. The editors believe that the public library can play an important role in the provision of health and welfare information, and hope that it will do so; indeed, there are promising signs that it will. Only a few important library information programs will be described, since extensive, well-documented works are already available, and because the concern here is primarily with the need for community information services and the conditions under which they are cost-effective, and only secondarily with the library as such. (In addition to existing works in this field, Carol A. Becker's *Community Information Service: A Directory of Public Library Involvement* has been published by the College of Library and Information Services at the University of Maryland.)

This book initially grew from the fusion of two projects. The first was Joseph Donohue's development of a monograph designed to collect and evaluate the information and ideas concerning public information service that he encountered in the course of the Public Information Center Project. The second was Manfred Kochen's interest in a plan devised to pool the resource files of several twenty-four-hour telephone answering services in a community to create a directory of agencies that could assist those in need. The project presented technical and organizational problems of some complexity, problems that Kochen felt should be addressed by information scientists. As chairman of the Special Interest Group on Behavioral and Social Sciences of the American Society for Information Science, he invited the attention of his colleagues to these problems, and a number expressed interest. The resulting panel discussion is presented as chapter 14 of this book. In April 1972 Kochen and Donohue decided to combine their projects and seek additional contributions.

Most of the contributions were originally written for this book, following extensive planning by the individual writers and both editors. If an author had published or was in the process of publishing an article similar to one in this volume, every effort was made to reduce redundancy and to design a chapter that could be readily integrated into the overall statement of the book. The editors did not require that all the contributions adhere to a given point of view or style, but rather, in the readings of the successive drafts, asked only for clarity. The range of views, styles, and orientations is stimulating, with some highly theoretical, some intensely pragmatic. The styles vary, as do their messages; it is hoped that the readers will find that variety as desirable.

Part I provides the necessary background for an understanding of the needs, the goals and problems, and the services that supply information to communities. It brings together contributions that help to identify and understand the needs of individuals and groups, traces the development of I&R services, and develops some points of view for discussing them.

Part II presents community information services already in operation. These services provide important practical lessons, as well as ideas, facts, and stimulation for needed research.

Parts III and IV deal with the present status of relevant research. Part IV offers commentary, conclusions, recommendations, and, to some extent, informed opinions, while Part III provides research results, techniques, and ideas.

Many persons contributed the ideas and labors that culminated in this book. Nettie Taylor, of the Maryland State Department of Education, provided early encouragement for the publication of such a book, and in connection with the idea, introduced Joseph Donohue to Herbert Bloom, Senior Editor of ALA Publishing Services. Mr. Bloom has been a major contributor to the conceptualization of the book and a real partner with the editors and other writers in bringing the idea to fruition. The authors have been industrious and patient in doing the successive drafts and revisions needed to bring the work as a whole into focus. Discussions with them have been enlightening and enjoyable. A revision of an earlier draft of this book benefitted greatly from a careful critique by Dorothy Turick.

The editors wish to express their particular appreciation to Dr. Flora Wallace, Joan Barth, and Barbara Badre, all of the Mental Health Research Institute, who greatly facilitated the task of Research Institute and greatly facilitated the task of improving the stylistic quality of this work.

MANFRED KOCHEN and JOSEPH DONOHUE
Ann Arbor and Washington

Part I

Background to Community Information Needs and Services

The reader is, undoubtedly, already aware of the serious problems requiring the help of community information systems, such as the drug problem, with its many facets relating to health, the family, the schools, the church, the police, and the courts. It illustrates the ways in which local government officials, as well as their constituents, need accurate knowledge. Urban managers must quickly learn the most up-to-date relevant facts; they must be kept apprised of both successful and unsuccessful programs, such as the studies reported in the survey report, *Drugs and American Youth* (Johnston, 1973).

In the larger framework of community health, Patricia A. Leo and G. Rosen (1969) maintain that "A sober look at our health care delivery system forces us to admit that there is no orderly, regulated, or comprehensive system in operation today; in fact, we have a non-system." It is, therefore, imperative that a city manager learn of the gap between welfare patients and other poor patients who are in debt; of methods allowing costs to be shared by various levels of government; of any possible systems for improved accounting, etc. It is equally important for the clients of health care systems to learn of the options available to them, of "traps" inherent in the system, of how to steer a wise course. How, then, can both managers and clients obtain this information quickly, painlessly, and in a way that will particularly stimulate the manager to arrive at wiser policies and procedures?

1

Part I should provide the reader with the proper orientation for the remaining chapters, an orientation based on actual problems he has doubtlessly encountered or contemplated. The next four chapters deal with the handling of any serious, urgent problem in urban communities. Where, for instance, can an ordinary citizen turn for help with his day-to-day problems? Chapter 1 begins with a conceptualization of "communities" and "information" in that context, designed to provide a point of view and a language for stating the problem.

The next two chapters specify two major aspects of the problem in greater detail. The first major aspect is the citizen's need for information. In chapter 2, results of two telephone surveys dealing with such needs are reported, with consumer affairs, public affairs, and health problems most frequently named. (It is interesting to note that another survey of community information needs [Turick, 1973] indicated that housing, employment, city services, health care services, and food had the highest priority.) Dervin's study is as important for its conceptualization and methodology as for its results. Clearly, it is difficult to validate general conclusions. The work serves as an example of the kind of applied research that is both feasible and necessary. It indicates the numerous difficulties involved in such research, while also providing some data and insights into the needs of the average citizen.

The second major aspect of the sample problem depicted in Part I deals with the needs of the community agency that is to help the average citizen. It can help him directly, as in the case of a clinic or a social work agency, or indirectly, by assisting those responsible for planning and decision making on matters that affect the citizen. In chapter 3, some of the needs of such agencies are discussed.

An agency designed to help citizens is likely to contain at least two kinds of agents: the *confronter*, the agent who advocates a particular position that may represent the views and values of a particular segment of the community, and the *negotiator*. The information needs of a confronter may differ considerably from those of a negotiator.

The confronter attempts to reach the best decision or policy by adversary proceedings, by probing for the weaknesses in his opponent's arguments and data. He hopes that, if each adversary constantly challenges and checks the other, each one will do his best to bring out the most relevant, significant, and valid facts and arguments, and in this way arrive at truths that might otherwise have escaped one unchallenged agent. An information system can help this agent by arming him with the facts needed to probe his opponent's position for weaknesses while bolstering his own defenses.

The negotiator, on the other hand, searches for ground he holds in common with his opponent, ignores differences in values and avoids issues where conflict is most intense, and tries to cooperate with his opponent on questions of mutual concern, where there is a chance of success. An information system can alert him to those issues to be avoided and those to be tackled, and to the methods that might increase the likelihood of cooperation.

Numerous methods are available for persuasion and negotiation. Kidd, for example, stresses case building. In its most radical form outside judicial contexts, case bulding is similar to advocacy, adversary proceedings, and confrontation methods. In its ultimate form, it becomes a contest of will and strength.

Persuasion and successful negotiation are not attained by logic, lucidity, and factual support alone. The following statement made by a university administrator to an academician proposing a curriculum revision illustrates the point: "You think, do you not, that you have only to state a reasonable case, and the people must listen to reason and act upon it at once. It is just this conviction that makes you so unpleasant."

For many conflicts, the case-building approach has proved useful. For conflicts with conflicting intragroup interests, however, it may not be the correct approach. Consider, for example, the "Prisoner's Dilemma," involving two potential adversaries, R (for row) and C (for column). R can choose either to admit to a crime of which both he and C are accused or to keep silent. C has the same two options. Figure 1 shows four contingencies. In the upper-left part of each contingency cell is the number of months in jail that R expects. The lower-right part of each cell gives the corresponding penalties for C in each contingency. If both keep silent, the outcome is equal for both parties, say 8 months. If R admits, his outcome is much more favorable if C keeps silent (1 month for R, 12 for C). If R builds his case, he persuades C to be silent while secretly he plans all along to "double-cross" C by confessing.

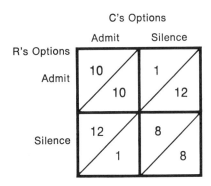

Figure 1. The "Prisoner's Dilemma"

But there are other ways of negotiating. The aim of the negotiator is to effect an outcome that is favorable to all parties, even if another outcome would be more favorable to one particular party. This means searching for the greatest common ground still acceptable to all parties. In the above example, that outcome is the lower right box, with both parties keeping silent. The key factor for success in using this approach is sincerity and trust. If members of a community or organization can learn to behave with sincerity and justified trust, rather than craftiness or strength, this method could work, and information supporting it should get top priority.

If nothing justifies either trust or distrust, perhaps because of insufficient understanding by the conflicting parties about one another, the old political maxim "be kind and cautious" is appropriate. While eyeing our adversaries warily, while extending an offer of peace and friendship, we gather information about them and the conflicting issues. Simultaneously, we must not fail to gather information to strengthen our case, to be armed sufficiently for victory in case of unavoidable conflict.

The information resources which help civic organizations build their cases in order to resolve conflicts should be supplemented by information resources designed to assist all adversaries to gain a deeper, clearer, and more common understanding of the problems and issues in conflict. Such information services should place problems in a new light and seek the greatest common ground acceptable to all parties. Both kinds of information resources together may increase the likelihood of success in conflict resolution, while reliance on either information resource alone may increase the likelihood of failure.

In many conflict situations the real sources of contention are emotional and sociological, rather than cognitive, and lie beneath the surface. Information, if it affects conflict resolution at all, is most likely to make its impact on the cognitive components of behavior. Thus intellectual arguments or data about embryology are not likely either to budge an antiabortion organization from its position or to persuade an abortionist group.

After chapter 3, the reader will have realized that a problem exists and will have some idea about its nature. The last chapter in Part I, by Long, then traces the history of the I&R center and presents the lessons to be learned from that history. Long's 1971 *Information and Referral Centers: A Functional Analysis* is still cited as an authoritative survey and analysis of trends. This chapter is an updated version of that review, with a suggested extension of the I&R center concept.

Poverty, ignorance, and prejudice, Long reminds us, are still the conditions of much of mankind, and are also the very conditions which block those afflicted by them from utilizing I&R services. Why? Pride is a factor. The causes of poverty and other undesirable human conditions are numerous. In some cases, trapping phenomena are at work.

Long apparently believes that a centralized assessment and referral service for all human services is eventually desirable, feasible, and likely. And, precisely because such a centralized system may develop, we should now seriously begin to ask if it is desirable. Each of the evaluation criteria is met at a cost: reducing problems of one kind creates problems of another. If a client complains to the central office about a local service, the former may honestly want to take the client's side, or may want to support its staff. In the latter case, the client may suffer even more the next time he has a problem. For example, if a client complains about the only local medical or police services to a superordinate body which is strongly (and secretly) supportive of its local agents, his complaints may backfire.

The threat to privacy is perhaps the gravest danger of a centralized, coordinated network. Centralization also threatens free competition and the informed choices available to clients, thus weakening quality and competition. It also widens the distance between the server and the client, making servers less responsive to clients and more to one another.

Insofar as the service system proposed by Long is aimed at helping the disadvantaged—i.e., those most in need of such help—it is plagued by the basic problem of distrust. For example, the most difficult thing of all to do for the poor is to give them money. Perhaps this betokens distrust of the disadvantaged, a fear that they would not spend money as wisely to help themselves as would professionals responsible for helping them. But health care delivery units, though supervised by such professionals, are more often unresponsive and of low quality than responsive and good. Coordination does not remedy this: those that want business either give poor care, are too expensive, or both. The rare good ones have more cases than they can handle.

The formulation of several focal problems thus emerges from the background provided by the first four chapters. How are citizens at various levels of sophistication to be made aware of the options among community resources available to them? How are they to be educated and assisted to make wise choices among them? And how are those who control the various collections of information going to make it available to those in need, at prices that will make it possible for the needs to be met?

References

Becker, C. A. *Community Information Service: A Directory of Public Library Involvement*. College Park, Md.: University of Maryland, College of Library and Information Services, 1974.

Johnston, L. *Drugs and American Youth*. Ann Arbor, Mich.: University of Michigan, Institute for Social Research, 1973.

Leo, P. A., and Rosen, G. "A Book Shelf on Poverty and Health." *American Journal of Public Health*, 1969, *49*, 595.

Long, N., et al. *I&R Services: The Resource File. 3rd ed*. Washington, D.C.: Administration on Aging, DHEW, 1973. 115p. (OHD/AoA 73–20111).

Turick, D. A. *A Proposal to Research and Design Criteria for the Implementation and Establishment of a Neighborhood Information Center in Five Public Libraries in Five Cities: Atlanta, Cleveland, Detroit, Houston, Queens Borough*. Final report to the U.S. Department of Health, Education, and Welfare, Office of Education, Bureau of Libraries and Learning Resources, Grant OEG–O–72–5168, March 1973, p. 2.

Chapter 1
Community Information Centers: Concepts for Analysis and Planning

by Joseph C. Donohue and Manfred Kochen

Ours is a generation of growing gaps. The generation gap, rifts among races, liberation movements of all kinds, the gulf between haves and have-nots, all these and more fragment our social fabric. Fragmentation differs from specialization. Specialization may be a healthy response to increasingly complex work loads, provided the specialized contributions hold together. Widening cracks in the system, all at once and in many places, can, however, lead to disintegration.

At the same time, ours is also a generation of unprecedented resources. Communities have, in most cases, more agencies than ever before dedicated to social welfare. Not all the numerous agencies, services, and products started only as institutional responses to need. There has been, in fact, a surprising degree of activity in anticipating need and in utilizing technologies to improve the quality of life.

Still, the ominous foreboding of impending crises pervades much of the society. The chasm between resources and needs may be seen as the greatest gap yet. What causes this chasm? Information helps change our perceptions, and these changed perceptions are a direct cause. We are more keenly aware now than at any previous time of the gap between what is and what could be. Our needs pain us in proportion to our awareness of their existence and of the necessity of the deprivation.

Information can also heal. Bridges of information can span the gap between resources and needs. If people in communities knew where to turn, they could be aided in making the needed connections, bringing together the splintered fragments.

Complexity and Information Need
The more complex our behavior becomes, the greater are our needs for information. Life in contemporary urban society is very complex;

so is our response to it. Merely to satisfy basic needs, a person must engage in complex behavior. Participation in social life and in formally structured organizations increases its complexity. Information is essential if we are to navigate well in a complex world.

Even in developing countries and the world's rural regions, technology has increased the information needs of people relative to their customary patterns of information use. In developed countries we take for granted being able to specify and obtain simple hardware items, such as nails, screws, pipes, wires, and tools. This can be an enormous problem for a community in Tibet or Indonesia. But we too, in our technologically developed urban centers, can be overwhelmed by the abundance of choices among nuts and bolts or plumbing fittings in a well-stocked hardware store. We find that considerable preparation and some specialized knowledge is thus required to deal with the complexity introduced by technology.

The relation between the need for information and the complexity of modern civilization is even more dramatically illustrated by the technologies of medicine and transportation; anyone who has encountered an occasion requiring assistance with automobile repair or a medical problem has been faced with the problem of where to turn. Not only do we need more information to cope with more complex problems, but we also need to take advantage of the more complex options, the embarrassment of riches in leisure, entertainment, and cultural activities available to us.

The Community as the Locus of Information Need

Although people in some occupations serve purely informational roles, much of the information necessary for survival has always been provided as a *secondary* function by agents whose primary roles are other than that of purveyors of information. In a tightly knit community, for instance, casual conversation and gossip provide a great deal of the information needed for survival. This is supplemented by information that community leaders transmit in the very process of exercising their powers: the rulers are always surrounded by people who energetically spread the word about what is expected of the governed. The members of the professions, including the oldest of them, are noted as transmitters of information not necessarily restricted to their areas of expertise.

Traditional social patterns are, however, constantly breaking down. People in a fast-moving city are cut off from many of the more leisurely social relationships that allow for informal exchange of important information. At the same time, the role of the professional has become more and more restricted to the exercise of his specialty. The disruptive effects of some of these social changes is dramatically shown in a documentary film, *Tell Me Where to Turn* (Public Affairs Committee, 1969), which demonstrates a series of critical human situations in which people lack knowledge of the resources available to them.

If predisposed to a nostalgic view, one could imagine that in an earlier and simpler society, the clergyman or the ward heeler may have effectively provided such help or direction. It is questionable, however, if these were ever adequate to the task, and many people today would not accept the implied need for gratitude to church or political party. In fact, many people in need will not approach agencies that are partisan or sectarian. Helping agencies that served an exclusive clientele a generation ago now attempt to play down their earlier religious or ethnic origins in an effort to gain wider support and a wider clientele. The services of such social agencies are deliberately being made less dependent upon narrow philosophical or ideological goals. Perhaps the least ideological of services is the information and referral type of agency, attempting to match need with resources in what seems a thoroughgoing pragmatic way. It exists solely as an informational function.

Recent Trends

Perhaps the most triking phenomenon of the last decade was the almost worldwide surge of soul-searching. An educated, idealistic new generation in search of justice, meaning, and purpose, unable to attain its goals through established institutions, became dissatisfied. Poor people, everywhere plagued with problems, were depicted on television. Rich nations realized age-old dreams of conquest in space, medicine, and engineering, and that was on television, too. The academic world became a focus of concern for a new use of resources, with students and professors alike demanding change.

John Platt was among the first to sound the alarm bell, when he gave the world an approximately even chance to survive for two more decades (Platt, 1969). He exhorted his fellow scientists to spend half their professional time on councils of urgent studies. Simultaneously, the Club of Rome and many other institutions and individuals issued similar calls and launched relevant research campaigns (Meadows, 1972). The resulting movement called for restraints on growth and the wiser use of dwindling resources in the face of rising demand.

Inspiring leaders such as Buckminster Fuller, John McLeod, Jay Forrester, William O. Douglas, F. Lappe, Murray Bookchin, Leslie Stevens, Arthur C. Clarke, B. F. Skinner, and Lewis Mumford enhanced the sense of crisis with their warnings, and several helped launch idealistic enterprises promising salvation. Some of the dire

9

predictions have, of course, failed to materialize, and some of the promises of salvation have proved equally disappointing. Was the great movement of this decade merely an attention-getting device, an outlet for the soul-stirrings of well-meaning and dedicated utopians, or was there a genuine problem underlying it? If the latter, what is the problem and what are its key issues? Platt gave us an appraisal of thoughts along these lines. Believing that a few vital ideas can change the shape of the future, he states that fresh and valuable ideas are always forthcoming and can offer hope, as they have in the past. These ideas need to be discussed, tried out, and evaluated. And it is quite apparent that information in communities—information about problems, about proposed solutions, about progress—is a vital factor.

The Rise of Information Services

In recent times we have seen a great increase in the number of agencies set up primarily or solely for the purpose of providing information. The term "information center" has become a cliché that is used to denote a motley array of things, ranging from a leaflet rack in a bank to a religious counseling office, to a computerized service that stores data for use by industrial or miliary decision makers. Although the function of all of these services is solely to provide information, it is apparent that their motives and goals are not independent of values and other functions to which information is a subsidiary.

The distinction between agencies that provide information as a by-product and those that do so as a primary function is important. Professional communicators sometimes overestimate their own importance in the communication process and underestimate the importance of the information that is transferred by others in the process of doing business, of work and play, of ministering and being ministered to. They need to be reminded that their professional outlook may tend to distort reality.

There are other useful ways of classifying information services. For instance, classifying services by the client group and support group are two particularly helpful methods used in analyzing the place of information services in society and their prognosis for survival. Where the two groups overlap there is, of course, always the danger of disseminating information that has not been critically analyzed. A corollary is that under such conditions the information provided will often be self-serving, such as the "news" supplied by press agents, public relations persons, and many government "Public Information Officers." In fact few information services are constructed without a strong motivation for serving a particular clientele, and the short life span of many such services may indicate that insufficient attention has been paid to understanding the nature of the client group's information needs. The same may be said about the need to understand and make explicit the needs and motives of the support group.

A very complex relationship may exist between the nature of the client group and that of the support group. There may be a high degree of overlap between the two, as found, for instance, in a referral center operated by a union for its own members. In such a situation, the relationship between operator and user of the service may be easier to ascertain than in a case involving a great disparity and distance between the support and client group. In the latter case, the motivation of the sponsor may be impossible to determine, despite official statements of purpose.

The relationships between the two groups will necessarily be critical, at least in times of scarce resources or whenever the purposes and goals of the two groups come into conflict. For this reason, it is important to explore the motivations and agenda of both from the start. It is not merely cynicism that encourages us to make explicit the admixture of altruism and self-interest that permeates human actions. The supporters, planners, and operators of information services, as well as the users, will have less cause for disappointment if all concerned know the expectations of those who provide the services.

Establishment and Counterculture

Information services in the vital areas of health, welfare, education, and employment have often been operated as adjuncts of parent institutions that are either official or officially sanctioned. They are part of the "establishment"—the state, the church, the quasi-official bodies—and they share the stability of those established parent groups. Like their sponsoring group, they tend to become bureaucratized. This condition may gradually alter their mode of operation in a way that serves no cause as well as the perpetuation of the organization itself. Voluntary, grass roots, or counterculture information services may be more daring and more responsive to the needs of clients as long as these services are operated in the heat of idealistic or ideological zeal, but such zeal is characteristically short-lived, and both the orientations and the cadres of such groups are apt to change rapidly.

Examples of the establishment's dramatic, if temporary, response to information needs of given segments of the population come readily to mind. During the 1950s and early 1960s the federal government responded to frequently expressed needs for scientific and technical information with substantial and expensive programs. By the late 1960s, however, many of these programs were required to become self-sustaining or be phased out. So, too, information services in the

11

areas of health and welfare, including legal services to the poor, were given substantial support by one administration, only to be dropped by its successor. For instance, the Economic Opportunity Act of 1964 attempted to move the decision-making powers from centralized federal bureaucracies to communities. The neighborhood service programs initiated in 1966 led to the establishment of a first generation of experimental service center cities. Fourteen cities were funded in July 1967, with seven being established as neighborhood corporations in order to evaluate the concept of community-run, not-for-profit corporations funded by the federal government. This eventually led to Model Cities, now also being discontinued.

With each such expansive program, an industry was built, personnel were recruited, facilities and equipment built or acquired, and systems developed. All of these were extremely vulnerable during the subsequent period of retrenchment. By far the most disruptive aspects of these programs involved the arousing of expectations that were not to be satisfied in the long run. It is probably of little social import that the defense industry is now deprived of some of the expensive special information services once provided it at great expense by the Department of Defense STINFO (Scientific and Technical Information) program, because the contractors so served are hardly without other resources. But to offer information services to the poor, the unemployed, and the disenfranchised and then abruptly to withdraw these services may have a more deleterious effect on the health of society as a whole than to have done nothing whatever. Motive power has been sapped, and cynicism encouraged.

Activists have helped to arouse consciences and spur corrective action. The establishment has responded in part to these outcries, and in part to the newly recognized needs, with a great variety of developments. In 1971 the Allerton Institute of the University of Illinois held a conference entitled "Libraries and Neighborhood Information Centers" (see Bibliography), and in Florida the Dade County Citizen's Information and Service Program was started. In 1972 the Kansas State Library started the Kansas Community Information Center Project, and the University of Toledo initiated its Community Information Specialist MA Program. In 1973 a 4.5 million dollar grant was awarded to New York City for establishing Citizen Urban Information Centers at fifty-five branch libraries in Brooklyn, a project headed by Beatrice Fitzpatrick. Although the city received this grant, the full amount was never allocated and the project was dead by the end of 1974. Perhaps its demise betokened the fiscal crisis faced by New York City as this book is going to press. I&R services were introduced into thirty branches and the main branch of the Detroit Public Library. This is but a small sampling of activities up to 1974.

Needs, Resources, and Impediments

Information agencies, like other social agencies, can either exist primarily for the benefit of those who operate them, or they can conscientiously seek to extend their services to the widest possible clientele. Even given good faith, there are impediments to this extension, some of the more common of which are:

1. The potential users' ignorance of the agency or of the availability of its service;
2. Alienation between the social group that the potential users belong to and the group providing the service, or distrust among potential clients of the motives of the agency's operators or sponsors;
3. Lack of sensitivity of agency personnel about the character of the user group, its needs, or the modes of operation needed to make successful contact;
4. Concern over possible breach of privacy, or resentment against attitudes of agency personnel;
5. The stigma of "welfare" or "charity"; and,
6. Financial failure. The voluntary agencies, whether grass roots, underground, or establishment, often lack a broad and stable financial support base. The tax-supported agencies are subject to the usual annual budget competition and in addition are constrained by their enabling legislation, as well as by the often restrictive attitudes of the electorate and officials concerning the proper limits of their functions.

A community "switchboard" which connects or couples resources with needs can aid in extending the services of both kinds of agencies—the substantive services type, as well as the specialized information type. It can:

1. Alert the potential users to the existence of a wide range of available services;
2. Act as liaison in situations in which the person in need of assistance is not likely to make effective contact unaided;
3. Follow up to assure satisfactory completion of the transaction;
4. Prod helping agencies where this appears needed; and finally,
5. Document and make public the instances where needed services are not available. By helping agencies to deliver services more effectively, such a switchboard type of service could in fact help them to better justify their existence to their sponsoring groups.

In building a switchboard or switching center, it is necessary to be well-informed concerning the existing patterns of communication in order to make the best use of what is already in existence. Professional system builders are sometimes unbelievably naive in this respect; they embark on expensive new systems for providing services already available to some extent. Sometimes this undertaking is due to ignorance, but other times it is due to a deliberate decision to ignore, and thus defeat, the existing service, competing with it for resources. At the very least the system builder should be aware of the consequences of such competition and confrontation. The new service may fail to attract sufficient continued support or even clientele. After a new service has acquired a clientele and raised the level of expectation, its developers may also move on to other activities, leaving a vacuum of leadership, with the previously existing service dismantled. The result can be the loss of both the old and the new service, with the final situation worse than the first.

Motivations

With such caveats in mind, it will be useful for those seeking to create information services to assess carefully their own motivations and ask searching questions about the need for such a service, questions such as: "Are we building only because we enjoy making things, or because informaton is our line of work and we need an outlet? If a need really exists, do we have substantial evidence that it is sufficient to warrant the service we envision? For how long will the service be in demand? Will the reward—whether financial or psychic—be sufficient to sustain those who must support and operate it? Are we on an 'ego trip'—playing God, seeking information, or being condescending do-gooders? Are we consciously or, of even greater danger, unconsciously using the cause for our own narrow self-interests?" Such questions must be considered, even if the answers are not readily apparent. In the innovative discipline of information science, and in branches of the social sciences relevant to it, sophisticated techniques have been developed to measure the degree of need for information. Methods to determine the types of resources people use to obtain the information they need are also available, to a lesser extent. Both kinds of tools are needed in the preliminary stages of designing public information services (Moore, 1971).

Need and patterns of information use must be assessed in relation to existing sources to justify the establishment of a new service. It is not realistic to expect that this will always be done in a thoroughgoing way. The creation of new information services often results from political pressures and zeal, rather than rationality and careful planning. But rational alternatives do exist.

In addition to asking questions about the conditions that appear to justify the formation of a new service and our motivations for starting one, we ought also to ask "What *can* we do?" In other words, what contributions are we really able and willing to make, at what cost, and for how long? How likely are we to succeed? Are we willing to fail and still consider the attempt worthwhile? What reward will we consider adequate for the investment we plan to make? And what will be the punishment for failure? For success? How important are particular individuals to the organization's success, and what assurance do we have that they will sustain their interest and involvement? If these persons are essential, are they likely to create a personality cult? Are there provisions to allow the pioneers to "cut the cord" at some definable point and allow the organization to survive or fail on its own merits? These questions obviously have no certain answers; yet to begin a new service without at least taking them into consideration is to invite eventual disappointments and troubles. To begin a business venture for profit without asking similar searching questions would be recognized as foolhardy; efforts at social melioration deserve equal care.

Choosing the Environment

The structure within which a new service is created determines, to a large extent, its viability. The system designer's prejudice for or against a particular kind of group or organization should not be allowed to bias the decision, but a home of some kind must be found or created for the service. Thus, the innovator is faced with a dilemma. The very fact that he is developing something new implies his judgment of the inadequacy of existing organizations, but if he decides that a radical departure is called for and divorces the new service from the establishment, he may also divorce the service from potential resources.

Radicalism in the literal sense (*radix*: "root") is an attractive notion, summoning up images of bold, inventive, fundamental changes, and not, by any means, necessarily through violence. One trouble with radicals, to paraphrase Justice Holmes's comment about the younger generation, is that "they haven't read the minutes of the last meeting." Radical new principles may be incorporated into a new system or service, but the designers ought to recognize that in the institutional, as well as the biological, sphere most mutations do not survive. Thus, if we have a limited resource base, and want to risk it all in a radically different approach, we ought to be reasonably certain of our chances of survival, and yet still willing to lose all, as should those who support the experiment and those who may be left without help in the event of failure. If, on the other hand, innovators are utterly convinced that moderate or conservative solutions are bound to be smothered by either the establishment or the bureaucratic vices of mediocrity and cautiousness, the radical solution *must* be chosen.

The designer must make that decision for the potential clientele, and it is a responsibility to be taken seriously.

In the social conditions that encourage radical measures, there appear to be rapid changes in political and social alignments. Revolutions, even peaceful ones, make strange and rapidly changing bedfellows. The system builder's choice of approach will be affected by these changes. For instance, the most innovative social service builder will likely find himself cooperating with elements of the establishment, as well as with dissidents, if his service is to survive. The implacable foe of the established order will mount a frontal assault on establishment services, in an attempt to replace them with newly created structures of his own making. Another, with radical aims, will nevertheless cooperate with others to obtain his means. The choice is intensely personal. In the area of information services, a rigid dogmatism would seem self-defeating; to serve clients well, one must keep all lines of communication open.

Many possible working environments can serve as the matrix for a community information service. The Health and Welfare Council has, up to this time, provided more of such services than any other type of sponsoring agency. H&W policy makers differ as to the appropriateness of a council's providing I&R services on a permanent basis. While some agree with this policy, others believe that an H&W council should implement such a service, assist it until it is self-sustaining, and then remove the council from an operating role. This kind of "turnkey" operation allows the council to emphasize its role as the innovator, coordinator, and research arm of the community's voluntary agencies.

The public library has been recommended as another potential basis for the community information service; Donohue, in his chapter on the Public Information Center Project, summarizes the reasons for that choice. In addition to the reasons he cites, the library has the potential to serve as a kind of citizen forum. It has often served this function by its provision of a wide range of documentary materials, by its informal programs of adult education, and by the presentation of public information programs, such as the dissemination, during World War II, of information on rationing, civil defense, employment, and other vital matters. In Great Britain, Citizens' Advice Bureaux, some of them located within libraries, operated as emergency information centers, and a few continue within libraries today. (A fuller treatment of this aspect is to be found in Carole Peppi's chapter.)

The library, although primarily supported by tax moneys, is usually governed by a board of trustees provided with some degree of independence from the direct political control of elected or appointed government officials. Because of that relative independence, libraries have successfully defied attempts to abridge their mission of education and information. The library, of course, is not concerned necessarily with the informational value of the documents it houses and circulates. It is unique among social agencies, in that its primary function is the selection, housing, retrieval, and provision of documents in many forms and media. Libraries and librarians differ as to the degree and depth of their interest in the contents of the documents. Some think that libraries may also be effective purveyors of information, irrespective of its format, while others believe that dealing with nondocumentary information weakens the library's primary role. If the library is to be successful as an *information center,* it must espouse the broader interpretation of its role, handling all media and concerning itself with the media's informational content in a critical manner. It must not stop with information found in recorded form.

The Epistemology and Ethics of Information Services

In theory, information may be thought of as ethically indifferent—i.e., a fact is a fact. In actuality, however, facts are formulated by people, who charge them with meanings, so that they cannot be free of ethical values. Certainly information, however factual, is not often supplied, received, or used in a moral vacuum. There is a continuum of means and ends that makes one man's end another's means, and vice versa. An information supplier may seek to dissociate himself entirely from the social or political content of his service or of the information it provides. He may even do so for ideological reasons, such as to remain impartial, unbiased, and truthful. But he can never really escape bias entirely. Merely to desire to inform is to judge that information is valuable and ought to be more freely available. In fact, that is perhaps in itself the most significant judgment, especially at a time when governments, industry, and social organizations appear increasingly able and willing to impose severe limits on the rights of the citizen to be informed.[1] The desire to provide unbiased information should not be construed as an indifference to values; rather it should be seen as a commitment to the recipient's right to all pertinent data, as well as the right to make his own judgment.

Whatever matrix is chosen for an information service, the extent

1. If the reader questions this judgment in view of such apparently liberalizing trends as the passage, during the past decade, of the Freedom of Information Law, he must consider the extent of the success of such formal efforts. This section was originally written at the height of the battle between Congress and President Richard Nixon over the right of the citizen and his elected representatives to know the business of government. Consider also the need for subsequent amendments to strengthen freedom of information in the face of intransigent officials of the executive branch.

of its ability to serve is highly dependent on the extent and nature of its contacts with the community. The number of contacts alone is not of primary importance—they must be lively, and continually used. They must span official, voluntary, and private organizations, of both general and highly specialized purposes. They must include groups that do not have true organization or recognizable structure, as well as individuals who do not participate in organizations, but who are nonetheless important because they know what is going on within a segment of the community, or because others who have need of information or action turn to them. The true leaders of opinion are not always the stereotyped well-educated, professional individuals active in official or voluntary work. Even in our nontribal society, counterparts of the tribal elders are still found—people who may not, from all standards, appear to be the best informed or wisest, but who are important contacts if they listen and are listened to.

References

Meadows, D. *The Limits to Growth*. New York: Universe Books, 1972.

Moore, J. R. *Information Sources for the Urban Dweller, an Exploratory Study*. Cleveland, Ohio: Case Western Reserve University, 1971.

Ogg, E. *Tell Me Where to Turn*. New York: Public Affairs Committee, 1969.

Platt, J. R. "What We Must Do." *Science,* 1969, *166,* 1115–16.

Chapter 2
The Everyday Information Needs
of the Average Citizen:
A Taxonomy for Analysis

by Brenda Dervin

Increasingly, social agencies are turning their attention to filling the everyday information needs of the average citizen. Indeed, "information" is becoming one of our society's power words. More and more, both agencies and the clients they serve are concerned with getting the right information at the right time for solving their problems.

The focus of this chapter is on this central concern—the average citizen and his information needs. The intent is to place these needs into a conceptual framework through which we can look at as many ramifications as possible for both future action and research. In particular, I propose to: (1) provide a taxonomy for the analysis of the information needs of the average citizen; (2) review briefly what is known about the process of filling these needs; (3) describe the implications of what is known for action agencies; and (4) identify still-unanswered questions amenable to future research.

Information and Control

As a starting point, I accept as an axiom that individuals want to control their own environments. In a modern, highly technological

This chapter is a revised and expanded version of the author's "Information Needs of Urban Residents: A Conceptual Context," in Edward S. Warner, Ann D. Murray, and Vernon E. Palmour, *Information Needs of Urban Residents*, the final report from the Regional Planning Council of Baltimore and Westat., Inc., of Rockville, Md., to the U.S. Department of Health, Education, and Welfare, Office of Education, Division of Library Programs, under Contract No. OEC–O–71–4555, December, 1973.

Dr. Dervin is Assistant Professor, School of Communications, University of Washington, and Associate Director of the Communications Research Center.

society such as ours, information is essential to that control. Without information, the individual cannot seek effective help or correct abuses, benefit from the protection and services the government offers, or get the most from his resources.

Communication theorists, in fact, suggest that information acquisition and its proper use are the basis of effective human functioning (Ascroft, 1969; Dervin, 1971; Hirschleifer, 1971; and Rotter, 1966). Studies show that information use is strongly related to an individual's ability to take risks, to make rational decisions and to achieve successful results (Bowes, 1971; Cangelosi et al., 1968; Hill, 1963; and Seeman, 1966).

Yet, the clearest picture that emerges from research studies on information needs is that, in spite of the abundance of information available, citizens are uninformed about public and private resources, facilities, rights, and programs (Kahn et al., 1966). They are frustrated in their attempts to get information required for everyday problem solving (Rieger and Anderson, 1968; Kahn et al., 1966; Mendelsohn, 1968; and Greenleigh Associates, 1965). The brunt of the evidence presents a clear picture of general inability to cope with information needs.

At the same time, new information agencies are reported as being rapidly overloaded with cases. Service agency representatives who make public appearances quickly have their switchboards jammed with requests. Governmental agencies become overloaded with requests for information that has nothing to do with their functions. I found that 186 general-population adults reflected 160 different information needs in just one survey questionnaire item (1973a). Another study (Kahn et al., 1966) estimates that certain five-block areas with 50,000 residents in New York City could keep an information center busy with 800 to 900 requests a month.

Recognition that a sizable number of citizens have a large number of information needs not being satisfied within the current information system leads to the obvious question: "What shall we do to meet this crisis?" The all too easy answer is, "Provide information services." Yet communication theorists have warned that "information" as such is not enough. Information needs to be managed and controlled in order to be useful and accessible (Dervin, 1971; Eisenstadt, 1955; Etzioni, 1969; Frey, 1963).

The increasing attention being placed on information delivery systems and information retrieval is symptomatic of the growing awareness of the need for controlling or managing information in a highly complex, highly diverse society (Allen, 1965; Brownson, 1962; Cole and Cole, 1968; Menzel, 1964; and Price, 1964). Such delivery systems do more than simply try to get the right information to the right person at the right time. They also deal both with the structure of the information system and with the structure of information. To get the right information to the right person at the right time, the information management or control process of the information delivery systems must have access to both appropriate information sources and appropriate information solutions. The system must be able to select from all relevant sources those who hold relevant information and must then select from all relevant information that particular subset that solves the particular need of the seeker. Access to a variety of sources provides the individual with a potential diversity of information types. Access to appropriate information solutions allows the individual to decrease that diversity by selectively choosing relevant information.

Taxonomy for Analysis

We can now pinpoint four elements of the information system within which the average citizen operates: (1) the individual citizen; (2) information needs; (3) information sources; and, (4) solutions to information needs. Figure 1 shows these elements and highlights six basic hypothetical two-element linkages.

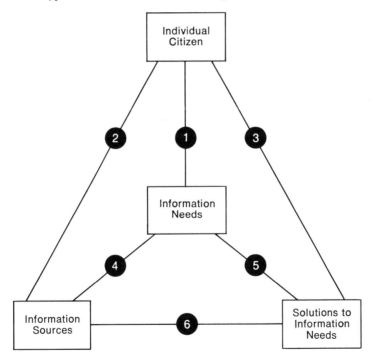

Figure 1.   Elements and Linkages in the Information System
             of the Average Citizen

Focus is on the linkage of the individual citizen (1) to his information needs; (2) to information sources; (3) to solutions to information needs; and on the linkage of (4) information sources to information needs; (5) information needs to solutions to information needs; and (6) information sources to solutions to information needs.

Activity would not necessarily have to occur along all possible linkages in any given individual's problem-solving processes. One of the tasks of both future research and action programs will be to pinpoint which linkages are relevant under what conditions.

The conceptual structure illustrated in figure 1 is used throughout the review to demonstrate the scope of what is known and what needs to be known (Warner et al., 1973).

LINKAGE #1: THE INDIVIDUAL CITIZEN AND HIS INFORMATION NEEDS

The linkage between the individual and his needs is basic to the design of programs intended to help citizens. Surprisingly, the questions that arise from analysis of this linkage are little researched. These questions include: (1) What constitutes the universe of average citizen information needs? (2) Which subgroups of citizens have which needs? (3) How do citizens perceive their needs?

A few studies have provided initial, if undocumented categorizations of citizen information needs. Kahn et al. (1966) and Voos (1969), for instance, refer to the logs of problems that have come into existing agencies. These studies of agency logs have not, however, been completed within the framework of a single classification scheme. Nor do they cope with the difference between the needs individual citizens may have and the needs that are actually recorded on an agency roster.

Other studies have looked at the users of particular document systems and the needs the users fulfill by using such systems. The most prevalent examples are library-use studies.[1] These generally ignore needs that are not met within the agency studied, i.e., the library, and by the primary informational format, which has been print media. These restrictions limit the expression of user needs to only those that are answered in print, thus eliminating many everyday problems (Voos, 1969; Zweizig, 1973).

---

1. For a recent and thorough review of library-use studies, see Zweizig, 1973. For examples of two classic library-use studies, see Berelson, 1949; Campbell and Metzner, 1950.

Not one single systematic study with a well-sampled population was found in the published literature that documents the nature of citizen information needs. Some comprehensive evidence is available, however, in government documents and in preliminary research reports. The first large-scale attempt to develop a content-analytic scheme for codifying average citizen information needs was completed in 1972 (Warner et al., 1973).[2] In this study of a large random sample of Baltimore adults, a basic content-analysis scheme was developed to categorize systematically the many needs named by the 1,000 respondents. I then expanded on the scheme that emerged from the Warner study. (1973a,b,c,d).

Essentially, our task was to develop a content-analytic scheme that taps the universe of average citizen information needs and is, therefore, transferable from situation to situation. The code scheme developed was an attempt to provide a set of mutually exclusive and exhaustive categories into which all citizen information needs could be classified.

Employing these procedures, general-population adults drawn randomly from the Seattle, Washington (Dervin, 1973a) and Syracuse, New York (Zweizig, 1973) phone books were asked if they had recently had any problems or questions for which they needed help or information. The respondents in these two phone surveys were asked to describe the nature of their problems.

All respondent answers from the two studies were then placed in an answer pool and categorized into 19 major categories (table 1), each of which was then divided into subcategories as illustrated in table 2. In total, the content-analysis scheme has 19 major categories and 154 subcategories (Warner et al., 1973).[3]

After solidifying the scheme on the two general population surveys, I then applied it to yet another body of data, a content analysis of the "problem-solver" columns in the two Seattle newspapers (1973b). Interjudge reliability was as good as that on the general population surveys, which was found to be 85 percent using the "exact code" as a criterion and 93 percent using "coding within a major category" as the criterion.

2. Study available only in draft form at the time of this writing, so that data from it cannot be cited. The present author was a consultant to that study, particularly on the development of content-analytic schemes for codifying citizen information needs.

3. A complete copy of the content analysis scheme as initially developed in the Baltimore study is available in Warner et al., 1973. A copy of the revised and expanded version is available from the author of this chapter (Dervin, 1973a).

Table 1.   A Brief Description of the Major Categories in the Information-Needs Content-Analysis Scheme.

Major Category	Brief Description
Neighborhood	Problems with neighbors, children, dogs in neighborhood, rats in neighborhood, city services, traffic and parking, vacant lots, abandoned cars, noisy airplanes, etc.
Consumer	Problems with product quality, product availability, best product information, service quality, service availability, where to get service information, prices, consumer protection, etc.
Housing	Problems with loans and mortgages, getting a place to live, landlords, public housing, housing insurance, selling a house, etc.
Housekeeping and Household Maintenance	Problems with regulations on home improvements, utility service, making repairs, do-it-yourself projects, car repair and operation, etc.
Employment	Problems with getting or keeping a job, changing jobs, on-the-job complaints, job training, unions, etc.
Education and Schooling	Problems with financial aid, adult education services, cost of education, the educational system, parent-teacher relationships, etc.
Health	Problems with mental health, health insurance, the cost of health care, getting health care, etc.
Transportation	Problems with inadequate bus service, auto insurance, auto financing, road maintenance, inadequate emergency services, etc.
Recreation and Culture	Problems with finding recreational opportunities, lack of supervision at playgrounds, high costs of recreation, etc.
Financial Matters or Assistance	Problems with taxes, getting credit or loans, retirement, investments, handling money, life insurance, etc.
Public Assistance and Social Security	Problems with unemployment compensation, social security, food stamps, Medicare, welfare, etc.
Discrimination and Race Relations	Problems with racial tensions, discrimination based on race or sex, etc.

Table 1.   (Continued)

Major Category	Brief Description
Child Care and Family Relationships	Problems of need for day care, high cost of day care, child behavior, need for someone to talk to about personal problems, etc.
Family Planning and Birth Control	Problems with family planning, birth control, etc.
Legal	Problems with legal aspects of marriages, contracts, need for legal services, documents, interpretation of law, etc.
Crime and Safety	Problems with lax law enforcement, crime, drugs, etc.
Immigration, Migration and Mobility	Problems with translation of documents, immigration, American citizenship, being new in area, etc.
Veterans and Military	Problems with veteran's benefits, rights, military service, discharges, etc.
Public Affairs, Political, and Miscellaneous	Problems with locating agencies and people, political issues and politicians, general government information, general factual information, travel, religion, news, current events, etc.

To date, the content-analysis scheme has been developed and tested on four data bases. What emerges is a scheme extensive enough and tested enough to suggest that it is at least transferable across urban situations. For instance, I also applied the scheme to a study of the problems actually brought in by clients during 1972 to a Chicano action agency based in Seattle. Preliminary results on this study (1973d) indicate that the scheme can be applied without modification to an actual agency data base.

The benefits of such a scheme are obvious. It answers, in part, the major objections made against prior research—that of the use of a constantly changing categorization scheme for the coding of needs. The scheme also allows for a systematic and reliable counting of the frequency of problems and a comparison of problem naming across different data bases, as shown in table 3.

For example, the newspaper content analysis shows lower frequency-of-mention percentages for most problems that we would generally typify as being "personal"—health, family, discrimination and child-care problems, for example. On the other hand, the newspaper study

Table 2. A Sample Subsection from the Information-Needs Content-Analysis Scheme

Code value	The needs
000–009	Neighborhood problems
000	Problems with NEIGHBORS—noisy, drunk, gossipy, etc.
001	Problems with NEIGHBORHOOD CHILDREN—noise, vandalism, etc.
002	Problems with DOGS IN NEIGHBORHOOD —loose, barking, into trash, not enough dogcatchers, etc.
003	Problems with RATS IN NEIGHBORHOOD —in house, in neighborhood, not controlled, etc.
004	Problems with CITY SERVICES IN NEIGHBORHOOD—trash removal, street maintenance, sewage, abandoned appliances, etc.
005	Problems with TRAFFIC AND PARKING IN NEIGHBORHOOD—noisy, speeding, not enough parking space, too little control, etc.
006	Problems with VACANT LOTS, ABANDONED CARS, ABANDONED BUILDINGS in neighborhood, etc.
007	Problems with NOISY AIRPLANES OVER NEIGHBORHOOD, etc.
009	OTHER NEIGHBORHOOD PROBLEMS— beggars, changing character of neighborhood, other animals (chickens, horses, etc.)

shows a markedly higher frequency of mention (24.2 percent of all problems named, compared to 6.7 percent for the general population study) for public affairs and political and miscellaneous problems. These results agree with what we ordinarily think of as being the focus of a newspaper. They also suggest the yet-to-be-tested notion that people who voluntarily write to newspaper "problem solvers" are probably more educated and more oriented to public affairs than the general population as a whole. The findings also suggest that more personal

Table 3. Comparison of Frequency of Problem Naming across Three Studies

The Need Categories	Proportion of all needs named		
	General population surveys		Newspaper content analysis
	Seattle (n=316)	Syracuse (n=460)	Two Seattle papers
Neighborhood problems	9.1%	3.0%	6.2% *
Consumer problems	16.8	14.9	26.2
Housing problems	7.4	0.7	2.0
Housekeeping and household maintenance problems	2.2	6.3	1.3
Employment problems	7.7	1.9	1.3
Education and schooling problems	9.1	2.6	0.8
Health problems	5.7	15.7	0.9
Transportation problems	6.7	0.7	9.7
Recreation and culture problems	3.6	3.7	3.4
Financial matters or assistance problems	5.2	1.5	5.4
Public assistance or social security problems	1.7	1.1	1.9
Discrimination and race relations problems	3.7	0.1	0.1
Child-care and family relationships problems	2.2	3.7	0.1
Family planning and birth control problems	1.5	0.1	0.1
Legal problems	4.7	4.5	9.3
Crime and safety problems	5.7	0.0	6.0
Immigration, migration, and mobility problems	0.1	2.0	0.3
Veterans and military problems	0.1	0.1	0.3
Public affairs, political, miscellaneous problems	6.7	37.7	24.2
TOTAL NEEDS NAMED	1471	298	1833

*The proportions listed here are calculated by dividing the number of needs named in a given category by the total of needs categorized.

problems may not be reflected on information agency lists in proportion to the frequency with which they actually occur.

The data presented above provide just an initial attempt to attack systematically the central question of interest to most information agency practitioners—what are the information needs of average citizens?

Simply identifying the nature of the needs of citizens, however, will not be sufficient for successful information handling. The entire definition and scope of an information agency depends, in part, on how people *perceive* their needs, since the differing perceptions of citizens may well act as barriers to information accessibility. An individual may not be aware of his information needs, or he may not be able to verbalize them. Or he may be aware of his needs, but not see them as "information" problems.

Thus, the problem of defining what is meant by an "information need" becomes crucial. The definition is clear when an individual seeks a simple fact (e.g., who was President in 1941?) ; when he seeks information about resources (e.g., where to get family counseling or emergency food dollars), however, the situation may become clouded. While an information counselor may consider his job done when he has answered the questions about resource location, the individual with the need is likely to be unsatisfied until the resource is actually delivered. Indeed, the individual with the need may consider the information counselor a failure *until* the resource is delivered. However, assurance by a counselor of the delivery of resources, as well as information, enlarges the counselor's role from that of informant to that of advisor and advocate. If people do not separate information from help or service, then the entire basis for objective information counseling is challenged.

Unfortunately, very little systematic evidence is available relating to this issue. Literature on Great Britain's Citizens' Advice Bureaux indicates that CAB services go beyond information to advocacy in as much as 40 percent of their cases (Bernard et al., 1968; Kahn et al., 1966; National Citizens' Advice Bureaux Committee, 1961; Ogg, 1969; Zucker, 1965). In fact, the very philosophical underpinnings of the CAB model were developed on the premise that citizens need advocates to protect them against growing government bureaucracies. In the United States, however, the information versus advocacy issue remains a controversial one, as documented by expressions of concern by active librarians and information counselors (Furman et al., 1962; *Wilson Library Bulletin,* 1970).

While no studies are available that directly address this controversy, tangential evidence (Bundy, 1972; Dervin, 1973a; Voos, 1969) suggests that, more often than not, the way people perceive their information needs leads the information counselor into the problems of advocacy and resource delivery. I found that, when asking for consumer information, 66 percent of a group of general population respondents wanted to know specifically "where" to buy a product and 33 percent wanted to know where to get the "best" buy (1973a). Problem statements were made in information terms in 54 percent of the cases in my content analysis of the two Seattle daily newspaper problem-solving columns (1973c). The rest were made primarily in "complaint or lament" terms—the individual was crying out against an error or injustice, only implying a request for more than information.

Such results suggest that information counselors who want to deal solely with information may have a difficult task ahead of them. Such "objective" information may not be possible in the arena of the average citizen's information environment; advocacy may be a necessary component of an information program. Conversely, it may be that information counselors can be trained to handle their interactions with clients in such a way that a more "pure" informant role is possible. These are questions that must be answered by future action and research.

LINKAGE #2: THE INDIVIDUAL CITIZEN AND HIS INFORMATION SOURCES

At the linkage between the individual and his information sources, the major questions include: (1) What sources are used by which individuals? (2) What are the characteristics of the sources being used? (3) What sources are seen as helpful by individual citizens? (4) Why do individuals use particular sources?

Of all the linkages posited in the average citizen's information environment, this linkage is the most researched. The use of information sources has long been a concern of several research traditions in communications research. Trust in sources has been a major concern of persuasion and attitude change research in social psychology. Recently, organizational researchers have begun to focus on the nature of source relationships with clients.

While a sizable body of relevant literature about the use of information sources is available, relatively little of it speaks directly to the problem of source use for everyday information needs. Generally it is concerned with source use in a topic-free sense or with source use solely on public affairs issues.

Most typically, the prior research is concerned with only one basic question—what sources are used, and how often? A capsule picture of the evidence suggests that most citizens in the United States live in a relatively homogeneous information environment that presents relatively little information for problem solving. The most used (and believed) mass medium of the average adult in this environment is television, though tangential evidence suggests that the electronic media lack the kind of information the citizen needs to help solve his everyday problems (Dervin and Greenberg, 1972; Greenberg and Dervin, 1970; Kline, 1971; Westley and Severin, 1964).

The most used sources of information on most topics for most people, according to research reports, are peer-kin network contacts (friends, family, and relatives). People meet, talk, and ask advice from people essentially like themselves (Dervin and Greenberg, 1972; Greenberg and Dervin, 1970; Katz, 1957).

The evidence further suggests that awareness of potential information sources is low (Block, 1970; Greenleigh Associates, 1965; Mendelsohn, 1968; Rieger and Anderson, 1968). Use of professionals and nonprofit agencies designated as information keepers is limited to the highly educated elite (Caplovitz, 1963; Dervin and Greenberg, 1972; Levine and Preston, 1970; Udell, 1966; Voos, 1969; Zweizig, 1973), who use these sources to solve problems that have reached the crisis stage, rather than for crisis prevention (Dervin and Greenberg, 1972; Levine and Preston, 1970). The research also suggests that a "law of least effort" is a strong factor in source use. People generally use sources and services that are close to their residences, preferring not to comparison shop (Alexander, 1968; Udell, 1966; Zweizig, 1973).

The capsule picture, then, is dismal, suggesting that for the average citizen, contact with information sources that are appropriate to optimum everyday problem solving is limited.

Unfortunately, much of the available evidence is indirect. Specific evidence is needed from both research and action programs on the nature and characteristics of information sources, with an analysis to indicate the specific sources used by a specific group of citizens for a specific set of needs. Content analyses are needed to determine (1) the actual nature of the information presented by different sources and (2) the relevance of the information transmitted for everyday problem solving.

Prior research on source use has focused primarily on how citizens relate to sources, rather than on the reciprocal question of how sources relate to citizens. The studies that are available on the reciprocal relationship present a bleak picture (Dervin, 1971; Furman et al., 1965; Greenberg and Dervin, 1970; Kahn et al., 1966; Levin and Taube, 1970; Mendelsohn, 1968; Pratt, 1969; Scott, 1967; Sjoberg et al., 1966; Stark, 1959). They suggest that the barriers to information accessibility that occur along the citizen-source linkage occur in both directions.

Some agencies intended to serve people's needs appear to prevent citizen access by establishing bureaucratic barriers and advertising too sparsely. Often agency practitioners are uninformed about the life styles of various citizen subgroups; they tend to stereotype their clients or, in some instances, relate to their clients in such a way that the clients feel humiliated. Some agencies may consciously, or unconsciously, withhold service from citizens with the most difficult (perhaps insolvable) problems in order to make their success records look better.

While findings such as these are depressing, they are also instructive. They suggest (1) the importance of examining the way agencies relate to people, as well as the way people relate to agencies; (2) some of the pitfalls that information agencies will need to avoid or overcome if they are to be effective in their roles; and (3) the importance of not always placing the burden of proof for the effectiveness of an information system on the users of that system.

LINKAGE #3: THE INDIVIDUAL CITIZEN AND
SOLUTIONS TO INFORMATION NEEDS

The linkage between an individual citizen and the solution to his needs raises such questions as: (1) What kinds of solutions do citizens see as helpful? (2) Which subgroups of individuals attempt to solve their problems in which manner?

No evidence is available for a satisfactory answer to the first question. On the second, clear and abundant evidence suggests that the more educated citizens are more likely to be information seekers, exposed to the print media, using more professional sources, more informed generally, and experiencing less trouble securing information (Hiltz, 1971; Parker and Paisley, 1966; Rieger and Anderson, 1968; Spitzer and Denzin, 1966; Tichenor et al., 1970; Zweizig, 1973). While the correlation between education and information use is well supported, no evidence has been found that clearly shows the extent of the advantage of education in the information environment of the average citizen.

Research showing a strong correlation between education and information seeking has essentially placed the onus for problem solving on the individual. If the focus is switched to how the information system is affecting the individual, another group of studies by researchers primarily interested in the concepts of self-esteem and personal competence (Bowes, 1971; Rotter, 1966; Seeman, 1966) indicates investigative directions for planners of information systems. These findings suggest that individuals who have failed in their attempts to secure information for problem solving in the past begin to believe that their problems have no solution and consequently stop trying. If failure in information seeking does lead to retreats from further attempts, planners of information systems should ask (1) how to reach those who have given up and (2) how to remove the barriers that stand between citizens and the solutions to their problems.

LINKAGE #4: INFORMATION SOURCES AND INFORMATION NEEDS

This linkage is usually concerned with the ability of information sources to handle particular information needs. Some questions raised here are: (1) What sources are being used for what needs? (2) How efficiently are the sources handling needs? (3) What sources are seen as "best" for what needs?

The small amount of literature dealing directly with this question is consistent in its findings. For instance, a great deal of inefficiency and noncommunication has been found in the information delivery system (Grunig, 1972; Kahn et al., 1966; Kurtz, 1968; Levine et al., 1963; Regional Health and Welfare Council, 1965; Sjoberg et al., 1966). Information sources located in the same problem area have different, and sometimes contradictory, preceptions of citizen problems. Although agency directors agree that more coordination and communication are needed among service information agencies, only a minority are actually willing to share their information. Other studies show that citizen needs are often handled by sources for whom the topic area is only a tangential or unrelated concern, and that people who atempt to seek their help face a frustrating maze of obstacles, including the necessity of contacting two, three, or more agencies before finally reaching a responsive source.

The situation, then, is one of inefficiency and lack of communication among various information sources. A great deal more must be discovered concerning: (1) the informational environment within which social welfare and service agencies operate—data which are not easily cataloged; (2) who the information "experts" are, and how they emerge in this environment; (3) how novice information practitioners learn who the expert sources are, and how different sources perceive the nature of needs; and (4) how to arrive at optimal alternatives in given contexts. Answers to these and other questions are essential components of more efficient and effective management and improvement of the information environment within which the average citizen operates.

LINKAGE #5: INFORMATION NEEDS AND
SOLUTIONS TO INFORMATION NEEDS

Understanding the linkage between needs and their solutions involves the questions: (1) What kinds of solutions do different needs have? (2) What problems lack solutions? and (3) What kinds of information are needed for problem solving?

No research was found that dealt directly with the first two questions. Tangential evidence suggests that practitioners hoping to establish information centers will necessarily be faced with two issues. One recognizes that some problems cannot be solved at all, given available resources, while the other makes a distinction between problems that have "information solutions" and those that have "resource solutions."

To provide some clarity in this issue, figure 2 suggests a 3-by-3 matrix within which, if the appropriate evidence were provided, any citizen need could be placed and the dilemmas that information providers face examined. The matrix indicates that a need can be solved by either information or resources, or both. In addition, it suggests that the information-resource environment may be such that either information and/or resources may: (1) not exist; (2) exist but be inaccessible; or (3) be accessible.

		Problem Solution Is Information Based		
Problem Solution Is Resource Based		Information does not exist	Information exists but is inaccessible	Information is accessible
	Resource does not exist			
	Resource exists but is inaccessible			
	Resource is accessible			

Figure 2.   Matrix of Information versus Resource Solutions

Of all the possible problem/solution combinations, one of the more serious is that in which the information does not exist and must be generated. The most serious situation, however, is one in which the resources for solving the ultimate problem do not exist. In such cases, the very concept of "information" may be irrelevant, and an information practitioner's attempt to deal with them simply futile. If, instead, the resources for the solution of some needs are so inequitably distributed that only a few citizens have access to them, the problem becomes less one of information and more one of power and advocacy. If both the existence and availability of information and resources, as perceived by different users, are examined, the points of greatest disorganization or dysfunction within the information system can be located. Little evidence is available that clearly makes this resource-versus information-based distinction. Yet any improvement of the information delivery system depends on the ability to make such distinctions.

Underlying this resource-information distinction is an even more complex issue on which little work has been done—that of the kinds of information needed in everyday problem solving. Increasingly, theorists (Ackoff, 1968; Dervin, 1971; Havelock, 1971; Morris, 1969) are suggesting that information, as an independent concept, must be divided into types and that successful information delivery depends on the ability to deliver not just "information," but the appropriate *types* of information.

For instance, in the discussion of Linkage #2 (between individual citizens and their information sources), evidence was presented suggesting that the electronic media are not useful sources for decision making. With its focus on types of information, Linkage #5 examines the reasons why. One explanation suggested by several researchers (Dervin, 1971; Wade and Schramm, 1969) is that the electronic media incorporate only "ends" information (information about goals) without presenting "means" information (information on how to attain the goals). I have suggested that at least three different types of "means" information are needed to satisfy everyday needs: (1) information about alternative means to achieving an outcome; (2) information about criteria with which to evaluate the means; and (3) data that allow criteria to be applied to means, so that a final decision can be made (1971). In addition, I pointed out at that time that information about information sources is needed in the decision-making process. Such typologies of information types will help practitioners collect and classify the at present elusive data in the social service information delivery field.

LINKAGE #6: INFORMATION SOURCES AND
            SOLUTIONS TO INFORMATION NEEDS

(1) What is the accuracy (correctness) and reliability (consistency across sources) of the information transmitted by sources? (2) What is

the nature of the accountability process in information delivery? and (3) What mechanisms are being used to improve solutions in the system?

The concern at Linkage #6 is for the quality of the answers provided by information sources. While no studies were found that addressed this question directly, inferences from the evidence presented for Linkage #4 suggest that a large degree of inaccuracy and unreliability exists.

At the root, this linkage raises the all-important question of the accountability of information delivery systems. At present, the typical system-effectiveness measure used to evaluate information agencies deals with such gross, institution-oriented concepts as library circulation (Zweizig, 1973). Such measures say little about the satisfaction of needs.

The eventual aim, of course, is to improve the quality of the answers in the system. This improvement will need to be based on a feedback process in which data on successes and failures are constantly sent back into the system. Such monitoring is a highly controversial, though crucial, issue. The rationale behind the establishment of information agencies for the average citizen is that they will reduce the inefficiency in the system (Davies, 1970; Furman et al., 1962; Roe, 1970). The question must constantly be asked: Do they?

Conclusion

The clearest generalization that emerges from this discussion is that huge gaps exist in the knowledge base relating to average citizens and their information needs. The list of unanswered questions is almost overwhelming. Two main conclusions emerge very clearly, however.

The first is that the frequently cited concept of information has received very little systematic attention, from either practitioners or researchers. More research that looks specifically at the nature of information and information needs is required.

Second, to deal effectively with the information needs of citizens will require a more interactive, or system, orientation. Most previous research has implicitly placed the onus of information seeking (and failure to obtain satisfying results) on the citizen, and yet this study suggests that the onus should be placed on the information keepers as well.

Clearly, then, an individual citizen's ability to cope with a given need is no better than the sources and solutions available to him. Thus, practitioners interested in helping the citizen with his needs must strive to identify information not as though it existed as an entity in itself, but as a process, defining its nature in the social context in which it exists.

References

Ackoff, R. K. "Toward a Behavioral Theory of Communication." *Management Science*, 1958, *4*, 218–34.

Alexander, C. *A Pattern Language Which Generates Multi-Service Centers*. Berkeley, Calif.: Center for Environmental Structure, 1968.

Allen, T. J. *Sources of Ideas and Their Effectiveness in Parallel R&D Projects*. Cambridge, Mass.: Massachusetts Institute of Technology, Research Program on the Management of Science and Technology, Report No. 130-65, July 1965.

Ascroft, J. "Modernization and Communication: Controlling Environmental Change." Ph.D. dissertation, Michigan State University, 1969.

Berelson, B. *The Library's Public*. New York: Columbia University, 1949.

Bernard, S. E.; Kurtagh, E.; and Johnson, H. R. "The Neighborhood Service Organization: Specialist in Social Welfare Innovation." *Social Work*, 1968, *13*, 76–84.

Block, E. "Communicating with the Urban Poor: An Exploratory Inquiry." *Journalism Quarterly*, 1970, *47*, 3–11.

Bowes, J. "Information Control Behaviors and the Political Effectiveness of Low-Income Urban Adults." Ph.D. dissertation, Michigan State University, 1971.

Brownson, H. L. "Research on the Handling of Scientific Information." *Science*, 1962, *132*, 1922–30.

Bundy, M. L. "Urban Information in Public Libraries." *Library Journal*, 1972, *97*, 161–69.

Campbell, A., and Metzner, C. A. *Public Use of the Library and Other Sources of Information*. Ann Arbor, Mich.: University of Michigan, 1950.

Cangelosi, E.; Robinson, D. M.; and Schkade, L. L. "Information and Rational Choice." *Journal of Communication*, 1968, *18*, 131–43.

Caplovitz, D. *The Poor Pay More*. New York: The Free Press, 1963.

Cole, S., and Cole, J. "Visibility and the Structural Basis of Awareness of Scientific Research." *American Sociological Review*, 1968, *33*, 397–412.

Davies, J. R. "The Problem of Information Exchange and Complete Information Center Concept." *The Information Scientist*, 1970, *4*, 39–45.

Dervin, B. "Communication Behaviors as Related to Information Control Behaviors of Black Low-Income Adults." Ph.D. dissertation, Michigan State University, 1971.

_____. "Report on Information Needs Survey—Seattle and Syracuse." Mimeographed. Seattle, Wash.: School of Communications, University of Washington, January 1973a.

_____. "A Content Analysis of the 'Problem-Solver' Columns in Two Seattle Dailies." Mimeographed. Seattle, Wash.: School of Communications, University of Washington, November 1973b.

_____. "Everyday Needs and Problems Coding Scheme." Mimeographed. Seattle, Wash.: School of Communications, University of Washington, May 1973c.

_____. "An Analysis of the Information-Resource Needs of Clients of a Chicano Action Agency." Mimeographed. Seattle, Wash.: School of Communications, University of Washington, December 1973d.

_____. "Information Needs of Urban Residents: A Conceptual Context." In *Information Needs of Urban Residents*, edited by Edward S. Warner, Ann D. Murray, and Vernon E. Palmour. Final report from Regional Planning Council of Baltimore and Westat, Inc., of Rockville, Md. to the U.S. Department of Health, Education and Welfare, Office of Education, Division of Library Programs, under Contract No. OEC-O-71-4555 (draft version), chapter 3, April 1973e.

_____, and Greenberg, B. S. "The Communication Environment of the Urban Poor." *Current Perspectives in Mass Communication,* edited by Gerald Kline and Philip Tichenor. Beverly Hills, Calif.: Sage Communication Research Annals, *1,* 1972.

Eisenstadt, S. N. "Communication Systems and Social Structure: An Exploratory Comparative Study." *Public Opinion Quarterly,* 1955, *19,* 153–67.

Etzioni, A. "Toward a Theory of Guided Societal Change." *Social Science Quarterly,* 1969, *50,* 3, 749–54.

Frey, F. "Political Development, Power, and Communications in Turkey." In *Communication and Political Development,* edited by L. W. Pye. Princeton, N.J.: Princeton University Press, 1963.

Furman, S. S.; Connell, S.; and Goldman, J. "The Indirect Values of Information and Referral Services." *Social Work Practice.* New York: Columbia University Press, 1962.

Furman, S. S.; Sweat, L.; and Crocetti, G. Social Class Factors in the Flow of Children to Outpatient Psychiatric Clinics. *American Journal of Public Health,* 1965, *55,* 12–18.

Greenberg, B. S., and Dervin, B. *The Use of the Mass Media by the Urban Poor.* New York: Praeger Press, 1970.

Greenleigh Associates, Inc. *Diagnostic Survey of Tenant Households on West Side Urban Renewal Area of New York City.* New York: Greenleigh Associates, 1965.

Grunig, J. E. "Communication in Community Decisions on Problems of the Poor." *Journal of Communication,* 1972, *22,* 5–10.

Havelock, R. G. *Planning for Innovation: Through Dissemination and Utilization of Knowledge.* Ann Arbor, Mich.: Institute for Social Research, 1971.

Hill, R. "Judgment and Consumership in the Management of Family Resources." *Sociology and Social Research,* 1963, *47,* 446–60.

Hiltz, S. R. "Black and White in the Consumer Financial System." *American Journal of Sociology,* 1971, *76,* 987–98.

Hirschleifer, J. "Private and Social Value of Information and the Reward of Inventive Activity." *American Economic Review,* 1971, *61,* 561–74.

Kahn, A. J., et al. *Neighborhood Information Centers: A Study and Some Proposals.* New York: Columbia University School of Social Work, 1966.

Katz, E. "The Two-Step Flow of Communication: An Up-to-Date Report on an Hypothesis." *Public Opinion Quarterly,* 1957, *21,* 61–78.

Kline, G. F. "Media Time Budgeting as a Function of Demographics and Life Style." *Journalism Quarterly,* 1971, *2,* 211–21.

Kurtz, N. R. "Gatekeepers: Agents in Acculturation." *Rural Sociology,* 1968, *33,* 63–70.

Levin, J., and Taube, G. "Bureaucracy and the Socially Handicapped: A Study of Lower-Class Tenants in Public Housing." *Sociology and Social Research,* 1970, *54,* 209–19.

Levine, F. J., and Preston, E. "Community Resource Orientation Among Low-Income Groups." *Wisconsin Law Review,* 1970, *80,* 80–113.

Levine, S. L.; White, P. E.; and Paul, B. D. "Community Interorganizational Problems in Providing Medical Care and Social Services." *American Journal of Public Health,* 1963, *53,* 1183–95.

Mendelsohn, H. *Operation Gap-Stop: A Study of the Application of Communication Techniques in Researching the Unreachable Poor.* Denver, Colo.: University of Denver Communication Arts Center, February 1968.

Menzel, H. "The Information Needs of Current Scientific Research." *The Library Quarterly,* 1964, *34,* 4–19.

Morris, C. "A Proposed Taxonomy for Communication Research." Mimeographed. East Lansing, Mich.: Department of Communication, Michigan State University, 1969.

National Citizens' Advice Bureaux Committee. *Advising the Citizen.* London: National Council of Social Services, 1961.

Ogg, E. *Tell Me Where to Turn: The Growth of Information and Referral Services.* New York: Public Affairs Committee, 1969.

Parker, E. B., and Paisley, W. J. *Patterns of Adult Information Seeking.* Stanford, Calif.: Stanford University, Institute of Communications Research, 1966.

Pratt, L. "Level of Sociological Knowledge Among Health and Social Workers." *Journal of Health and Social Behavior,* 1969, *10,* 59–65.

Price, J. L. "The Use of New Knowledge in Organizations." *Human Organization,* 1964, *23,* 224–34.

Regional Health and Welfare Council. *5,400 Inquiries and Those Who Made Them.* Kansas City, Mo.: Regional Health and Welfare Council, December 1965.

Rieger, J. H., and Anderson, R. C. "Information Sources and Need Hierarchies of an Adult Population in Five Michigan Counties." *Adult Education Journal,* 1968, *18,* 155–77.

Roe, A. "Communication Resource Centers." *American Psychologist,* 1970, *25,* 1033–40.

Rotter, J. B. "Generalized Expectancies for Internal Versus External Control of Reinforcement." *Psychological Monographs,* Whole No. 609. 1966, *80,* 1.

Scott, R. A. "The Selection of Clients by Social Welfare Agencies: The Case of the Blind." *Social Problems,* 1967, *14,* 248–57.

Seeman, L. "Alienation, Membership, and Political Knowledge." *Public Opinion Quarterly,* 1966, *30,* 353–67.

Sjoberg, G.; Brymer, R. A.; and Farris, B. "Bureaucracy and the Lower Class." *Sociology and Social Research,* 1966, *50,* 325–36.

Spitzer, S. F., and Denzin, N. K. "Levels of Knowledge in an Emergent Crisis." *Social Forces,* 1965–66, *44,* 234–37.

Stark, F. B. "Barriers to Client-Worker Communication at Intake." *Social Casework,* 1959, *40,* 177–83.

Tichenor, P. J. et al. "Mass Media Flow and Differential Growth in Knowledge." *Public Opinion Quarterly,* 1970, *34,* 159–70.

Udell, J. G. "Prepurchase Behavior of Buyers of Small Electrical Appliances." *Journal of Marketing,* 1966, *30,* 50–52.

Voos, H. *Information Needs in Urban Areas: A Summary of Research in Methodology.* New Brunswick, N.J.: Rutgers University Press, 1969.

Wade, S., and Schramm, W. "The Mass Media as Sources of Public Affairs, Science, and Health Knowledge." *Public Opinion Quarterly,* 1969, *33,* 197–209.

Warner, E. S.; Murray, A. D.; and Palmour, V. E. *Information Needs of Urban Residents.* Final report from Regional Planning Council of Baltimore and Westat, Inc., of Rockville, Md., to the U.S. Department of Health, Education, and Welfare, Office of Education, Division of Library Programs, under Contract No. OEC–O–71–455, December 1973.

Westley, B. H., and Severin, W. J. "Some Correlates of Media Credibility." *Journalism Quarterly,* 1964, *41,* 325–35.

Wilson Library Bulletin. *Voice of Experience.* September 1970, 45–53.

Zucker, M. "Citizens' Advice Bureaux: The British Way." *Social Work,* 1965, *10,* 85–91.

Zweizig, D. "Predicting Library Use: An Empirical Study of the Role of the Public Library in the Life of the Adult Public." Ph.D. dissertation, School of Library Science, Syracuse University, 1973.

Chapter 3
Determining Information Needs
of Civic Organizations and
Voluntary Groups

by Jerry S. Kidd

Civic organizations and voluntary groups are those groups, whether permanent or ephemeral, that have overt objectives with respect to the public life of the community. Thus strictly social organizations, such as country clubs, recreational groups, study groups, and so forth, can be excluded from this definition. Groups that use community concerns as a rationalization for social activities (e.g., some "charity" groups), and organizations that start as recreational or vocational associations and migrate into community action under force of circumstance or by accident, present problems of ambiguity with regard to classification. Such ambiguity is easily tolerated, however, on the grounds that conclusions about such organizations will be valid to the degree to which these organizations commit group resources to community concerns.

A minor ambiguity in the analysis concerns the position of commercial organizations. Most such organizations would not be included. However, those that should be included are ones which tend to be pivotal in the degree of influence they exert on the life of the community as a whole. For example, a large industrial concern can obviously influence general conditions of community life by its personnel policies, by its public relations program, and by the way it uses its capital resources. Similarly, banks, mortgage lending institutions, so-called developers and construction firms can have an extensive influence on the overall configuration of a community. Insofar as commercial

Dr. Kidd is Professor, College of Library and Information Service, University of Maryland.

organizations take what might be called a self-conscious stance with regard to community affairs, they are candidates for inclusion in the main set.

A crucial indicator for identifying those candidates for inclusion is the operation of some more or less formal and well-structured planning activity within the organization, directed toward explicit consideration of the organization's interdependence with the community. For example, if a given industrial concern has both a planning department and a community affairs office, and if these units work together, it would represent a clear case for inclusion. Most developers having any but the most modest scope of operation would qualify. The general criterion for inclusion is involvement in the community process in some consistent and coherent manner. In particular, organizations can be classified on the basis of whether organizational actions change the character of community life.

Agencies of community government can be used as archetypal models for determining the inclusion of organizations. The rule would be that the more an organization resembles a department or agency of local government, the more likely that it would be included. The most relevant attributes of community government organizations are their sanctioned and sustained *controls*[1] over conditions of community life. While much of the output of governmental agencies relates to the maintenance functions of the community and is, in a narrow sense, conservative rather than change inducing, the significance of the control aspect can be appreciated when, for example, the consequences of *not* keeping the sewerage system in repair are contemplated. Along with control, other significant features of government agencies are their provisions for rational planning and the relatively explicit nature of the decision-making process. Increasingly, this latter aspect is overt, self-conscious, and open to public view and review.

Thus, civic organizations form the present domain of interest. Local governmental agencies constitute the archetype, but legitimate inclusions could be found in certain forms or parts of commercial and social organizations and groups, such as neighborhood associations, PTA groups, civic betterment committees, and so forth. Perhaps the best example of such an organization is the League of Women Voters (McKay, 1968).

---

1. For example, civic government controls the use of various parcels of land within its jurisdiction by means of zoning regulations and the operation of a zoning board or commission. Zoning decisions have the force of law and can, in the ultimate test, be enforced by police power.

With the broad outlines of the clientele established, similar consideration of organizations that provide information services is needed. Just as governmental agencies are used as archetypal civic organizations, the public library can be employed as the archetypal provider of service. Any alternative forms of information service will be influenced by the precedents provided by the public library, and some new forms of information service might be direct subsidiaries.

A special problem involved in the use of the public library as a model is the historical indifference of public libraries to the aggregate, or organizational, client. The public library is by tradition strongly oriented toward service to the *individual* citizen. A few leaders in the public library field have started to advocate a more structured analysis of the clientele and more services for organizations (Gregory, 1968). Given the declining patronage of some urban public libraries, such a shift could have multiple advantages. The individual client should not be neglected, but a more balanced approach to organizational clients seems possible.

The Objective

An analysis of the information needs of civic organizations has several practical objectives, the most central being the clarification of the bases on which decisions that effect community development are made. Community development includes such things as education and vocational training for citizens; housing, including such programs as urban renewal; commercial and industrial expansion and change; and modifications in municipal services such as transportation, police, sanitation, fire protection, and other systems. Such developments usually involve capital budgeting and are often manifest in the reallocation of land use, and other community capital resources.

Decisions regarding community development issues are usually made under conditions of uncertainty and ambiguity; usually no explicit method of predicting the full range of consequences of any set of decision alternatives is possible. For example, a community may be confronted with the prospect of being host to a major recreational facility, such as a "Disneyland." It *can* be anticipated that such a facility will generate broad changes such as more cash flow, more vehicular traffic, increased demands for solid waste disposal, enlarged police department, etc. However, the magnitude of such changes, and the complete configurational outcome, are not predictable. Even more to the point, the question of whether the community will be, on balance, better or worse off cannot be answered completely.

When the prospect of a commercial recreational facility coming into a community is considered, what stands out most clearly is that some citizens will see advantages for themselves and others will see disadvantages. These individual projections can be quite accurate. If advantages and disadvantages are perceived to be substantial, the community can become polarized, creating a basis for controversy and conflict. In such situations, ambiguity of the net, or configurational, outcome can contribute to the intensity of the disagreement. Fortunately, mechanisms for resolving such controversies are well-developed in today's society. These mechanisms involve the construction of a logical "case" by the contending parties. Once formulated, the cases are reviewed and adjudicated by some body representing the community at large.

While outcomes may be beyond full specification, the cases as presented involve expressions of both value *and* fact. Indeed, the critical arguments are likely to be dependent upon assertions of fact. The factual content of the case must be assembled. The raw materials are information items. In the example used here, information about the experiences of other communities that have allowed the establishment of large-scale recreational facilities would be vital to all contending parties. How is such information to be garnered?

Problems of availability, intelligibility, and cost are involved in information acquisition. If one set of parties to the deliberations has the means for surmounting these problems, while another set of interested participants does not, a substantial subversion of the accepted mechanisms of community development exists. If community information resources are improved, however, the subversion can be eliminated, or at least ameliorated.

The question of the ways and means of improvement now comes to the fore. It is contended here that determinations of ways and means are best made from an appreciation of the nature of the information service needs, and the requirements of the full range of groups engaged in community development issues.

The Approach

Precedents for an analysis of the information needs of organizations in the community come from the basic social sciences (e.g., Katz and Lazarsfeld, 1955; Allen and Cohen, 1969; and Deutsch, 1963) and from market research (Engel et al., 1968; Kuehl, 1972). Grunig's work (1972) on information support for collective economic decisions provides a bridge between the two areas.

These lines of study all involve some form of observations in the field which can be used to form the basis for change. Such analyses can launch new procedures for providing public services and, indeed, for restructuring entire systems of public service (Churchman, 1968).

The approach is called "functionalism," and its application is called "system engineering." It is possible that the concepts and methods of functionalism, as represented by system engineering, might be brought to bear on the problem of information service development with good effect.

Methodological Issues

The traditional method of studying information needs has been unobtrusive observation of information-seeking behavior or self-descriptions by patrons of their behavior in the library or at the terminus of a document delivery sequence. There are obvious advantages to these modes of inquiry, and they can produce valuable findings. Inferences can be made about preferences for alternative media, channels, and conditions of the information exchange process. Determinations can be made with respect to satisfaction with alternative modes of service. The subject can reveal to the researcher by his or her overt behavior something of the subject's solution strategies. Such findings can be used to make resource-allocation and service-priority decisions in the administration of the information service operations.

However, there are limits to such techniques, The population of individuals from which the cases are drawn for study is limited to those who *are* patrons of a particular facility or service channel. Moreover, the more intensive the transaction rate of a given patron, the more likely he or she is to be chosen. The researcher is constrained to observe a captive audience which is self-selecting. One obvious bias is toward a general positive response on the part of the subject toward the facility, system, or service in question.

In a similar sense, the patron is a captive of the particular facility. He or she can respond only to what is available at the time of the transaction. This condition generates a bias in favor of the status quo, or toward marginal adjustments at best. It ignores the nonuser or potential user of the facility or service; it tends to omit the prospect of substantial, or even radical, innovations in the mode, channel, or conditions of information exchange.

The alternative to studying the behavior of patrons in an information delivery transaction is to seek out patrons and potential patrons in their own operational environments. Here again, the sampling procedure is constrained, but only by the conceptual boundaries of the target audience (and the usual statistical conventions) .

The problem-solving behavior of the subject is the focus in this alternative method of study. Here the elements of problem generation, as well as the cognitive and behavioral responses employed by the subject to cope with the problem, are considered. Mechanisms of instigation (e.g., a person's "boss" gives an order) and goals and achievement criteria of the subject (i.e., how the subject defines "success" in his or her enterprise) are examined.

The most common technique for implementing this alternative approach to the study of user needs is by questionnaire. The classic instance of the use of questionnaires was by the American Psychological Association (APA, 1963 and 1965), a program which has since been followed up by the principals working separately on other target audiences in the science and science-related professions (Garvey and Griffith, 1972). The use of questionnaire techniques within this general method has the advantage of providing extensive coverage and relatively large sample sizes at relatively low cost. However, the questionnaire technique has limitations in applications involving audiences or organizational settings that are not thoroughly understood beforehand by the researchers. The most appropriate variation on the questionnaire technique for overcoming such limitations is the interview technique, a procedure that has many variations (Kidd, 1968).

Perhaps the most elaborate application of the interview technique occurred in the Hamline Library Project (Johnson, King, and Mavor, 1970), wherein faculty members in a small, liberal arts college were interviewed periodically for a total of three to six hours. The specific variant was called "user task analysis" by the researchers. The idea was to have respondents characterize their operational aspirations and day-to-day activities at such a level of detail that very precise prescriptions for information service inputs could be formulated. This idea worked well in the general sense that a very substantial increase occurred in the perceived value of information services and in the particular sense that perceived relevance of the information products increased. The catch, of course, is the higher cost of this procedure in its opening stages. However, once momentum is achieved, the need-sensing function can be fulfilled in less costly ways by direct participation on the part of service providers in the client's day-to-day operations.

An intermediate stage of this general approach is exemplified by a project in the Baltimore metropolitan area (Warner, 1973), the objective of which was to find or develop new or improved services on the part of the public libraries in the region—based on explicit data covering citizen needs and priorities. Semistructured interviews lasting about one hour each have been conducted with approximately 1,000 householders. A key ingredient in the interview protocol was that the word "library" was not mentioned by the interviewer. The idea was to elicit a picture of information transfer covering all topic-by-channel combinations without bias toward the more formal channels.

An earlier study (Kidd, 1969) in the Baltimore-Washington corridor area used a similar technique but is even more relevant to this discussion, since respondents were chosen on the basis of their organizational affiliation. In particular, planning officials were a major component in the study sample.

A major proposition which can be derived from these precedents is that the final prescriptive stage of information-need assessment is best supported by study techniques that reach out into the operational environment of the user. The more sophisticated version of these techniques, involving detailed task analyses, might be too costly for large-sample studies, but the less expensive variants are both feasible and productive for use in determining information needs tied to organizational affiliations.

The Urban Social System

As indicated previously, the main focus of this analysis is an arbitrarily defined set of prospective clients, composed of members of 'civic organizations in their roles as organizational participants. A major implication that arises from this specification is that the functional domain of such organizations is political, in the sense of affiliations based on common values. This implication, in turn, suggests that the main thrust of the analysis is focused on how organizations realize *their* values among competing values. In other words, attention is focused on persuasion and negotiation behaviors. These behaviors involve a process which can be called "case building," in which arguments are constructed and used in behalf of the organization. The mechanisms can include case presentation via the mass media, pamphleteering, and quasi-educational proceedings, such as seminars and briefings, hearings before commissions or legislative bodies, and so on into formal juridical operations where the official advocates are attorneys. The extreme instance is represented by a civil proceeding before the Supreme Court. However, when the courtroom as the scene of action is removed, a grey area is entered, in which substantive expertise is a critical ingredient. Even in the most formal juridical proceedings, expert witnesses may be called to testify. In such proceedings as legislative committee hearings, the subject matter expert may predominate. If the issue is a matter for public debate, the journalist can be a dominant figure. Finally, in many instances of civic action, it is the articulate but otherwise unspecialized layman who must carry the argument. The opposite end of the continuum from a Supreme Court hearing might feature a confrontation between two opposing factions in a neighborhood PTA meeting. In such a situation, although there might not be an attorney within miles of the scene, the conditions of competition between alternative values and actions are present. The point is that while case building and case presentation are functions which the legal profession has as its special prerogatives, all citizens engage in these functions to some extent. A collateral point is that such functions can be more or less successfully carried out, depending on the information resources of the participants.

The phenomena can be illustrated by examining a specific area of social discourse; for example, the problem of public housing in metropolitan areas (Goodall, 1968). The history of public housing, for purposes of this discussion, begins with the deliberations of the United States Congress in the 1930s which culminated in the Housing Act of 1937. This statute provided for federal loans and subsidies to local agencies to acquire and clear land and to construct and manage public housing units. It is critical to note that these local agencies were not and could not be integral units of local government. This arrangement was imposed because of problems related to statutory debt limitations of local governments, and was welcomed as a means for keeping public housing "out of politics." While the arrangement did buffer the line of control between elected officials and crucial economic decisions, the removal of public housing operations from the domain of politics (in the larger sense of that term) was not possible because divergent values *were* involved. In the early stages of public housing, the alignment of opposing organizations put the contractors, developers, bankers, and realtors on one side as representatives of the private housing market, and welfare professionals, politicians with low-income constituences, and parts of the liberal establishment on the other. The issue was mainly defined by one side in terms of unfair competition by subsidized housing against private housing interests, and by the other in terms of negative consequences of substandard housing for the entire community, with slums placed in the role of breeding sites for delinquency, broken families, etc.

Two factors are particularly noteworthy in this situation. First, the people most affected by the outcome were not direct participants in the controversy. The slum dwellers were but feebly represented by elected officials. Second, neither side's argument turned out to be valid. Public housing at peak production was never a significant factor in the housing market, and neither has it been a significant influence on the behavior patterns of the urban poor. The net effect has been, perhaps, marginally beneficial in the matters of fire hazards, sanitation, and general structural factors. Even in the area of aesthetics it could be argued that the barracks-like appearance of most public housing is no great improvement over a slum, which at least has some variety of architectural form.

It is pertinent to speculate about what might have emerged if the slum dwellers themselves had been organized, and if all parties to the public housing controversy had had effective access to relevant and valid information.

Aspects of Structural Analysis

The structural aspects of community organizations must be considered along with the processes of decision making and conflict resolution. The structures of community organizations are even more complex than the processes, and abstractions in these matters can easily constitute oversimplification. Nevertheless, an attempt must be made to look at structure.

Several framing dimensions can be suggested. A first consideration is the composition of the group. How large is the group? What are the common attributes of membership? What are the criteria for eligibility? Under what circumstances do individuals leave the group by either voluntary or coercive routes? If the organization is large with rather simple or indifferent membership qualifications (i.e., a political party organization in a local jurisdiction), it can be predicted that internal governance will be in the hands of a core component. The core unit will operate on the basis of endorsement mechanisms that are often implicit, rather than explicit.

A second major factor is the durability of the group, as reflected in its life history and life expectancy. In other words, some civic organizations are created as intentionally permanent entities. The expectation is that the group will survive its individual members. Organizations such as local Chambers of Commerce are examples of this type. At the other extreme are what might be called ad hoc organizations. They are avowedly transient, usually the product of jointly perceived crises. Their raison d'être is the crisis itself, and when the crisis terminates, the group dissolves.

There are several variations along the continuum of durability. For example, there is what might be called the "sleeper" organization. Typically, this is a neighborhood association that is nominally permanent, but which functions in a highly superficial mode most of the time. It is often an organization in name only. However, the membership is highly accessible to mobilization in a crisis (i.e., members share a locale). Structural features, such as role assignments, are present so that the group can begin to function quickly as a real organization when a significant instigation appears.

Another variant is illustrated by the long-range consequences of voter registration drives among the economically disadvantaged. Prior to such drives, little if any semblance of civic organization existed among the target participants. Once organized to vote, however, many groups tend to persevere. The main factor appears to be the emergence of an indigenous leadership. When a local leader is invested and recognized, he or she provides a point of cohesion—it is not difficult to provide for continuation of the group beyond the voter registration deadline. Thus purportedly ad hoc organizations can occasionally become permanent, while a purportedly permanent group may really function in an ad hoc mode.

A third factor is the position of the organization relative to the sources of real power in the community. While a long discourse on power, or the absence of power, with respect to community organizations would be out of place here, the reader may find it useful to refer to the contributions of Banfield (1970), Downes (1961), Coleman (1957), Gamson (1966), and Pettigrew (1972). A paraphrase, "Knowledge is . . . contributory to . . . power" repeats the main theme of this analysis.

Need Specification

Throughout the array of community organizations there has been a major trend toward rationalizing the case-building process. Either explicitly or implicitly, there has been a growing tendency to employ at least an approximation of scientific or scholarly research methods in preparation for deliberations or confrontations. This is not to suggest the dawning of any utopian era; research is no panacea, and some value issues simply do not yield to scientific inquiry—but the trend provides openings for innovation.

This trend is most pronounced in the more formal organizational units. Symptomatically, governmental planning agencies have become increasingly "professionalized," partly as a consequence of subsidy and the strings attached to such subsidy from the federal level. The staff complement of official planning bodies is now much more likely to include economists, civil engineers, and others trained in some aspect of research.

In the less formal organizations the intensity with which research techniques are applied declines, but it is reassuring to find organizations such as the League of Women Voters, for example, undertaking empirical studies of population growth in order to influence the selection of sites for new school buildings (Biddle and Biddle, 1965).

In all, there is a strong suggestion of a research-oriented component emerging in many organizations, even the more informal and transient ones (Rogers, 1961). For example, an ad hoc neighborhood organization in Baltimore, Maryland, recently successfully delayed the incursion of a superhighway through the neighborhood by adopting some of the research resources and findings of the highway engineers who had planned the route. In such instances, the research component is likely to be strongly connected to the leadership of the organization, so that even in relatively diffuse structures, the research function has coherence.

Given the emergence of research-like activities in civic organizations and the centrality of these activities, a very close approximation of the conditions specified by Lazarsfeld in the two-step model of information diffusion is provided (Katz and Lazarsfeld, 1955). Even more precise specification by Allen (Allen and Cohen, 1969) of what he calls the "gate-keeper" process can sometimes be met.[2] In other words, the presence of a very explicit *channel* between information service providers and ultimate recipients can be perceived. An example of this is provided by the Community Resource Information Center described in chapter 13. Instead of the organization presenting a boundary as a barrier to transaction, it now begins to present a particular pathway for communication. Furthermore, the pathway is likely to be not just open, but beckoning. That is, it is more likely that there is an active, seeking aspect to the pathway than the indifferent acceptance or lack of attention that might characterize a channel based predominantly on the formal leadership component or the membership-at-large of the organization.

The full specification of the needs of a particular client involves a description of the optimum content, mode, language, and format of the messages to be transmitted, as well as the optimum channel. With many types of target audiences, such descriptions would require detailed empirical inquiry along some of the more expensive lines previously suggested under methodological considerations. However, the civic organization as a target audience permits an inferential process to become a partial substitute for the empirical, and this option offers a substantial economic advantage to service-providing facilities.

In this regard, organizations, particularly voluntary civic organizations, must literally broadcast critical descriptive characteristics. Individuals would have neither the inclination nor the means to transmit such data to service providers. In the individual case, then, if the service provider wants data, a specific study must be mounted; but in the organizational case the service provider can draw similar conclusions from less costly procedures. In a sense, a "study" must also be mounted to assess needs for organizational clients, but the study can be less expensive. The procedures for such study are simple enough that the most modestly endowed service facility can proceed

2. A "gate-keeper" in this usage is an intermediary or linking agent in the information transfer process.

with one. The scope can be controlled as well: for instance, it would be useful to begin with only a single target organization if resources were quite limited. The procedure would include the following steps:

1. Selection of the subset of target organizations (selection criteria could include accessibility, impact, social value considerations, etc.) ;
2. Review of the organization's self-descriptive materials;
3. Identification and direct contact with the organizations' "linker" personnel (e.g., operatives in the research component) ;
4. Assessment of the organizational demands and capabilities with regard to mode, language, and format of information products;
5. Establishment of a project-content monitoring mechanism (see discussion below) ; and
6. Specification of content to be provided.

Probably the most critical step in the sequence is project monitoring. Many civic organizations operate in a form of crisis mode. Urgency may be a critical factor in many information service transactions with civic organizations. On the other hand, crash mode responses may not be compatible with the economic operation of the service. Efficient and lasting arrangements can depend on some form of advance notice between the target organization and the service facility. Such a time buffer can best be instituted by the service provider by a form of program or project monitoring. (An assumption can be made in this regard about the mode of operation of many organizations: that is, that the organizational activity often occurs in "blocks" that can be designated as organizational projects.) The idea is that if such projects can be recognized by service providers while the projects are in their formative stages, specific information content needs can be anticipated and service actions can be undertaken in a timely way. Service continuity can likewise be enhanced by periodic monitoring of the progress of the project.

This monitoring is made feasible by two attributes of civic organizations. First, their own charters will tend to specify, at least in broad terms, a content domain. For example, a citizen's housing association will clearly portray a small set of what might be called thematic orientations: rehabilitation, rent control, building code enforcement, etc. Second, there are usually definite signals that precede critical events for which informational services would be required. For example, the initiation of a new project will involve recruitment of members to form a project team or task force. The recruitment message will almost inevitably contain clear data on the topical thrust of the project. If the information provider can detect such messages, the classic mechanisms of search, retrieval, selection, and packaging for dissemination can be put in progress almost before the target organization realizes it has an information problem.

The specific configuration of the monitoring mechanism will depend upon the details of particular situations, but it could be as simple as a periodic phone call from the information provider to the linker, or vice versa.

Conclusions

Since the early 1950s there has been a concerted, but often unofficial, effort to rationalize the processes of community governance. This effort is evident in provisions of the Demonstration Cities and Metropolitan Development Act of 1966, and in the Intergovernmental Cooperation Act of 1968, both of which supported the creation of regional Councils of Government with direct subsidization of professional planning staffs. Support was also provided directly and indirectly to the professionalization of planning at state and local/municipal levels.

In local affairs it is possible for the techniques of research to be adapted and made usable by a broader constituency (Abramson, 1969; Edelston and Kolodner, 1968). There is no fundamental barrier between citizen participation and the use of research methods and findings in developing programs and policies at the local level. It is not inconceivable to have something like participatory rationalism in civic governance. But it is clear that for a community to do so, its local information services must be of high quality and must be superbly efficient in delivering relevant information to the right person at the right time.

The spread of rationalistic problem solving from national to local governance is related to the development of research aims in a wide variety of civic organizations. This development is now taking place at the level of neighborhood associations. That is, it has spread from formal government to governance, which includes all forms of political operations (Rogers, 1961).

The appropriate operational scenario for relating civic organizations to information service facilities appears to derive from the conceptual frame of need arousal exchange via contact agent, and case assembly. The problematic aspects of the scenario lie predominantly with the mechanisms of service provision. In contrast, those parts of the process which are within the purview of the recipient organizations are either spontaneous (i.e., the emergence of gate-keepers or linkers) or are developing under their own dynamics (e.g., self-conscious attempts at rationalistic persuasion). These organizational processes will occur with or without the explicit contributions of public information agencies. They can only be made more effective, less awkward, and less costly if the information agencies do their job well. The major step in doing the job well is simply to recognize that it exists, and that it is feasible to do.

The information provider can just as easily be deterred from rendering service by the complexity of the community organizations as the public librarian might sometimes be put off by the apparently inchoate form of service demands by individual clients. Actually, the job is easier with organizations because they are fewer in number— but it is still difficult.

In this regard, there are, of course, certain costs associated with the achievement of an orderly procedure. The saving condition is that the situation to be faced is not an all-or-nothing situation. A cost-graded strategy *can* be formulated.

The first step in such a strategy is the creation of an organizational file, analogous to the preparation of a list of prospective customers. Many public libraries possess lists of local civic organizations, but the criticality of such a file, and the allocation of effort to keep it current, have not often been recognized. Moreover, the inclusion of a file entry which identifies the key liaison person in the target organization is rarely provided.

The second step is maintenance of contact, which includes some marketing in the sense of advertising specific services and capabilities (Berenson, 1969).

The third step is the actual inquiry into needs. This can become very costly indeed if it is done by observation or by depth interviews, where the end product is a task-analytical prescription for information delivery. This level of approach must probably be limited to a few demonstration projects. What appears to be most economical at the present time is some kind of organizational penetration on the part of the providers of information services. The simplest form of penetration would be for the provider organization to send a staff member to attend open meetings of at least some sample set of the target organizations. Barring this as still too expensive, the fall-back position would be to negotiate with the liaison or linker personnel, so that transcations between the information provider organization and that person could become a two-way exchange. In other words, the provider facility would keep the linker up-to-date on services, and the linker in return would keep the provider organization informed about changes in program and activities of the target organization. Such a relationship could, and probably should, become explicit.

In brief, there are good prospects for both parties to the transaction if community information service providers, such as public libraries, would become more oriented toward organizational clients. Most of the requisite conditions for fruitful transactions exist because of the natural trends toward rationalistic procedures on the part of all forms of civic organizations and the highly probable presence of linkers in such organizations. The ingredient which must be added is a higher level of mutual awareness. The contribution of this ingredient is the responsibility of the service provider.

References

Abramson, J. *A Neighborhood Finds Itself*. New York: Harper, 1959.

Allen, T. J., and Cohen, S. I. "Information-Flow in Two R and D Laboratories." *Administrative Science Quarterly*, 1969, *13*, 71–83.

American Psychological Association. *Reports of the American Psychological Association's Project on Scientific Information Exchange in Psychology*. Washington, D.C.: APA, 1963 and 1965.

Banfield, E. C. *The Unheavenly City: The Nature and Future of Our Urban Crisis*. Boston: Little-Brown, 1970.

Berenson, C. "Marketing Information Systems." *Journal of Marketing*, 1969, *33*, 16–23.

Biddle, W. W., and Biddle, L. J. *The Community Development Process*. New York: Holt, Rinehart and Winston, 1965.

Churchman, C. W. *The Systems Approach*. New York: Dell, 1968.

Coleman, J. C. *Community Conflict*. Glencoe, Ill.: The Free Press, 1957.

Deutsch, K. W. *Nerves of Government*. New York: The Free Press, 1963.

Downes, B. T. "Issue Conflict, Factionalism, and Consensus in Surburban City Councils." *Urban Affairs Quarterly*, 1961, *4*, 477–97.

Edelston, H. C., and Kolodner, F. K. "Are the Poor Capable of Planning for Themselves?" In *Citizen Participation in Urban Development*, edited by H. B. Spiegel. Washington, D.C.: NTL Institute for Applied Behavioral Science, 1968, pp. 225–40.

Engel, J. F., et al. *Consumer Behavior*. New York: Holt, Rinehart and Winston, 1968.

Gamson, W. "Rancorous Conflict in Community Politics." *American Sociological Review*, 1966, *31*, 71–81.

Garvey, W. D., and Griffith, B. C. "Communication and Information Processes Within Scientific Disciplines: Empirical Findings for Psychology." *Information Storage and Retrieval*, 1972, *8*, 123-36.

Goodall, L. E. *The American Metropolis*. Columbus, Ohio: Charles Merrill, 1968.

Gregory, R. "The Search for Information about Community Needs." *Library Trends*, 1968, *17*, 14–21.

Grunig, J. E. "Communication in Community Decisions on Problems of the Poor." *Journal of Communications*, 1972, *22*, 5–25.

Johnson, H. G.; King, J. B.; and Mavor, A. S. *A Feasibility Study for the Establishment of an Information Switching Center at Hamline University*. St. Paul, Minn.: Hamline University, (PB192944–NTIS), 1970.

Katz, E., and Lazarsfeld, P. *Personal Influence*. New York: The Free Press, 1955.

Kidd, J. S. *Interview Methods for Determining User Needs*. Invited Paper, American Society for Information Science Annual Meeting, Columbus, Ohio, 1968.

_____. *Plan for a Query-Controlled, Integrated Data and Document Retrieval System for Urban Studies*. Invited Paper, American Society for Information Science Annual Meeting, San Francisco, 1969.

Background

Kuehl, P. G. "Marketing Perspectives for 'ERIC-Like' Information Systems." *Journal of the American Society for Information Science*, 1972, *23*, 359–64.

McKay, O. "Community Involvement in the Solution of Urban Problems." *Adult Leadership*, 1968, *17*, 6–13.

Pettigrew, A. M. "Information Control as a Power Resource," *Sociology*, 1972, *6*, 187–204.

Rogers, W. C. "Voluntary Associations and Urban Community Development." *International Review of Community Development*, 1961, *7*, 135–45.

Warner, E. Personal communication, 1973.

Chapter 4
Information and Referral Services: A Short History and Some Recommendations

by Nicholas Long

During the past fifteen years, a new kind of social service has blossomed on the American scene, one known by a variety of names, the most popular of which is "information and referral." I&R services are symptomatic of the complexity of present service modes, and reflect a relatively conventional response to the problems created by such complexity. This chapter is intended to clarify the concept of I&R services, and to suggest the potentials and limitations of these services in the context of other human services, as they are currently delivered.

It is important to distinguish between the activities carried out under the title of information and referral and the settings or manner in which such activities are discharged. Settings and functions are, in fact, often confused, leading to discussions of whether I&R services should be part of a multiservice center or a freestanding center, or whether they should be centrally located or delivered through neighborhood centers. Such discussions are generally based on data concerning the location of present I&R services, rather than on data concerning the service itself.

The research and preparation of this chapter were undertaken at InterStudy under a grant from the Administration on Aging, U.S. Department of Health, Education, and Welfare (Grant No. 93–P–75051/5). Earlier versions of the historical analysis have appeared in C. L. Kronus and L. Crowe, eds., *Libraries and Neighborhood Information Centers* (Urbana, Ill.: University of Illinois, 1972), pp. 1–14. A revision appears in the *Social Service Review*, 1973, *47*, (1), 49-62. "Coordination of Service Agencies" appeared as "A Model for Coordinating Human Services" in the Spring 1974 issue of *Administration in Mental Health*, a publication of the National Institute of Mental Health, U.S. Department of Health, Education, and Welfare.

Dr. Long is in the private practice of clinical psychology in Minneapolis, Minn.

Background

Historical Analysis

Agencies that refer to themselves as I&R centers often: (1) develop and update files about community resources in the area of human services; (2) provide telephone information about resources and formal referrals to service agencies; (3) perform follow-up functions with clients and agencies to determine if the service was obtained, and provide case advocacy if the service was not obtained and the client still desires it; (4) provide counseling or casework services, escort services, and out-reach or case-finding services; (5) participate in community education; (6) prepare statistical reports on service requests for other agencies and undertake research on community needs to help planners; (7) engage in advocacy for the development of new service programs; and (8) operate holiday or Christmas clearinghouses and volunteer bureaus.[1]

Although this listing is probably incomplete, it does give an overview of the activities that are undertaken in many I&R centers. As some of these activities are also undertaken by other agencies, however, it is difficult to identify what is uniquely an I&R activity. An examination of the background and auspices of agencies providing such services may help clarify this problem.

ORIGINS OF INFORMATION AND REFERRAL CENTERS

Information and referral services have been developed by both voluntary and public agencies.

Private sector. The antecedent of present-day I&R centers is the social service exchange, which had its origins in the charity organization movement of the 1870s. For a variety of reasons, the social service exchange has virtually disappeared from the social service scene. Although recently its purpose, in theory, has been to facilitate communication among agencies in order to enhance service coordination, the original intention was to prevent duplication of relief. Thus, this pioneering source of information and referral was organized to prevent, rather than to facilitate, access to human services (Williams, 1964).

In 1972 the United Way of America listed some sixty I&R centers in operation under its auspices in the United States and Canada. The history of many of these centers can be traced directly back to social

---

1. For further discussion, see Long et al. (1971).

service exchanges. Initially, these centers restricted the contents of their files to social welfare resources, but with the development of the Public Health Service Chronic Disease Program in the early 1960s, many of them began to expand their resource information to include the fields of health and aging as well (Lester, 1969).

In 1966 the National Easter Seal Society adopted the delivery of information, referral, and follow-up services as its basic program for all Easter Seal Society affiliates (Long et al., 1971). Since that time, approximately 10 percent of its affiliates have taken steps toward developing such programs.

In addition to these programs, which are identified with a central coordinating body, there are numerous local I&R centers sponsored by special interest groups, such as labor unions, churches, and societies dealing with mental retardation, mental illness, and alcoholism. Also, numerous "Action Line" programs are sponsored through newspapers and radio and television stations. One of the best organized of these is "Call for Action," sponsored by the Urban Coalition (Daniel, 1969).

Public sector. After World War II, the Retraining and Rehabilitation Administration of the Department of Labor sponsored the development of community advisory centers, popularly known as Veterans Information Centers, which were modeled after the British Citizens' Advice Bureaus. There were over 3,000 centers in operation immediately after World War II, but most had closed by 1949 (Kahn et al., 1966; U.S. Department of Labor, 1944, 1946).

The next push from the public sector came from the Public Health Service, particularly through funds authorized by the Community Health Services and Facilities Act of 1961, which provided for "grants to state agencies and to other public or nonprofit agencies or organizations for studies, experiments, and demonstrations looking toward the development of new or improved methods of providing health services outside the hospital, particularly for chronically ill and aged persons" (U.S. Department of Health, Education, and Welfare, Public Health Service, 1967). Twenty-eight grants were given under the broad area of activity called information and referral during the six-year period 1962–67.

The Social Security Administration, through its various offices, has maintained an interest in the provision of I&R services and, from time to time, has conducted studies to determine the extent and quality of such services in selected offices (Haber, Schmulowitz, and Cormier, 1971; Larson, 1961; Townsend, 1957). However, the Social Security Administration has not been an advocate of the extensive provision of such services because of its heavy work loads. In 1972 this position was reexamined in light of the Nixon administration's interest in providing I&R through social security offices (Nixon, 1971).

The Administration on Aging of the U.S. Department of Health, Education, and Welfare is a more recent sponsor from the public sector. Several projects with an I&R component have been funded under Title III of the Older Americans Act of 1965. Other projects, with a greater emphasis on research, have been funded under Title IV of that act. The Administration on Aging has stimulated careful investigation and definition of such services under its Title IV projects in order to better define the scope and limitations of such services as they may apply to older Americans. Title III of the 1973 Admendments to the Older Americans Act requires the states to "provide for establishing or maintaining information and referral sources . . . to assure that all older persons in the State . . . have reasonably convenient access to such sources."

In addition, a number of other federal agencies have had an interest in I&R services. These include the Community Services Administration of the U.S. Department of Health, Education and Welfare, the Office of Economic Opportunity, the General Accounting Office, which sponsors over twenty-five federal information centers around the country, and the Department of Housing and Urban Development.

Given the multiplicity of activities of I&R centers, the checkerboard auspices of agencies engaging in such services, and the overlap of these activities with those conducted by other agencies which do not designate themselves as I&R centers, it is not difficult to understand why confusion may exist as to just what I&R services and centers actually are. The primary theme appearing in the activities of most such centers involves access to the service system, as Kahn (1969) defines it. From the perspective of settings or auspices, the centers seem to be associated primarily with the disabled, the chronically ill, the aged, and the facilities that serve them.

A recognition that these are not the only categories of individuals who need help in gaining access to human services is now receiving attention. There is also an understanding that such "access" is not a simple service to provide. In the remainder of this chapter, therefore, a program for I&R services will be described, and the strengths and limitations of that program examined in relation to other human services.

An Information and Referral Program

OBJECTIVES

The preceding description permits an overview of the current situation and provides a limited understanding of how that situation came about. What is missing, of course, is a clear statement of program objectives.[2] An examination of the literature on I&R (Bolch, Long, and Dewey, 1972) reveals no conceptualization or definition of such services in terms of program objectives. The program for services outlined in this section has two primary purposes: (1) to increase the accessibility of human services and (2) to maximize the utility of I&R center data for the planning of human services.[3] The program is designed to be compatible with existing practice within the constraints of accomplishing the two primary objectives.

In brief, the program envisages the I&R center as the provider of one or more discrete modules of functions designed to facilitate access to human services. These modules include resource file development and maintenance, information, referral, systematic follow-up, escort, and outreach. The basic service of telephone-oriented information and referral is the core to which each of the other modules may be added. It is suggested that each of these additional service modules will help in a unique way to improve an eligible individual's access to the service(s) he needs. In addition to these discrete modules of service functions, the program requires that all centers participating in it be coordinated through the use of identical procedures with regard to information stored in the resource file and information gathered on center users.

Because the words "information and referral" have come to have a variety of meanings, the following definitions are offered to circumscribe this discussion:

Resource file. The resource file is an organized, cross-indexed file of all services and programs in the area covered by the center (Long, Reiner, and Zimmerman, 1973). This file is updated and modified on a continuing basis. The initial development of such a file usually requires from three to six months, depending on the number of resources and the personnel available in the area. Failure to allow sufficient time for resource file development has been a common error in new centers (Hampton Roads Health Information-Referral Planning Center, 1968; Health and Welfare Council of Metropolitan Saint Louis, 1967; Sigler, 1964).

Information-giving. Information-giving consists primarily of providing information about services and programs. It should include

2. A more detailed explication of these objectives is contained in the publication *Information and Referral Services: Evaluation Design for a Network Demonstration* by Long and Yonce (1974). See also Long (1972).

3. The approach taken here follows that of such students of program evaluation as Suchman (1967) and Wholey et al. (1970). The author also acknowledges indebtedness to the following colleagues at the Institute for Interdisciplinary Studies for their contributions in the formalization of the program objectives that appear in this section: Eleanor Bolch, Steven Reiner, Diane Tessari, and Leslie Yonce.

some effort to obtain background materials about the inquirer to determine his potential eligibility for a specific agency. However, this should be only a crude screening procedure; actual eligibility determination should be left to the service agency (Tessari et al., 1974).

Referral. Although referral may be thought of as including concepts such as "direction" or "steering" to agencies, the term is limited here to the process of actually making an appointment for an inquirer with a person in the service agency. Obviously, not all inquirers will need this level of referral (Tessari et al., 1974).

Follow-up. For purposes of definition, complete follow-up is restricted to those calls for which a referral is made. Follow-up requires contact with both the inquirer and the agency to which he was referred, in order to determine whether he got to the agency, whether the referral was appropriate, and whether the inquirer received the service requested. Partial follow-up with inquirers alone might be carried out for those individuals who were given only direction or steering, not formal referral. The decision to provide partial follow-up would be left to the judgment of the local center specialist (Institute for Interdisciplinary Studies, 1971a).

Escort. Escort services consist of two components: (1) the provision of transportation for initial interviews with other agencies and (2) the provision of a temporary companion to help the inquirer complete forms and answer questions at the service agency in the initial stages of contact. This service may be entirely operated by volunteers, or it may be paid for through the center's budget (Institute for Interdisciplinary Studies, 1971b).

Outreach. Outreach consists of a case-finding activity in which an active effort is made by the center to reach out to the community to stimulate the use of existing programs and services by persons not using them (Cushing and Long, 1973). There have been only a few experiments with outreach through I&R centers (National Council on the Aging, 1970; Orris, 1970; Putter and Malzberg, 1969; REAL Service, 1969). Nevertheless, findings from these experimental programs suggest that outreach is a very valuable and potent activity for facilitating access to services.

If the potential contribution of I&R centers to the planning process is to be fully realized, a carefully designed research activity must be built into the center's program (Bellamy, 1968; Hampton Roads Health Information-Referral Planning Center, 1968). The outreach module also serves as a mechanism through which to implement survey research for the purposes of planning. Many centers indicate that they see identification of service gaps and areas of unmet need as one of their functions (Bloksberg and Caso, 1967). However, careful analysis suggests that such work is poorly conceived and carried out by most centers. The data collected are often from biased samples and rarely representative of the needs of the community at large.

Many of the activities necessary for an outreach program are also key components of survey-research methodology (e.g., the use of census-tract data to determine the areas to be canvassed; door-to-door canvassing procedures; the use of interview skills). An outreach service could accomplish objectives of both direct service and survey research without compromising either.

This design for I&R services circumscribes a set of activities that are related to each other and lead toward the common goal of facilitating access to human services. Until further research and evaluation is undertaken, the utility of this particular program with regard to the service-access goal cannot be asserted. However, the program provides a basis for research, and should permit the addition or subtraction of component activities as they are found to enhance or detract from this goal. Data are presented in the final report of the Information and Referral Center Study that bring into question the provision by an I&R center of some of these service components (Long, 1975).

The program is designed to work within the existing structure of human services. It poses no threat to the way in which such services are now delivered, and thus should meet little resistance upon introduction into the human services spectrum. However, it is also designed to be flexible and readily amenable to change.

A major limitation to this program is that it formalizes I&R services as another specialized human service, and thus contributes to fragmentation of the service system. An obvious illustration of this weakness is found in the medical field. Specialization has become the major mode of responding to health problems, so much so that general practice has been renamed "family practice" and added to the list of other "specialities."

Given the complexity of the tasks involved in facilitating access to other human services, it is difficult to imagine that I&R will escape gradual development into a very specialized human service. The program previously described is not intended to bring about change in the delivery of human services in any direct manner. It is unrealistic to expect that such change can be brought about through I&R services.

While some view the I&R center as the ideal place for an advocacy program (for changing the system), such a role is very difficult for an I&R center to perform while still maintaining vital positive relationships with the service agencies to which it refers people (Helling,

1971). The media's "Action Line" approach has tended to create the image of the center as advocate, but Action Lines are not I&R centers in terms of the model described here, and they are unlike most I&R centers in operation throughout the country.

It is, of course, possible, even desirable, to test an aggressive advocacy program as a module to be added to the model previously described. However, the effect of this component on other activities should be carefully evaluated before it is recommended as part of a center's program. It is possible that the advocacy role can be carried out more effectively if it is lodged in an entirely separate structure and simply relates to the I&R center as one information source among many.

A final limitation of this program involves the role which center data might play in the planning of human services. Although a fairly elaborate system has been described for data collection and research, it must be noted that such data, and the reports generated from them, play a limited role in the overall planning activity. Determination of priorities and allocation of limited resources are heavily influenced by the quality and quantity of lobbying by population subgroups on behalf of specific programs.

Although the data obtained through a coordinated network of centers might be used to strengthen the lobbyist's position, the direct effect of the I&R data on decision makers would be necessarily limited. The intent of building a fairly sophisticated mechanism for data collection and analysis into the I&R model is to maximize the potential of this component of the planning process and to make it responsive to the needs of service consumers. Evaluation data regarding the planning process are needed to determine the extent and limitations of this function of an I&R service. On the basis of such an evaluation, a more rational decision can be made about whether the cost of the function is justified.

COORDINATION OF SERVICE AGENCIES

It is obvious that steps must be taken to improve the access of all people to human services. It is also obvious that major revisions of the ways in which human services are delivered are necessary. I&R services may be able to bridge the gap between these two needs. With regard to the issue of access, an underlying assumption about I&R services is that human service agencies are able to help individuals with their problems once they begin to receive services. Although this is valid in many instances, there remains a significant number of individuals who cannot be reached by services currently offered. These are the people who either move from agency to agency or finally drop out of the social system that supports such services.

With regard to the problem of revising the ways in which human services are delivered, I&R services may be able to play a more central and coordinating role among the direct service agencies, provided the power structure, both public and private, has the desire to bring about such coordination. Human services remain largely inaccessible to a great number of people in need of them. The barriers that prevent the utilization of services—such as poverty, ignorance, and prejudice—are not easily overcome. The means for removing such barriers fall primarily into the human-services area, so that the problem becomes circular: to obtain help in changing one's condition, one must have an adequate income, education, and a means for combating discrimination. But if one does not have these resources, the probability that help can be obtained to reach such resources is greatly diminished. *The dilemma of I&R centers at the present time is that, although they may possess data that could be used for aggressive advocacy to stimulate coordination, they cannot use those data in such a manner without endangering their primary function of facilitating access to services.* Evidently a revolution in the delivery of human services or the development of an entirely new approach to their delivery is necessary, an approach completely outside the present structure.

If a superordinate body were to be established to bring about change in the delivery of human services, it is certain that the functions of an I&R center would be of critical importance in facilitating such change. However, the functions would be greatly expanded, and perhaps, for the sake of clarity, a new name would be given to this set of activities. From a historical point of view, I&R centers may be only a transitional step toward a centralized assessment and referral service for all human services.

Centralized Information Service

In this portion of the chapter, the information and referral center concept is extended toward that of a centralized assessment and referral agency for all human services. This agency, called "Model A," is designed to increase the amount and kind of participation among the consumers of health and social services in (1) assessment of problems, (2) assessment of the quality of service rendered to solve or cope with the problems, and (3) economic power to back up the evaluation of the services rendered. Incentives that could reinforce cooperative behavior among the facilities that deliver services are described. Through the administration of such incentives, Model A may be able to improve the coordination and accountability of human service providers. The program operations of Model A are designed to disturb the present human-service-provider complex to the minimum possible extent consistent with the achievement of program objectives.

Background

In a recent article, Schulberg (1972) discusses his thoughts about the evolving context of human services in which psychological services will be delivered in the 1970s. In the evolving human service system, the practitioners will "seek to provide comprehensive and coordinated assistance to clients." Demone (1975) is cited as having identified four alternatives for insuring comprehensive human services: (1) the I&R center, (2) the diagnostic center, (3) the multiservice center, and (4) the human service network. Model *A* combines several of Demone's alternatives to achieve the goal of coordinating human services in order to provide efficient, comprehensive services to all individuals seeking help for health and social problems.

ASSUMPTION

The following discussion is based on the assumption that existing human services do deal effectively in helping those with various health, social, and personal problems. That is, the major deficiency in the provision of human services is due to the lack of coordination of different service elements rather than to the possibility that the services are not relevant or suitable for the solution of problems. There are some who may challenge this assumption, but it should be accepted, at least for the moment, to facilitate examination of an approach to coordinate, and thus improve, services as they now exist. Additional research to confirm this assumption may well be warranted.

HYPOTHESES

Based on the assumption just discussed, the following hypotheses are suggested for consideration:

1. The current service system does not work adequately because it is not really a system. It is, instead, a set of discrete facilities, offering a variety of services essentially independent of one another. If the various facilities worked closely together, the results of service delivery would be better. Hence, if there were a proven mechanism for coordinating the delivery of services, the current "nonsystem" would be more effective in accomplishing its goals of helping individuals to improve the quality of their lives.

2. The various service facilities are not as responsive to the stated problems of their consumers as they might be. Professionals in the facilities tend to redefine (i.e., diagnose) client problems and then provide services for the redefined problems. Some professionals tend to redefine ("diagnose") the stated problem into one they feel more comfortable or competent to handle. Hence, if the services rendered were made more compatible with the stated problem, consumers or

clients would be more likely to perceive the services rendered as useful, helpful, and generally more valuable.

3. Both of the above hypotheses (better coordination among agencies and a shift in focus to the consumer for the rendering of services) may be viewed in the context of improved communications. That is, if the client communicated his problem more effectively to the service facility, the situation would improve; if the facility communicated its concern (i.e., delivered the service requested by the client) and stated its limitations more effectively, the situation would improve; and finally, if facilities communicated more effectively with each other, the client would be better served.

Another aspect of improved communications in this context should be the client's evaluation of the service he has received. This evaluation should be given both to the service facilities involved and to the community as a whole, since it supports the service facilities through public and private funds. This evaluation can be viewed as the accountability of the service facilities to the public they serve directly and indirectly.

CHARACTER OF MODEL A

The model for improving the coordination of the present service delivery system which follows incorporates the assumption and hypotheses previously mentioned. The mechanism for the model may be crudely conceptualized by considering its analogous relationship to the American Automobile Association. The AAA serves as a coordinating mechanism for services relating to the health and welfare of automobiles and travelers. It identifies facilities that provide services in these areas (automotive garages, repair services, highways, hotels, and eating facilities). These facilities are evaluated, and the evaluation is communicated to the potential consumer in the form of ratings. In addition, the AAA guarantees, to a degree, that the evaluated service will be delivered as stated and at the cost stated. The AAA acts as a broker between the consumer, who can report satisfaction or dissatisfaction with the services rendered by member facilities, and the service facilities. The AAA constantly reevaluates the quality of services being delivered by member facilities and takes action when the services fall below a specified level of acceptance. The AAA also refers individuals to member facilities (trip planning, hotel reservations, etc.).

In summary, these features are present: the assumption that the present service delivery system is adequate; communication of consumer needs to a central office; evaluation of consumer needs by a "professional"; and referral of the client to the appropriate facilities. If the client is not satisfied with the service rendered, he may communicate this to the central (or branch) office, which then assumes some responsibility for investigating the failure of adequate service delivery. The service facilities are held accountable to the central office and the consumer. To the extent that a service facility fails to please the consumer, the consumer may stop using its services, and the central office may stop recommending that the facility be utilized by potential clients. Thus, the AAA is attentive to client needs, organizes and evaluates the service facilities that exist to meet those needs, communicates information about these facilities and refers clients to them, evaluates and holds member service facilities accountable for the services they deliver, and is interested in, and utilizes feedback from the consumer about, the quality of the service that he receives.

The analogy between this field of service and that of health and social services cannot, of course, hold up in a close, careful comparison. Membership in the AAA is voluntary and paid for by the consumer. If the consumer is dissatisfied, he may terminate his use of the service at will. The consumer of human services does not have such a choice. Furthermore, nondelivery or poor performance in the area of human services may have life and death consequences.

Let us hypothesize another agency which has the functions and responsibilities listed below. For purposes of discussion, let us refer to that agency as Model A (a prototype—the first step toward a more streamlined, efficient model). The characteristics of Model A would include at least the following:

1. General intake and assessment of a client's problems.
2. Extensive knowledge about the service facilities participating in a coordinated human services network.
3. The responsibility for referring clients to appropriate service facilities, based on an initial intake assessment.
4. Responsibility for a formal contract between the client, Model A, and the participating service facilities. This contract would be in terms of the services to be provided by each facility, as determined from the initial assessment and the client's agreement to or desire for the suggested service.
5. Responsibility for evaluating the quality of the service rendered to the client, based on the following:
   a. The client's evaluation of services rendered;
   b. The service facility's evaluation of services rendered;
   c. Model A's evaluation of the solution to the assessed problem,

as defined in the initial intake procedure, and the client's subsequent status after the service has been rendered.

6. Follow-up at various intervals to obtain the information necessary to execute an adequate evaluation (#5 above). The follow-up must include information from both the client and the facilities delivering the service.

7. Responsibility for administering funds for the operation of participating service facilities. These funds would be primarily incentives to be given to participating facilities for excellence in the delivery of the services which they contract to render.

8. Responsibility for researching areas of unmet needs and gaps in the service delivery system. This is conceptualized not as a mere tabulation of requests for service that cannot be met, but rather as a part of an aggressive outreach program to identify unmet needs of those persons who are not currently utilizing services. This research activity should be viewed as a new service function, with resources sufficient for it to be undertaken.

9. Model *A* is accountable first of all to the consumer. Its primary responsibility is to get the client to the most appropriate service facility. This implies knowledge of the services different agencies offer, of eligibility requirements of different agencies, and of the waiting list for the agencies—that is, how soon the service could be delivered. In essence, these are the functions of the typical I&R center.

10. Model *A* is secondarily responsible to all direct service facilities making accurate assessments and appropriate referrals. Model *A* would serve as the liaison among all participating direct service facilities, and would have the responsibility to encourage cooperation among these facilities through its administration of incentive funds.

METHODS FOR COORDINATION OF SERVICES

Given the premise of Model *A*'s existence, the following steps would be undertaken to improve coordination among participating service agencies:

Step 1: Development of a network of participating facilities. Model *A* must have sufficient funds to create an incentive for the existing facilities to become "participating members" of the network. At present, an obvious source of such funds would be those currently provided through public welfare departments for the delivery of social services and through private providers of moneys for health and social services such as United Funds, Community Chests, and the like. In essence, these bodies would be advised by Model *A* on how best and most effectively to distribute such funds according to detailed and public schedules. Based on knowledge of existing budgets and resources available for each agency in the community which may participate in the network, Model *A* would develop incentive schedules for distributing funds. Once these schedules were developed, officials would then approach each service facility and present a plan to its officers. This step would be similar to the development of a resource file by a traditional I&R center, but with the additional component of obtaining a commitment from the facility to participate in this new program.

Commitment for participation must include an agreement to allow Model *A* to serve as an initial intake-assessment agency and an agreement to accept appropriate clients on a contractual basis. It is vital that service facilities not be threatened with budget cuts, etc., lest the effort collapse at the very beginning. Incentives should be provided for the simple act of agreeing to participate in the network; these would continue as long as the service facility continued to fulfill certain minimum obligations and would be separate from incentives given for excellence in service. Assuming a suitable diversity of facilities willing to participate, the next step of the program could be developed.

Step 2: Designation of responsible service facilities. It is unlikely that any one facility will be able to serve most individual clients in all potential problem areas. This, obviously is one reason for developing coordination methods. The key issue is to give one facility the responsibility to plan a service program for a client who is likely to require many different services, and for that one facility to have the authority to encourage cooperation from other facilities in carrying out the service program.

The following mechanism is recommended: initial intake and assessment by Model *A*; contractual assignment of the client to a Responsible Service Facility (RSF), which has both the responsibility and the authority to develop a client's entire service program and to subcontract to other Ancillary Service Facilities (ASF) to carry out parts of the program. However, the RSF will retain final responsibility for seeing that the total service program, as initially contracted by Model *A*, is carried out. The RSF will be accountable to Model *A* for delivering the services initially contracted (or for providing different or additional services, if needed), either directly or through subcontracts to ASFs.

The common goal of Model *A*, the RSFs, and the ASFs is to structure a service program that truly considers the client as a whole person. The Model *A* is a repository of information about service alternatives that are available for specific problems and combinations of problems that a client may present. The RSF could draw on this information in the development of a service package for the client. As the client's broker and advocate, the RSF could negotiate the optimum package of services and service delivery mechanisms to meet the total complex of problems presented by the client. The RSF would continue in this role until the client's initial contract was successfully fulfilled, a new contract was negotiated, or the contract was terminated by the client.

A special incentive package would be developed for performing this broker-advocate function. It would be available only to those facilities which choose to participate in the network as an RSF. This incentive package would be administered separately from the initial incentive package for participation in the network and would serve as a source for additional revenue to support the RSF, thus providing built-in incentive for facilities to become RSFs. However, assumption of this responsibility would be voluntary. That is, the facility would be motivated only by the positive incentives for performing this new task, and not by threat of funding cutbacks, etc.

Incentives would not be given to become or participate as an RSF (as in the instance of agreeing to participate in the network), but only as a consequence of performance of broker-advocate activities. Start-up funds, or funds for expanding staff or facilities to undertake this function, would not be made available. Thus, the facilitiy's commitment to the new concept of coordinated services would be tested at the beginning of the program. It is likely that existing multiservice facilities, with a diversity of professional staff, will be the prime candidates to become the first RSFs.

Ancillary Service Facilities, which are more limited in scope of service and staff, could be encouraged to expand their programs to become RSFs at some future time, if data indicate the need for more RSFs. Guidelines should be developed for Model *A* to identify potential RSFs in the existing system. However, any facility that wished to become an RSF could do so on its own initiative. The criterion for remaining an RSF would be the successful accomplishment of the tasks specified for an RSF to carry out: namely, those tasks which result in the efficient delivery of coordinated services.

Step 3: Operationalization of Model A. Assuming that Steps 1 and 2 are successfully accomplished, Step 3 would involve the operation of Model *A* in the community. The basic requirements for the operation of this new facility are the following:

1. An accurate resource file on participating facilities and procedures for updating this file on a frequent, ongoing basis.
2. An adequate tool for assessing the problems of clients who come

into Model A. The assessment tool may result in a relatively gross assessment of the problem (e.g., that the potential client has a mental health problem, without necessarily stating which problem) or it could be more detailed. The tool should be functionally related to the services provided by the participating facilities: e.g., housing, health, transportation, or employment. It should be relevant to the consumer: a self-assessment tool would be ideal if it were sufficiently clear so that the client could identify his problem himself, thus optimizing the fit between his expectations of the service he needs and those that he actually receives.

3. Adequate tools for client follow-up through contacting the client and the facility, and resources for doing this.
4. Adequate tools for evaluating the outcome of services rendered, in terms of the initial contract or its client-approved revision, conducted by Model A and in cooperation with the client. Separate tools would be needed for use by (a) the client, (b) the RSF, and (c) Model A.
5. A comprehensive incentive scheme that permits sliding fees to the RSF based on the degree to which the presenting problem was satisfactorily resolved by the RSF (in essence, a performance contracting arrangement).
6. Funds to implement the incentive scheme.

Step 4: Evaluation of the system. The last step in the program would be the assessment of how the entire system functions. The following aspects should be taken into consideration:

1. Overall reduction in problems of one kind or another among the target population (s). This would require base-rate information about the use and attitude toward specific services and facilities by the population (s) *before* implementation of the program.
2. Changes in utilization rates and/or attitudes about human services in the population (s).
3. Changes in the cost and outcomes of the services rendered by participating service facilities.
4. The attrition rate among participating facilities.
5. The evaluation data collected on each case going through Model A.
6. The development of new facilities.
7. The closing of existing facilities.
8. The utilization rate of Model A by the target population (s), as well as practitioners and service facilities.

Conclusion

Model *A* is obviously a very ambitious solution to the problems created by the lack of coordination of human services. It explores the extension of incentive principles into a social system beyond a clinical setting to stimulate discussion. What is really needed before discussion ensues, however, is empirical evidence of whether or not such a model can be made to work.

It is this author's view that the chaos in the delivery of human services is approaching a crisis state. The developmental tradition of human services has been to respond to crisis situations, rather than to engage in rational and long-range planning. Perhaps when a state of crisis is reached, the approach suggested here for the coordination of human services will be demonstrated in an actual test. In this way, needed empirical evidence can be obtained to determine, on a scientific basis, whether or not such an approach to the coordination of human services is feasible.

References

Bellamy, D. F. *A Study of Information and Referral Services for Metropolitan Toronto.* Toronto: Social Planning Council, 1968.

Bloksberg, L. M., and Caso, E. K. *Survey of Information and Referral Services Existing within the United States: Final Report.* Contract PH 108–65–198 (P) , Public Health Service. Waltham, Mass.: Brandeis University, Florence Heller Graduate School for Advanced Studies in Social Welfare, 1967.

Bolch, E.; Long, N.; and Dewey, J. *Information and Referral Services: An Annotated Bibliography.* Minneapolis, Minn.: Institute for Interdisciplinary Studies, 1972.

Cushing, M., and Long, N. *Information and Referral Services: Reaching Out.* Washington, D.C.: U.S. Government Printing Office, 1973.

Daniel, J. "Call for Action!—New Voice for the People." *Reader's Digest,* 1969, *95,* 207–12.

Demone, H. "Human Services at State and Local Levels and the Integration of Mental Health." In *American Handbook of Psychiatry,* edited by G. Caplan. Vol. 4. Boston: Little, Brown, 1975.

Haber, L. D.; Schmulowitz, J.; and Cormier, R. H. *Information and Referral Services in SSA District Offices: A Pilot Study.* Social Security Publication 34–71 (4–71) . Washington, D.C.: U.S. Department of Health, Education, and Welfare, Social Security Administration, Office of Research and Statistics, 1971.

Hampton Roads Health Information-Referral Planning Center. *Annual Report (March 1, 1967–June 30, 1968).* Norfolk, Va.: United Communities Health-Welfare-Recreation Planning Council, 1968.

Health and Welfare Council of Metropolitan Saint Louis. *The Organizational Period: Quarterly Report Number I (February 1, 1967–March 31, 1967) Information and Referral for Older Persons.* Saint Louis, Mo.: Health and Welfare Council, 1967.

Helling, R. A. "Some Definite Opinions on Information and Advocacy." *Canadian Welfare,* 1971, *57,* 3–4, 28.

Institute for Interdisciplinary Studies, *Information and Referral Services: Follow-Up.* Working draft. Washington, D.C.: U.S. Department of Health, Education, and Welfare, Social and Rehabilitation Service, Administration on Aging, 1971a.

_____. *Information and Referral Services: Volunteer Escort Service.* Working draft. Washington, D.C.: U.S. Department of Health, Education, and Welfare, Social and Rehabilitation Service, Administration on Aging, 1971b.

Kahn, A. J. *Theory and Practice of Social Planning.* New York: Russell Sage Foundation, 1969.

_____, et al. *Neighborhood Information Centers: A Study and Some Proposals.* New York: Columbia University School of Social Work, 1966.

Larson, N. "Collaboration between OASDI and Central Information and Referral Services." Paper presented at the National Conference on Social Welfare, Minneapolis, Minn., May 1961.

Lester, N. Personal communication, 1969.

Long, N. *Information and Referral Services.* InterStudy Information and Referral Center Study, v.1. Minneapolis, Minn.: InterStudy, 1975.

_____. *WIS: An Information and Referral Network.* Minneapolis, Minn.: InterStudy, 1972.

_____, et al. *Information and Referral Centers: A Functional Analysis.* Washington, D.C.: U.S. Government Printing Office, 1971.

_____, Reiner, S.; and Zimmerman, S. *Information and Referral Services: The Resource File.* Washington, D.C.: Government Printing Office, 1973.

_____, and Yonce, L. *Information and Referral Services: Evaluation Design for a Network Demonstration.* Minneapolis, Minn.: InterStudy, 1974.

National Council on the Aging. *The Golden Years . . . A Tarnished Myth.* Washington, D.C.: National Council on the Aging, 1970.

Nixon, Richard M. "An Address by the President to the White House Conference on Aging, December 2, 1971." *Washington Bulletin,* 1971, *22,* 117–20.

Orris, M. S. *Factors Which Contribute to the Social and Economic Independence of People over 60.* Saskatoon: Social Planning of Saskatoon, 1970.

Putter, H., and Malzberg, A. *Helping to Serve the Aging in Their Own Homes: The Effectiveness of Information and Referral Services for Meeting Home Health and Housing Needs of Aging Persons.* New York: Community Council for Greater New York, 1969.

REAL Service. *Information, Counseling and Referral: An Action, Research and Demonstration Program—Final Report.* South Bend, Ind.: United Community Services of Saint Joseph County, 1969.

Schulberg, H. C. "Challenge of Human Services Programs for Psychologists." *American Psychologist,* 1972, *27,* 566–73.

Sigler, J. *The Trial Run: A First Quarter Report.* Kansas City, Mo.: Regional Health and Welfare Council, 1964.

Suchman, E. A. *Evaluative Research: Principles and Practice in Public Service and Social Action Programs.* New York: Russell Sage Foundation, 1967.

Tessari, D., et al. *Information and Referral Services: Information-Giving and Referral.* Washington, D. C.: Government Printing Office, 1974.

Townsend, R. E. *Report of a Study of Referral Services by Old-Age and Survivors Insurance District Offices.* Washington, D.C.: U.S. Department of Health, Education and Welfare, Social Security Administration, Bureau of Old-Age and Survivors Insurance, 1957.

U.S. Department of Health, Education and Welfare, Public Health Service. *Classification of Approved Community Health Projects by Broad Areas of Activity.*

Washington, D.C.: Bureau of Disease Prevention and Environmental Control, 1967.

U.S. Department of Labor, Retraining and Reemployment Administration. *Community Advisory Centers Face the Future.* Washington, D.C., 1946.

_____. *To Organize—To Operate Your Community Advisory Center for Veterans and Others.* Washington, D.C., 1944.

Wholey, J. S., et al. *Federal Evaluation Policy: Analyzing the Effects of Public Programs.* Washington, D.C.: The Urban Institute, 1970.

Williams, K. I. "Social Service Exchanges." *Social Work Year Book,* 1964, *15,* 731–34.

Part II

Experience with
Operational
Systems

Part II relates some of the facts concerning the basic conceptual problems experienced in building information centers to the kinds of needs outlined in Part I. Universities have recently become increasingly involved in this activity, both as a public service and as a new kind of research activity (see, for example, Sutherland, 1973). The bibliography at the end of this book also indicates the recent increase in activity in the library world as it responds to the need for community information.

In chapter 5, Donohue presents a strong case for the public library as an agent in providing information and referral services. One frequently mentioned rebuttal to this view is that public libraries are wedded to a middle-class clientele, rather than the groups most in need. In recent years, however, library systems have done a great deal to extend services of all kinds to citizens who were previously not library users. The federal government provided funds to the states through the Library Services and Construction Act to help the disadvantaged, institutionalized, and physically handicapped who previously had not been library users. System Development Corporation (SDC) has recently completed a study of programs of this kind (Black, Seiden, and Luke, 1973). A summary (Luke, 1974) notes that nearly 1,700 such projects, aimed at providing library services to persons not previously served, could be identified. Most operate in more than one location; some libraries in ghetto areas utilize storefronts. Federal funding is spent primarily for materials and services, rather than for facilities. Volunteers, by operating special programs, transporting materials, etc., represent community involvement. The following examples provided by Luke illustrate a range of outreach efforts.

Hopi and Navajo Indians on reservations in Arizona are reached by an LSCA-funded project that provides bookmobiles which travel to locations so distant that they stay out for a three-day period each week, visiting one settlement or trading post after another. Indians drive the mobile units, and materials on Indian culture are included in the materials that the bookmobile provides, along with other material on health, child care, vocations, and small businesses. Users may request material on any topic in which they are interested.

Approximately six nursing homes in Tacoma, Washington, are served by another such project, a mobile unit that visits the homes every one or two weeks. Persons in the homes can request any materials they want: high on the list of requests are travel films that library personnel show to the patients, as well as phonograph records and books. Here, one member of the city's library staff is entirely supported by LSCA funds. He devotes all of his time to the project; when he is not assembling materials, visiting homes, or directing the work of his assistants, he is out in the community encouraging local organizations to contribute funds or materials toward the project. He promotes the service himself, by visiting patients in the homes. Many of the users of the project's services depend heavily on it as their major source of entertainment and information.

In a barrio in San Diego, a project has recently been initiated to encourage greater library use by Mexican Americans in three branch library areas. The head librarian has placed in each of these branches a personable, bilingual librarian who has had a hand in selecting Spanish language books and other materials that he or she feels will be of interest to the Spanish-speaking members of the community. Publicity is the key to the success of many such projects, and here it has been generated through fiestas held at the library on Sunday afternoons, with plenty of advance notice, complete with decorations, mariachi music, and other attractions.

The SDC study reported extensive efforts by libraries to assess the needs and wants of the unserved, their potential clients. These signs of increased concern to extend their clientele give reason to believe that public libraries may break out of the stereotypes frequently imputed to them—that of being confined to a literate middle class or of restricting service to the library's own building or conventional media. With an expanded view of service, information and referral would seem a natural next step.

The magnitude and quality of work along these lines by public libraries is well indicated by the recently concluded project on the neighborhood information center concept (Turick, 1974). This consisted of activities by libraries in Cleveland, Detroit, Atlanta, Houston, and the borough of Queens. Each library was asked to describe its sites, existing neighborhood information resources at those sites, citizen involvement, statements of the library's role and objectives in meeting neighborhood information needs, evaluation of service needs, gaps, overlaps, and a plan.

The Detroit Public Library has been notable for extending this service to all branches and for maintaining a central office and clearinghouse—over and beyond the requirements for this particular grant. Detroit calls its service "TIP" for The Information Place. Turick has pointed out that every public library needs to study and determine its service goals for the next decade and summarize them, as the Dallas Public Library did with *Library Service Goals 1972–1982*, for only then will program objectives be set forth and evaluated to formulate a strategy for public library change.

An even more recent and significant project, launched in January 1974, is "Benchmark." This is a program aimed at improving the usefulness, quality, and accessibility of the knowledge used by an urban region in planning. It is part of the Academy for Contemporary Problems, funded by Battelle and Ohio State University. A prototype program exists in Columbus. The Columbus Community Conference, which consists of public officials, neighborhood leaders, and researchers, guides the continuing design of community analysis programs and focuses attention on the "vital signs" that are the "benchmarks" for continuing appraisal of community institutions. Benchmark/Columbus also has a "Community Analysis Assistance Group," which has four missions: (1) survey research and evaluation, (2) synthesis and presentation of community data for use by residents, (3) preparation of handbooks for civic leaders and the public for need assessment and planning, and (4) liaison with similar community groups elsewhere. The program, as of May 1974, appears to have attracted very dedicated, enthusiastic, and capable graduate students from Ohio State, and appears to be succeeding in its missions.

The monthly Newsletter of the Alliance of Information and Referral Services[1] gives an accurate indication of the vigor with which the entire area is expanding. New York's Citizen Urban Information Center in the Public Library is another example of public library involvement at a very significant level of funding that was started in

1. B. Thies, ed. For information write to 621 S. Virgil Avenue, Los Angeles, Calif. 90005.

1974 by Beatrice Fitzpatrick. Though the Brooklyn Public Library has had a neighborhood outreach program since the early 1960s, the plan to introduce I&R services into the fifty-five branches and evaluate their impact was new. By the fall of 1974, however, it became clear that the mayor's office of New York City was reluctant to release the funds for this project, and it was not continued in 1975.

The services developed at Baltimore and Philadelphia, described in chapters 5 and 8, respectively, provide some interesting contrasts. The Philadelphia Center, a Model Cities project, was clearly identified from the start as being in business to serve health- and welfare-related information needs, and featured a telephone service, whereby it was possible to link the client with an agency while the center remained on the line to assure that effective contact had been made. The service developed at Enoch Pratt Library, on the other hand, provided similar information as part of a more general question-answering service, on both a walk-in and telephone basis. The Philadelphia Center has since been disbanded for lack of funds, while the Baltimore Center has been incorporated into the overall reference function of the library.

Differences between the two services are, apparently, largely the result of different stances toward already existing agencies that have similar or related functions. One strength of the Philadelphia operation was that it was clearly identifiable as the link between helping agencies and their potential clients, i.e., clearly an I&R service. The Baltimore service is not identified as such. It shared the functions of an I&R center to some degree, but also attempted to help other library departments and branches, as well as the social agencies.

Still other organizational models are found in chapter 6, which describes the British Citizens' Advice Bureaux, and in chapter 9, which describes the crisis information services that have been organized to meet the needs of young people. All these experiments show a variety of staffing and training patterns. The organizational needs for the approximate mix of talents are treated in detail in chapter 7, based on the experience of one I&R service operated by a health and welfare council. It is instructive to compare these varied responses to common problems.

On the whole, there is currently a great deal of activity in the area of community self-help which Part II can only sample. The concept of community participation is, of course, not new in the United States. What is new is the recognition that classical social service structures are of limited effectiveness in dealing with contemporary problems; that today's social problems require more responsive mechanisms and some redistribution of power.

Steven Lorch (1969) has traced the history of the Neighborhood

Service Program to shed more light on the problem of how to improve social service structures. The Neighborhood Service Program is a forerunner of the Model Cities Program, and it is an experiment with neighborhood corporations. Lorch concludes that despite many failures, the program has clarified many issues. He feels that community leaders should be educated to understand bureaucratic structures. Decentralization without education confronts the poor person with a new structure just as alien to him as the old one, leaving him in an untenable position. The program also provided the lesson that there are many potential resources, such as underground service systems, that must be understood and tapped. The community must learn to integrate all these resources with those from various levels of government and academia. Above all, the persons who operate these branches must learn to listen to one another with empathy.

References

Academy of Contemporary Problems. *Benchmark Brochure*. 1501 Neil Avenue, Columbus, Ohio 43201, 1974.

Black, D.; Seiden, H.; and Luke, A. *Evaluation of LSCA Services to Special Target Groups: Final Report*. Santa Monica, Calif.: System Development Corporation, 1973.

Lorch, S. Private communication, 17 January 1969.

Luke, A. W. *Bringing the Library to the Unserved*. Santa Monica, Calif.: System Development Corporation, 1974.

Sutherland, R. L. *Social Service of Our Cities*. Pamphlet. Austen, Tex.: University of Texas, 1973.

Turick, D. A. *The Neighborhood Information Center Concept: A Talk*. Cleveland, Ohio: Case Western Reserve Graduate School of Library Science, 20 February 1974.

Chapter 5
The Public Information
Center Project

by Joseph C. Donohue

The past twenty years have seen the rise of many specialized information centers. Like libraries, they collect and maintain documentary materials. Unlike libraries, they do so only as an adjunct to providing information. Freed from the concern of maintaining a collection, an information center is often able to provide intensive information services within its restricted subject area. Since there is a continuing need for an agency that maintains documentary materials and assists in their use, the information center cannot replace the library; but as an adjunct or supplement to the library the information center has been found very useful, especially in scientific and industrial applications. Efforts have been made in recent years to apply the information center concept to problems of daily life in society, such as those of health, welfare, education, employment, and the like.

This chapter reports on both a study and planning project conducted by the author, and an information service that was instituted at Enoch Pratt Free Library as a result of the project. Both have been referred to in library circles as the Public Information Center, or PIC. This has been a source of some confusion. In this chapter, an effort has been made to show the conceptual development and its partial implementation in the chronology in which they occurred. While it might have been clearer to the reader had the two—the project and the resulting service—been more clearly separated in the retelling, that would have obscured the reality. The conceptual development, the planning, and the work of building and doing interacted from the early stages of the project. It is useful to keep in mind that what is reported here is both a developmental project and the work of putting into practice some of its recommendations. The former began in 1968 (officially 1969) and ended in December of 1970. The latter began in October 1970 and continued until 1974, when it was officially phased out as an operating unit and its functions taken over by the Library's General Information Department.

Dr. Donohue is Library and Management Information Scientist, Bureau of Foods, Food and Drug Administration, Washington, D.C. He was Director of the Public Information Center Project in 1969-70.

One such effort was the Public Information Center (PIC) Project, sponsored by the Enoch Pratt Free Library and the University of Maryland School of Library and Information Service. Its purpose was to find out whether or not a public library could be a comprehensive information center. The project originated with a suggestion from Paul Wasserman, Dean of the University of Maryland library school, to the library's director, Edwin Castagna, and its assistant director, Grace Slocum, that such a study might be conducted at the Pratt Library. Federal funds in the amount of $25,000.00 had been made available for improving services in Maryland's five metropolitan library systems. At the request of the Enoch Pratt Library, and with the support of Nettie Taylor, State Director for Library Development, the directors of the respective systems elected to apply these funds to the PIC project. The library then contracted with the school for the half-time services of a faculty member, the author, as director of the project, and other persons as needed in the study and planning of the service.

The library's interest in sponsoring the effort may be seen as a recognition of the changing conditions of urban life, and of resulting changes in the support base of libraries. The book-using middle class has, to a significant degree, deserted the city, leaving the continued viability of the urban public library in question. Nevertheless, people continue to need information; indeed, many kinds of information vital to survival in the urban environment cannot be found in books, and some important information is not in published form at all. It was, therefore, appropriate for the library to extend its scope, in order to become a clearinghouse for information, regardless of the format in which such information is to be found. Where the information needed was of a factual kind, such as could be obtained from publications, the center could direct the inquirer to such literature, either directly or through the appropriate department of the library. If what was needed was substantive help, the center could direct the inquirer to the social agency, organization, government department, or individual able to provide that help. In thus acting as a broker between people with needs and people with the resources to answer the needs, an information center would, it was thought, learn much about which kinds of needs are satisfied and which are not—data that would be useful to planners, officials, and voluntary citizens' groups.

Orientation and Planning

Over a period of several months, project persons from both the library and the library school met frequently, identified and reviewed useful documentary materials, and interviewed people in the community who had special knowledge of existing social welfare problems and services. While there is no dearth of potentially related literature, there seemed at the time very little that related directly to problems of setting up a service of the type envisioned. The most valuable reading was a report by Kahn and others (1966), *Neighborhood Information Centers,* which explored the potential value of several types of services, including the British Citizens' Advice Bureaux. Given the lack at that time of empirical research such as is represented by Dervin's chapter regarding the kinds and extent of information types needed by citizens, it was necessary to construct such an array a priori. After a study of relevant literature, Samuel Markson, then a graduate student at Case Western Reserve University, developed the following outline of subject areas. It has since been circulated among some members of the "invisible college" concerned with public information services and has been found to be of such usefulness that it is reproduced here, with the permission of Mr. Markson, who is now Public Services Systems Coordinator at the University of Massachusetts Library.

1. Government in General
   Legislative bodies in a given jurisdiction: how elected, their powers, structure, and operation. *Office holders:* responsibilities, committe assignments, powers, pay, how appointed. *Courts:* how judges get their jobs, their responsibilities, powers, and jurisdiction of respective courts. *Taxes:* kinds, how they are set, how collected, how earmarked for spending, how disbursed. *Constitutions, charters, laws:* which are extant, their import, how interpreted, how they may be changed. *Influence:* means of influence open to individuals, to groups, how lobbyists work, where they are registered.

2. Agencies
   Responsibilities (of respective agencies), their normal work and normal clienteles, powers permitted to them and those they are required to exercise, their methods of operation, supervision, and control. Procedures to follow in order to get an agency to act on a problem, procedures for complaints about an agency.

3. Police
   Citizen rights and obligations in dealing with police, and conversely the rights and obligations of police. How to get a lawyer to help in dealing with police. Bond procedures. Kinds of problems appropriate/not appropriate for police to deal with. Relationship of police to other government agencies.

4. Housing
   Landlord/tenant relations: leases, and rights of those who sign them, limits of lease. Rights in the absence of a lease. Deter-

mining ownership of a building. Getting landlord to make repairs. Rent strikes. *Public housing:* who qualifies, how to apply, who runs it, and by what rules and procedures. *Urban renewal:* effect on citizens, redress against actions under renewal programs. *Housing codes and laws:* coverage, impact, who enforces, how to get action under them, operation of rent control, of fair housing laws. Significance of condemnation, of receivership. *Housing purchases:* how to find an appropriate house to buy and how to buy it, problems and dangers in purchase. Significance of condominium and cooperative ownership, their respective advantages and disadvantages. True cost of purchasing. Insurance needed. Taxes on houses. *Rented housing:* deciding on desirability of rental property, responsibilities of landlord, and tenant maintenance. Types of heating; determining degree of congestion in a building or rental neighborhood.

5. Employment
Training: where to get training, what is available and at what cost. *Apprenticeships:* how to obtain, their conditions, requirements. *Employment agencies:* availability of public agencies, private agencies, profit/nonprofit. What the agencies will/will not do, costs. *Job hunting:* education, skills, other requirements for particular jobs. *Unions:* purpose, who needs to belong, how to join, laws governing unions, regulations of unions. *Unemployment, disability, and workmen's compensation:* who qualifies, how to apply, types of benefits. *Social Security:* how it operates, Compensation benefits. Appeal. Redress in unfair treatment. *Labor laws:* what laws exist, who enforces, how to get action under them. *Labor statistics:* on city, state, national level. Numbers of people employed, by job, by industry. Jobs available, growth trends.

6. Education
Courses, programs available (all levels). Entrance requirements, costs, scholarships, loans, and other support. *Tutors:* where to find, at what cost. *Schools:* how supported, their organization, curricula, local, regional, state control, governance. *School districts:* how they are set. Accreditation, availability of special schools and courses, e.g., for handicapped, etc.

7. Welfare
What public/private aid agencies exist and whom do they serve? Kinds of problems they handle. Eligibility to receive help.

8. Health
Medical problems: how to find a good doctor, how to determine competence of doctor. *Public programs:* clinics, hospitals avail-

able, health education programs, pollution control programs and agencies. *Private programs:* what services are available, their cost, how financed, who run by. *Health insurance:* costs, coverage, limits, and conditions of payment.

9. Business and consumer affairs
Credit purchasing: interest charges, finding true interest, laws governing credit buying, who enforces laws, repossession for nonpayment. Differences in borrowing from bank vs. finance company. Collateral, cosigners *Prices:* determining fair prices, comparison shopping. *Workmanship and service:* how to get redress. *Reputation of stores or products:* how to determine. *Establishing your own business:* laws governing new business, help available from public/private sources, financing, costs, and profits.

Determining Needs and Resources

Given the limited time and resources of the project, and the determination of the library director to develop a useful service as soon as possible, it was necessary to severely restrict the study phase. In addition to a literature review, this phase consisted of interviews with a series of persons involved in official and voluntary agencies and citizen groups. By far the most informative of these interviews were with the staff of the Health and Welfare Council. Its Information and Referral Service (I&RS) was already operating on a 40-hour-a-week basis, giving referrals and advice, mostly by telephone. It was found that the capabilities of the I&RS and those of the library were complementary, though they overlapped in important areas. Much of the work of I&RS is beyond the competence of the library, involving as it does highly sensitive casework, sometimes of a medical or psychiatric nature. However, other aspects of its work are purely informational, involving the identification, collection, analysis, organization, and dissemination of information. Much of what the I&RS and the council's member agencies do in this area is really library work, involving operating their own special libraries, devising indexes, keeping data files, and the like.

The suggestion was made during discussions with council representatives that the library should do more to assure the availability of the publications needed by the council and its member agencies, thus relieving them of the need for their own special libraries. This would require close liaison between the library and the social agencies to assure the permanent availability of important planning materials, however ephemeral their form. The I&RS also scans newspapers and other publications for information about changes in the availability of social services in the community, thus to a large extent duplicating files kept in the library. Plans were made to reduce such duplication while assuring the ready availability of needed materials. Also, it became clear that the library could do a great deal more to inform its clientele of the availability of social services in response to particular needs. Its central and branch libraries could offer many points of initial contact for persons who could be referred to appropriate agencies either through the I&RS or directly, as appropriate.

Technical Resources

At this time, there was general agreement on the need for an efficient system for gathering, processing, and retrieving data on the availability of official and voluntary services. Some studies were made to determine the feasibility of computer methods or other electronic or mechanical aids, but at the time these were not available to the project or to the library at acceptable cost. Instead, plans were made to adopt the "extract-clueword" system developed by the Battelle Memorial Institute in Columbus, Ohio, for use by its own information analysis center. It had been successfully adapted to the needs of the Columbus (Ohio) Regional Information Service, an agency similar in some ways to the service envisioned by Pratt. The extract-clueword system is particularly well suited to the needs of a small, specialized information center lacking computer support, where the information is to be derived from many formats and where a high value is placed on exact, timely, and accurate data. It is remarkably simple and economical, and provides a format that allows easy transfer of data to machine-readable form for automatic processing. It has been described as an expansion of the card catalog format, which makes for acceptability in the library environment; through well-chosen extracts it also provides more substantive data than does the conventional catalog, thus greatly reducing the need for referring to the original documents.

The first input to the central file was the data from current files of I&RS. Most important of these is the file that the council uses to update its *Directory of Community Resources,* a guide to social services in Maryland, used heavily by caseworkers, educators, and others in making referrals. The PIC project took on the task of preparing the index for the next edition. A computer program was written to sort and list the indexes by type of service, agency, and geographical area served.

Study of the British Citizens' Advice Bureaux

An unexpected but highly beneficial opportunity arose to study a model of citizens' information service that has operated since World

War II, the Citizens' Advice Bureaux. This was made possible when Ms. Carole Peppi, the project's Administrative Assistant, returned for a visit to her native England. With CAB cooperation, she was able to study the system intensively and actually to work for some days in several of the local bureaus. Among the matters that she studied, the following were considered most important in the context of PIC planning:

> *Structure:* Enabling legislation, funding, governance, legal authority, legal vulnerability.
>
> *Administration:* Staffing, training, centralization/decentralization, communication patterns, both internal to CAB and external; relation if any to public libraries.
>
> *Services:* Extent and nature of services, clientele; problems of special types of clients; experience under normal and stress conditions, follow-up methods.
>
> *Technical support:* Facilities, communication, and cooperation with other agencies; types of documentary resources; files (types, structure, maintenance, integration), special talent, "resource persons."

Ms. Peppi returned with a great deal of information that proved helpful to us in the planning. A report of her findings was published as part of the project's final report, and has been rewritten as a chapter in this book. The reader familiar with British institutions will surely recognize the influence of CAB on our recommendations for expanded services at Enoch Pratt, but as Kahn and others have recognized, it will be necessary for agencies here to develop approaches particularly suited to the nature of our society. Especially problematic are issues such as (1) the effective scope of service, (2) the degree of centralization or centralized support of services, and (3) the appropriate contribution of volunteer workers.

Meanwhile, planning continued at the library, with a number of managerial structures being devised and considered, and suggestions being received from members of a professional seminar conducted by the school in connection with the PIC project, on the subject of community information services. The seminar brought together library school students, experienced librarians, social workers, and city planners in an exchange of ideas that served to stimulate interest beyond those immediately concerned with the project. Also during the course of the project, two one-day institutes on public information services were held, to acquaint members of the professional community with the range of problems and opportunities attendant upon the project.

Recommendations

The project team made many recommendations to the library for the creation and operation of an information center. These have been fully documented in the final report of the project, published in 1971. The most important of these are summarized here.

The project team recommended to the library that it set up a new department which would be a special information unit, under the full-time direction of a senior librarian and located in the most prominent place possible in the central building. Its function would be to assist its users, both individuals and organizations, to find information and information sources in answer to particular needs, especially those of a health and welfare nature. It would become the point of entry for users who were unsure of how to use the library, and a court of last resort for those who had exhausted the library's resources.

The information center, it was recommended, should continue to identify urgent information needs of the city's populace, including those people who do not use the library. Conversely, it should seek to identify resources, both documentary and institutional, and to develop excellent day-to-day liaison with the agencies that could serve in this capacity. It was envisioned that in addition to providing extensive information-handling capability to support these agencies, the library could serve as a point of referral, with its branches acting as feeders to I&RS where appropriate. It was recommended that since I&RS already operated a telephone service, the library's information center should, at least initially, emphasize in-person services, though it should answer phone queries as received. The center would not build a document collection, but would extract materials and pass the publications themselves on to the library's appropriate departments, maintaining within the information center itself only a file that could lead to information sources, wherever found.

With respect to organization, it was recommended that (1) the center be created as a department of the library, under the direct supervision of a senior librarian, the peer of other department heads, who would be responsible *only* for the center; (2) the staff should be composed of both librarians and others, such as persons with expertise in social work, to complement the skills of a bibliographic and technical nature that the library's regular personnel would provide; and (3) it include technicians whose principal duty would be the maintenance of the files and the answering of routine questions. All staff members of the service should regularly participate in the selection of input and in preparation and use of the files, in order to maintain a current knowledge of the files and how they might best be used.

It was further suggested that librarians from other departments and the branches who had an interest in PIC-type services should be recruited to work full-time for periods of from three months to a year in the center. This would help to spread an understanding of the center to the staff generally. It was emphasized that the center should be staffed by people with good general education, the ability to learn quickly and adapt to the fast-changing requirements of an evolving service, a commitment to service, and a healthy respect for people. Training was recommended along the following lines: (1) the city and state, their political and social organization, and the organization of social welfare service; (2) the library, its structure and operation, goals, and services; (3) the center itself, the reasons for its existence, special features of its service; (4) information needs of the urban setting; (5) interview techniques; and (6) systems of information handling.

It was recommended that the library not attempt to be an ombudsman or advocate, except to assure the citizen free access to information.

In late July 1970 these and other recommendation were made in an interim report to the library administration, which, agreeing that such a service should be instituted, began the necessary internal planning and training. The project team did not participate in this internal planning or in selection of staff for the center. At the request of the assistant director, the project team did set up and conduct the training course it had planned, and completed the development of the resource file that was to be used jointly by the library and the Health and Welfare Council. In addition, the team completed work on the index for the *Directory,* to be published by the council, and spent the remaining time documenting the entire project, delivering the final report to the library on December 31, 1970.

Implementation

As recommended, the new service was given the desired prominent location in the central building. No direct telephone service was provided, as it was at that time the library's policy for *all* calls to enter the system through the telephone Reference Service. The service area was identified by a sign that indicated only that this was an "information" desk. At no time was the unit identified to the public by any distinctive title such as "Public Information Center."

A leaflet was prepared and distributed, indicating that the library now had established closer ties with the Health and Welfare Council and could, therefore, provide more information in that area of need, but no indication was given that such service was localized in a particular unit of the library.

It may seem strange that after so much planning and effort, no publicity was given to the new service. It should be understood that given certain budgetary stringencies imposed about that time, there was doubt whether the new information service would begin at all. The decision was made by the library administration to go ahead with plans, but to do so in such a way that, if necessary, the new unit could be reabsorbed into the preexisting structure with a minimum of difficulty. With this in mind, no publicity was provided at the beginning of the service. At that time, it seemed to the author that the important thing was not what the service unit was called, or whether it would have any fanfare, but rather what it would do; it seemed that if the staff began to provide information and referral services to even a few people a day in an active way, the word would spread. Anyway, the lack of publicity was then expected to be temporary, until the service could get onto its feet and establish itself internally within the library.

The staff chosen to operate the information service was comprised of four college graduates[1] from the Library Auxiliary Service, all of whom had shown high aptitude for library work and who had expressed special interest in the new concept of an expanded information service. They responded well to the special training provided and brought much talent and a high degree of motivation to their new assignment. At a later time, a clerical assistant was added.[2]

The service was not established as a department; rather it was placed directly under the office of the assistant director, and was supervised by her administrative assistant, Mr. Robert Kinchen, who supervised it as a responsibility added to others, such as general administration of the central building. These circumstances precluded his spending the time needed to establish the desired liaison with city, state, and regional government and voluntary agencies.

In addition to serving as a general inquiry point, the new information service was given the task of making all photocopies required by the library staff and patrons, as well as providing general directions about the building and the neighborhood. Thus, with the exception of maintaining the specialized information file on community health and welfare agencies, and querying that file in response to the few queries that required it, the new service became outwardly in no way distinguished from the kind of general information desk that had long been found in most large libraries. A study made of questions addressed to this information desk in the first year of its existence showed that less than 2 percent were related to health or welfare problems. Nevertheless, the staff continued to maintain the currency of the community resource file and for a time made weekly visits to the

1. Roberta Busky, Peggy Cook, Jolanta Szulinski, and Fawn Van Allen.
2. Beverly Spande.

Health and Welfare Council, working side by side with its I&RS staff contacting social service agencies in order to keep data current. Subsequent reductions in the staff resulted in these visits being discontinued. In 1974 the library's General Reference Department was renamed General Information Department, reflecting the growing commitment to information service, which had been earlier seen in the creation of the Telephone Reference Service, a pioneering effort, and which had been continued in the PIC experiment. At the time of the restructuring of the General Information Department, the remaining staff of the information service (PIC) were incorporated into it. The service location that had been set up inside the front door was vacated, and a large desk was placed in the center of the hall to serve all types of information requests, including those for catalog assistance. The resource file was placed at that desk, and continues to be used upon occasion by personnel of the General Information Department in answering queries made by patrons in person or calling the Telephone Reference Service. Plans are under way now (February 1975) to perform a complete update of that file.

Conclusions

The Public Information Center Project cost $25,000.00 for salaries of personnel from the university and the expenses of travel, training, equipment, and overhead. The library may well have contributed at least an equal amount in the salaries of its staff members who were involved in planning, training, and implementation. Today there is no visible evidence that the project ever existed or that a service resulted from it, except for the card file. Persons who have read earlier descriptions of PIC have inquired about its fate, and have asked in effect, "What went wrong?"

From the end of the project to this writing, more than four years have elapsed, during which time the author has not had official contact with the library nor any opportunity to observe closely the subsequent history of the service initiated as a result of the project. The following comments must be considered with those limitations in mind.

PIC was an experiment. It is in the nature of experiments that some of them fail, and PIC was one that failed. It may be useful to try to understand why, because there are still people who believe in the concept, and some may be in a position to try a similar experiment.

It is not possible to say to what extent each of the following deficiencies was responsible for the failure. A postmortem may be of some value to others who, like the author, are convinced of the validity of the PIC concept. Therefore, some of the deficiencies in both the project and the resulting service are sketched out here.

The officials of Enoch Pratt undertook a pioneering effort, attempting to create a new service under less than ideal conditions. The failure of the service initiated is in some measure a result of inadequacies in the planning, for which the author is responsible.

Confusion about mode of service. During the planning, there was a long period of discussion about whether PIC should be a telephone service, a "walk-in" service, or both. There was some concern about duplicating the telephone access service of Health and Welfare's I&RS, while leaving other potential needs unmet. Further, since the library had gone to great lengths to consolidate all incoming calls in Telephone Reference Service, there was a reluctance on the part of the administration to cause further confusion by introducing a new telephone service. The resulting decision to begin operating almost exclusively in a walk-in mode represented at best a compromise solution, since it made it difficult to present a clear and forceful image of the new service to either the library's staff or to the public. In retrospect, our concern over jurisdictional problems seems to have been unnecessary and vitiating. Experience of the I&RS indicates that the demand for telephone service is very elastic. Promotional programs, such as television spot announcements for I&RS, regularly produce such response that they must be carefully spaced to avoid creating a demand beyond the service capacity. In short, there appears to be no reason to avoid competition in delivery of telephone service. The experience of both the I&RS and the library indicate that few people are inclined to come to a downtown building with questions of the health and welfare type; the convenience and anonymity of the telephone service has greater appeal. However, knowledgeable persons at Pratt expressed the belief that if such information service were available in person at the neighborhood branch libraries it would be used.

Restriction on PIC-type development in branches. The library administration elected to concentrate efforts on setting up the central information unit. Community leaders in one branch area expressed considerable interest in starting a small PIC-type service at that branch. The administration agreed to make space available, but not to permit any other dedication of library resources. No one can say for sure what would have been the result if the branch had been allowed to participate fully in such an effort, but failure to do so seems like an opportunity lost.

Organizational structure and placement. It now seens clear to the writer that it would have been better either to have created a PIC department as recommended, or else to have placed the new service in an existing department. Operating as it did for several years as a special project reporting to the assistant director's office, and under a part-time supervisor, it could not establish itself and its role satisfactorily. In the opinion of this author, the most crippling blow to the implementation of the unit was the failure to appoint a full-time professional with adequate time and the clear mandate to represent the new service to the library staff, to the cooperating civic agencies, and to the public; although the unit's staff were talented and well motivated, as paraprofessionals they could not perform the necessary liaison function satisfactorily. They did not have sufficient authority, and they did not have the necessary credentials in a society and an occupation that are, to an ever-increasing degree, obsessed by credentials.

It should be understood that though the staff of Pratt were, in general, interested and sympathetic to PIC, the project was to some extent resented as a dilution of traditional library resources at a time of retrenchment.

In the early months of the PIC project, each step was documented in "Project Notes" that were provided to the library for wide internal distribution, in the hope that these would generate wide discussion and input of ideas from the staff. After some months, it became apparent that, for whatever reason, these notes were not being read by the staff generally and were demonstrably ineffective as a communication medium. They were therefore discontinued as a poor use of project time.

In another attempt at internal communication, a number of meetings on PIC were held with the library's staff. Unfortunately, these were too large and too highly structured to encourage two-way communication. Perhaps small meetings would have brought out better discussion among staff members and more suggestions from them, which could have been incorporated into policy discussion and planning. A complex organization such as Pratt cannot possibly include everybody in all its activities, but it now seems clear that too little was done along these lines.

Failure to publicize. The new service unit was opened without publicity, a decision of the library to which I did not object strenuously because I believed—and still do—that if the will to serve is present and resources are allocated to serve, the use of such a service will quickly grow through personal referral. Given all the other impediments to PIC's development, I now believe the decision a mistake. Even if publicity had temporarily swamped the library's resources, it would have been preferable to a stillbirth. In the absence of demand and without demonstration of the value of the service, there was no effective motivation for the library to continue the operation of the unit or to devote adequate resources to it. The investments that had been made in conceptualizing, studying, planning, and developing were, to all intents, written off as bad investments without the product having been tested or marketed.

By the definition of survival, PIC was a failure. Its planning and execution were inadequate and/or inappropriate to the Pratt Library at the time. That does not invalidate the concept of providing greater depth of information services through the medium of the public library system. The public library has a traditional responsibility to provide documentary materials. If libraries do not do this, they are failing as libraries. If they do not serve this function, it is questionable what agencies in our society will do so. But the world is becoming inundated with documents. Only a few of them are relevant to a given problem or a given library user. There is great danger that a library's preoccupation with collections and its relative neglect of information services may render those very collections progressively less relevant to the needs of its patrons. In short, the quality of even the collection itself is subject to continued improvement through use.

Today's citizen needs information of many kinds just to survive. To supply information related to survival, such as was envisioned in PIC, is to build up the library's capability to supply other kinds of information and documentary materials, including those more traditionally provided by a library.

Some traditionalists are concerned that the library's role as champion of literate culture will be diluted or cheapened by making it also an I&R agency for a public sometimes indifferent to literacy or high culture. But culture, in a deeper sense, is not divisible into "high culture" and the other things that people do, including basic survival; it is all a single fabric. The citizen who can approach the library with confidence in seeking survival information will be more receptive to the library's potential as an educator.

In the view of this writer, the provision of comprehensive information services remains a valid function for the public library. The public library, more than any other agency, is suited to the task. While many kinds of agencies distribute information, the public library is unique in our society in combining the following features:

1. Its primary function is to provide information and informational materials.
2. It exists to serve the entire community.
3. Its subject scope is virtually unlimited.
4. Its operators are specialists in document and information handling as such.
5. It is in principle impartial, being dedicated to the interests of society as a whole, rather than of a particular element of society.

6. While generally supported by public funds, its customary form of governance provides some measure of freedom from direct or partisan political control.

There is significant precedent for I&R service in public libraries. Librarians have long maintained informal files of "resource persons" to call upon when the library, with all its books, could not answer a question. In some communities, especially in periods of mass immigration, economic depression, or wartime, public libraries have served as liaison between official and voluntary organizations and the citizens.

But even though a rationale and clear precedents can be presented for the PIC, the creation of the information service along the lines attempted at Enoch Pratt is still a somewhat radical departure from tradition—at least in emphasis. It cannot be done successfully without a sizable commitment of resources. It is a mistake to begin it unless the commitment is strong enough that it is likely to be continued in lean times, when to do so might mean retrenchment elsewhere in the library's program.

Like all institutions, the public library seems certain to change greatly in the near future. How it changes, and what its place will be in the society of the future, will depend in large measure upon how effective it is in providing comprehensive information and referral services.

Chapter 6
The Citizens' Advice Bureaux

by Carole E. Peppi

The code of the Citizens' Advice Bureaux (CAB) is: "To make available to the individual accurate information and skilled advice on many of the personal problems that arise in daily life, to explain legislation, to help the citizen to benefit from and to use wisely the services provided for him by the state, and in general, to provide counsel for men and women in the many difficulties which beset them in an increasingly complex world."[1]

The CAB fulfills the need for a *general* advice service. It is a free service, offered to all people who care to use it. One of the great achievements of the CAB service is that it has become recognized as a service that people of all classes feel they can use—all are treated with courtesy and consideration and without discrimination by race, creed, or politics. CAB has attained a reputation for its impartiality.

CABs are established *for* citizens *by* citizens, often by ad hoc committees representative of the principal interests in the locality. When the CABs were begun during World War II,[2] it was realized that such advice centers could be successfully established only with local support and participation. Where there existed an active council of social service, the bureau was set up under its auspices; otherwise, leading citizens in many walks of life—employers, workers, councilors, and representatives of the church and the principal social work organizations in the area—were contacted and brought together to sponsor the

The cooperation and assistance of the officials and staff of the Citizens' Advice Bureaux is gratefully acknowledged.

Ms. Peppi was Administrative Assistant of the Public Information Center (PIC) Project throughout its duration.

1. From the CAB service's pamphlet "Aims and Methods," 1968.

2. The Citizens' Advice Bureaux (CAB), which has offices throughout England, Wales, and Scotland, was established by the British National Council of Social Service in 1939 and is financed by the Ministry of Health.

new service, and unless and until such representative support was obtained, the bureau was not established. This policy has continued ever since.

A Citizens' Advice Bureau is, then, a service established by the citizens of a locality, with the support of a national movement, for the citizens and visitors of that area. Its function is to give advice and information on any problem that the inquirer cares to bring. Wide in range and variety as these problems are, they are, in the main, problems of daily living in a highly complex society. It is important that such an advisory service remain independent and that it be known to be independent of central or local government control. Thus, although many bureaus receive financial and other help from local authorities, the independence of the CAB service is recognized and respected by statutory bodies. This independent status is a valuable asset to the bureau worker when seeking to discover what the individual's problem or grievance is and in bringing it to the notice of the appropriate authority, as well as in interpreting an official ruling to an aggrieved or bewildered citizen.

The nongovernmental status of the CAB service, which is so important when the matters to be considered concern the relationship between citizen and state, is also of value when the issue raised is between citizen and citizen. In all questions of civil law and related issues, the organs of the state must remain neutral and must avoid favoring one citizen over another. Hence, while a government official can appropriately give information, the situation changes when what is asked for is advice as well. The difference here lies in the fact that advice involves interpretation. An informant confines himself to presenting the facts; an adviser helps the inquirer to interpret the facts and relate them to his own particular situation. He does not, however, direct the inquirer to a particular decision. Adviser and inquirer may together seek a solution of the difficulty, but the choice as to which possible alternative should be adopted, or whether a solution is accepted or rejected, remains the inquirer's; this must be clearly understood by both sides.

There are, however, situations when something more positive is needed—action as well as advice. Some such actions are well within the compass of an adviser, as for example, drafting a letter for an illiterate person, or putting his case forward in a way which would be beyond his own capabilities. However, when more extensive help is asked or needed, the nature of the service changes from advice to a form of casework. The question of referring these types of problems to social casework agencies depends upon three things: (1) the availability of a professional welfare agency; (2) the willingness of the inquirer to go to one; and (3) the nature and urgency of the difficulty presented. Duplication of effort is avoided wherever possible, but the CAB workers themselves, as a result of their knowledge and experience, can handle many of these casework problems effectively and without difficulty. In general, it is felt that CAB workers can best serve both their clients and the community at large by making full use of, and cooperating fully with, the statutory and voluntary organizations in the area.

A CAB thus forms the link between the individual in need and an extraordinarily wide range of services, and as such it is an antidote to the prevailing tendency toward specialization in social and professional work. Whereas the main purpose of a CAB is to answer individual questions and to deal with individual difficulties, this is not its sole function. Inquiries made by the public to CAB sometimes reveal hardships caused by legislation imperfectly thought out, badly drafted, or operating in ways that were not foreseen. In such a case, the CAB has a duty, not simply to its clients, but to all citizens, to accumulate and sift evidence as objectively and impartially as possible and to make the facts known to the appropriate authorities. The bureaus often recommend action on a local and national basis. The National CAB Headquarters obtains data from the monthly reports sent in by each CAB and takes action where needed in cooperation with voluntary organizations and departments of the central government.

The CAB Council accepts responsibility for the maintenance of standards in all bureaus. Without the acceptance of centralized responsibility it would be impossible to retain the confidence of governments and professional organizations or to maintain the high quality of service. The national headquarters provides an information service to all the local CABs in the form of monthly newsletters and leaflets to keep them abreast of changes and developments in legislation, agencies, personnel, etc. They also provide a complete program for training all CAB workers, including basic training courses for new volunteers, refresher courses for experienced CAB staff members, and lecture series that are required for all CAB personnel. Finally, the national headquarters has established regional advisory committees. The committee members serve as consultants to the local bureaus and act as liaison between the local and the national organizations. The regional committee also convenes annual meetings of all workers within the region for the purpose of review and planning.

The regional advisory committees also help with the organization of a new CAB, that is, in finding and furnishing suitable premises (usually of a shopfront type in the center of the community), the recruitment, selection, and training of workers, and publicity and public relations. The time taken to establish a CAB is approximately nine to twelve months from the date of the initial public meeting. A

bureau in a large center of population may require the full-time services of paid staff in addition to a roster of voluntary workers. In many
cases, however, the bureau can be run by voluntary part-time staff. The
same careful selection is exercised in the case of voluntary workers as
in the appointment of paid staff, and all are expected to participate in
the continuous process of training, which is an integral part of the
service. No distinction of duties is allowed between voluntary and paid
staff; they all perform exactly the same tasks in the bureau—interviewing, counseling, filing, and the like. One of the values of the
training and lecture series is that it provides an opportunity for CAB
workers, local social workers, and government officials to meet and
discuss how each can complement the work of the other, thus laying
the foundation of the good relationships essential to the success of
the work.

The Local Authority Bureaux

There are two separate types of bureaus in the CAB structure: the
regular independent bureaus, of which there are more than 450, and
the few remaining "Local Authority Bureaux" (LAB), of which there
are about 20. These LABs are governed by local authorities and have
full-time paid staff instead of volunteers. The CAB headquarters provides them with the regular information bulletins, and the LABs, in
turn, submit a monthly statistical sheet to the headquarters on the
inquiries they have received.

A visit to a LAB situated in the central branch of a large public
library was arranged by officials of the National CAB Council. This
particular LAB was started during the war and has always been housed
in the central library building. The town is self-governing, having its
own local council and offices of national government agencies in the
Town Hall. In the 1950s, when CABs were experiencing a decline in
use, it was decided that the local council would take over the running
of this particular bureau. It was hoped that the services would be more
widely used if the bureau were made an integral part of the library
and managed by a regular, full-time, paraprofessional staff. The LAB
was renamed "Advice and Information Centre" (A&IC) and three
full-time and one part-time workers were appointed to operate the
center. The A&IC was placed just inside the main entrance of the
library. Its facilities consist of one large office and two smaller interviewing rooms. The center is regarded as a division of the Reference
Department of the library and works very closely with that department. The reference librarians are encouraged to work in the A&IC
in order to familiarize themselves not only with the operation of the
center but also with the types of questions asked by the public. The
regular staff members of the A&IC are nonlibrarians, but have had

some experience with social and government work. If a client asks a question of a kind that is usually handled by one of the library's regular departments, he is asked to visit the appropriate department.

Approximately 65 percent of the inquires are about civic, local, or national government matters. The other 35 percent range from communications and travel inquiries to problems of buying a house. This particular LAB answers about 2,000 inquiries a month. It is open to the public on the same schedule as the library. There are many leaflets on display which are available to the public either free of charge or, in a few cases, at a minimal cost. These leaflets, brochures, and pamphlets cover an enormous range of subjects, from a list of local government offices, their telephone numbers, addresses, and a complete breakdown of their services, to consumer advice. This material is supplied by the National CAB Council, government departments, tourist agencies, local manufacturers, and other sources.

Every inquiry received is recorded and every month a statistical report is prepared and sent to the National CAB Headquarters, as well as to the various departments of the library system. The majority of the inquiries (75 percent) are made by people who personally visit the A&IC; the remainder are made by telephone. It is the policy of this particular LAB not to participate in casework of any kind. If social casework is required, the problem is immediately passed on to the appropriate government agency *if* the inquirer agrees to this action. Letters are written and telephone calls are made where necessary if the inquirer requests it or if the staff member suggests such action.

Since all members of the staff perform exactly the same duties, it is posible for the A&IC to be run smoothly and efficiently even if a staff member is absent for reasons of sickness or vacation. The exception is the organizer, who performs extra duties such as issuing the monthly and yearly reports and training the staff.

There are, then, two important differences between this kind of bureau (the LAB) and the independent bureau (the CAB), which is under the direction of the National CAB Council. One is the degree of local autonomy; the other is the pattern of staffing. The LABs employ paid workers, unlike the CABs who consider its volunteer structure essential to its successful operation. These differences perhaps account for the decision of the National Council not to sponsor any additional bureaus of the LAB type.

A Visit to a Local CAB

The CAB which was visited is situated in the northwest section of Greater London and covers four boroughs, which location provides the bureau with a good cross section of the community.

The bureau has twenty volunteers and one full-time, paid organizer.

Each volunteer works approximately four hours per week on a rotating schedule, working one morning and one afternoon shift each week. Volunteers come from many walks of life—a retired bank manager, a nurse, a schoolteacher, housewives, civil servants, lawyers, and several blue-collar workers. All attended the twenty-four-week training course and are required to attend refresher courses which are held annually. Each is familiar with the area and with the government and local agencies serving the community. There appears to be a good rapport between the CAB staff and these agencies and a great deal of complementarity among their roles.

This CAB has two local lawyers available to advise on legal questions and legal aid cases; availablity of legal advice is common to most of the CABs. The bureau also has a consumer adviser available.

The bureau is of the shopfront type, comprising one large front office and two smaller interviewing rooms. It is bright and informal, with many leaflets and brochures on view for the public to take, free of charge. There is a large selection of pamphlets explaining the latest government social services and the circumstances for eligibility.

Most of the volunteers specialize in some area of government work, for example, taxes, National Health Insurance, maternity and child benefits, and housing, to name but a few. If a volunteer is asked a complex question on a particular subject and his information is insufficient to answer it, he will refer the inquirer to the worker most able to deal with it.

This CAB deals with some 250 inquiries per month. It has been open for only a year, but the staff is confident that its use will continue to grow. The problems brought to the bureau are many and varied, the largest proportion dealing with family and social questions and with landlord and tenant inquiries.

The Role of Volunteers

Volunteer workers, about 4,500 of them, from virtually every walk of life make up about 90 percent of the total work force. The volunteers contribute six to eight hours a week, a work pattern that enables a typical CAB office to absorb and appoint approximately ten to thirty staff members, thus obtaining a varied fund of knowledge and experience.

There must be careful selection; people are found who are willing to give their time to the work and the extensive training. This training involves not only the learning of a great deal of substantive information, but also learning to use a variety of reference materials.

CAB volunteers must bring to their work both objectivity and human warmth. They must be able to appraise objectively both the problems and their own limitations, refraining from undue personal involvement. The workers should also have the ability to put people at their ease so that the client's story emerges spontaneously, even if slowly and mixed with many concerns which are not relevant to the solution. Informal observers who were consulted felt that the majority of CAB workers are mature people with considerable life experience and a fund of knowledge at their disposal that they have the ability to relate this knowledge to the problems of those who come to them for help, yet somehow remain "quite ordinary people." The volunteers are expected to communicate effectively with people who are slow in understanding and expression, as well as with people who are highly sophisticated.

Most of the volunteers are recruited through "Help Wanted" advertisements in the local newspapers. Applicants are asked at the initial interview to supply the usual information required for employment on a paid basis, relating to relevant experience, qualifications, and availability, and they are asked to give two character references. A few people object to this and are heard of no more; it is felt by CAB authorities that if they are unwilling to respect this procedure they are probably no loss. Those remaining, who may number anywhere from 20 to 120 in any one town, are then invited to a meeting at which the work of the CAB and its training are described by an officer from the CAB Headquarters. Those who are interested enroll at the end of the meeting for a very basic training course, which is later supplemented by frequent programs devoted to new developments.

The preliminary course is organized locally by the CABs management committee under the guidance of an officer from CAB Headquarters. It comprises twelve to sixteen lectures, the first being an introduction to the goals and principles of CAB. There follows a series of lectures by local professional social workers and statutory officers providing a brief outline of existing social services.

Finally, there is a lecture on the day-to-day work in a bureau, including interview techniques, information resources, the filing system (which is standard in all CABs), and the recording of inquiries. It is a very brief course but serves to introduce the workers to the fabric of the social services and to some relevant principles of social work. Especailly stressed are the concepts of confidentiality, impartiality, respect for the individual, and the need to help people make their own decisions.

Apart from the obvious value of the training program in equipping the volunteers for work, it also helps to build a good relationship between the CAB and the local officials and professional people who give the lectures in the preliminary and local courses. The volunteers learn to respect the knowledge and skills of the professionals and soon understand the boundaries of their own work and how to make satisfactory referrals. Moreover, the local lecturers soon find themselves serving as the consultants to the bureau, and it is for this reason, and because some of the Headquarters and regional staff are professional social workers, that CABs have earned the reputation of being a professionally guided service.

The preliminary course serves also as a sifting device, wherein some candidates will either drop out or will be asked to stop attending because it is apparent that they are not suited for this type of work. The candidates who finish the course are then interviewed by two or three members of the local committee and a Headquarters officer, who make the final selection. Typically, a training course will prepare from ten to forty volunteers who are then ready to work in a local CAB office. Although the requirements placed upon CAB volunteers are rigorous, there is seldom a shortage of applicants. The CAB authorities attribute this to the fact that they treat their recruits in a businesslike manner and expect a substantial contribuion from them in regular weekly duty. The standards of work and training are such that volunteers look upon work in the CAB as a privilege. This attitude is in direct contrast to the view that still exists in some quarters—that a volunteer is due special respect and should be given special privileges because he *is* a volunteer. To accord volunteers special privileges could easily cause many irritations to clients and fellow workers.

Until recently, only bureaus in large towns and cities employed salaried organizers, who often were professional social workers. However, the demands on the organizers have increased to the extent that the National CAB Council recommends the appointment of a full-time or part-time salaried organizer in towns with a population of 40,000 or over. It is clearly stressed, however, that an organizer in a local CAB must allow the volunteers to think and act for themselves and must not let them rely too heavily upon the professional worker, for such dependence could lead to a decline in the volunteer's interest and satisfaction in the work.

There is a special skill needed when working with and using volunteers which is based upon a combination of training and trust. The secret appears to be to need them, to equip them by training, and to make heavy demands on them—using them not as cheap labor or second best, but as respected contributors whose work is its own reward. It must be remembered that many of these available volunteers are of such status that CAB could not get them for money—they just would not be available on that basis. There are many people who want to give their time, energy, and talent for the benefit of their fellow man. CAB recognizes the responsibility of the management and officials in the social services to make available to them the opportunity to do so.

Chapter 7
Staffing and Training Patterns for an Information and Referral Service: The Baltimore Experience

by Ruth W. Mednick

Information and referral services, since their inception during World War II, now serve most large metropolitan communities in this country. Such services may be autonomous or part of a community service agency or planning council. Some are part of government-supported agencies, but most are voluntary or privately supported. They are still few in number and, as they are staffed by only a small number of workers, there is no organized training program. On-the-job training is the rule, with many workers seeming to "fall into" the work more by accident than by intention. And, since services have developed to meet the specific needs of their own sponsoring agencies and communities, there is a great variation of structure and operation from one service to another.

Efforts have been made for a number of years by the administrators of the major I&R services in the country to hold annual meetings and workshops at which they may exchange information, discuss problems, and establish professional standards for this subgroup of the social work profession. At the 1972 annual workshop, part of the National Conference on Social Welfare, the Alliance of Information and Referral Services was founded. A committee of the alliance, aided by a staff member of the United Way (parent organization to all United Funds, Community Chests, Planning Councils, etc., in the United States and Canada), prepared for publication *National Standards for Information and Referral Services* (United Way, 1973). There are several hundred I&R services that are not affiliated with United

Ms. Mednick is a Planner at the Health and Welfare Council of Central Maryland, Inc., and was previously the Director of the Information and Referral Service.

Way agencies; some eighty of the largest community services are affiliated. If they all adopted the national standards, their operations could be affected. The alliance initiated a newsletter for the exchange of information among services between workshops, and a number of committees were established to work on specific problem areas. Among these is a Classification Committee, which is investigating the numerous classification systems in use by the many services in recording their statistical data. Its goal is to determine the feasibility of a standardized classification system for use in all services to provide comparable data and to insure that any newly established computerized systems can be related to one another. The alliance is still a loosely structured organization, without staff or facilities (other than the contributions of time and effort by its members), and thus has not as yet taken up such operational problems as the staffing of I&R services or training program content.

The training of I&R personnel has no general-purpose, comprehensive textbook. The Institute for Interdisciplinary Studies (now called InterStudy) began, in 1970, to publish helpful special purpose materials (U.S. Dept. of Health, Education and Welfare, 1971) for use on an experimental project for the U.S. Department of Health, Education and Welfare in Wisconsin. (*See* the bibliography in the chapter by Long, page 73.) Our own manual, prepared for the Social Security Administration in 1972, is the only other known to us. Neither of these efforts was intended for general use by I&R services; they were written with specific training situations in mind, and nowhere is staffing for a service spelled out.

In this area then, written guidelines are few. The purpose of this chapter is to share our experiences, providing a description of the Baltimore Information and Referral Service, its history and developing expansion, its growing staff needs, and a comprehensive training program of information and referral.

Information and Referral in Baltimore

The Health and Welfare Council of Central Maryland (earlier known as the Council of Community Services, and then as the Health and Welfare Council of the Baltimore Area) has had an I&R service as a component since 1962. Its purpose is to provide the public and the professional community a central source of information about community resources, and to provide a professional referral service to help link clients in need with the appropriate community resources to meet these needs. A more recently recognized function of the service is the provision of statistical data which can be utilized as a planning tool for the Planning Department of the Health and Welfare Council and other community agencies. Staff members also lend their expertise to other agencies in consultations, training programs, and special assignments, such as the preparation of the training manual for the Social Security Administration.

The I&R Service of the Health and Welfare Council now serves the Baltimore metropolitan area, with a population of roughly two million people. The service handles about 16,000 calls annually from its single Baltimore office location. For about three years (1970 to 1973) a specialized branch, I&R for the Aging in Maryland, served aged residents of the entire state of Maryland through the use of a Wide Area Telephone Service (WATS) system. That unit, however, had to be discontinued when funding expired, and its work and its staff were both absorbed by the main I&R service.

The challenge of running an expanding service over a number of years—growing pains—and the awareness that the service was certainly needed by far more citizens than it had then reached, stimulated the Baltimore I&R staff to study and search for improved techniques and methods of operation several years ago. There is, for instance, a never-ending struggle to develop satisfactory files and filing systems for the storage and selective retrieval of community resource data. This effort was, at that time, furthered considerably through the establishment of a working relationship between the social work staff of I&R, professional librarians, and information scientists of the University of Maryland School of Library and Information Science, and Baltimore's Enoch Pratt Library. In 1969 and 1970, a joint Public Information Center Project (PIC) (Donohue and Peppi, 1971) developed a method for producing a computerized index to the resource data files and a thesaurus of subject headings designed to fit both the I&R files and the *Directory of Community Services in Maryland* (Health and Welfare Council of Central Maryland, 1972), which is published biennially. While PIC itself was never fully implemented due to budgetary cutbacks, I&R had acquired a system for its resource files and for the *Directory,* and this greatly facilitated the computerization of the resource data three years later.

FRISBY AND COMPUTERIZATION

In April 1974 a demonstration project was added to the I&R Service. It was part of Baltimore's Youth Services System (YSS) known by the acronym FRISBY—Fast Referral Information Service for Baltimore Youth, under the administration of I&R, and using its facilities. The Mayor's Office of Manpower Resources (MOMR) sponsored it. It was to provide: a central referral service for youth of Baltimore City, using a special telephone line (the FRISBY line); expanded daytime office coverage; an answering service at night; preparation of the

BYSS index of Youth Services and Programs; a directory of resources serving youth and their families, which has been programmed onto a computer and which will issue a computer-produced directory to participating agencies three times a year; and the initiation of a tracking process to follow clients referred by participating agencies, which will provide a profile of each client and daily agency reports on referred clients. An on-line terminal used for making accurate referrals by matching the eligibility factors of a client with the resources available in the computerized directory. This computer system will also provide resource and service data information for community planners.

FRISBY has provided the initial financing for computerizing the bulk of I&R resource files. It will also provide an opportunity to test an almost instantaneous client-tracking system for the major agencies serving youth in a large metropolitan area. It provides technology to produce the Health and Welfare Council's biannual *Directory of Community Services in Maryland.* It also added three full-time staff members to the I&R service. Of the ninety-seven YSS projects throughout the country funded by the Office of Youth Development of the Department of Health, Education and Welfare, Baltimore's is the only one that has contracted with an I&R service, or the Health and Welfare Council; most others are associated with correctional or other kinds of community agencies. It is also the only one that has provided computerization of the project data.

In 1974, a plan was initiated to develop the statewide I&R plan for all state welfare agencies under federal law. To derive the benefit of the three years of I&R staff experience with the statewide Information and Referral for the Aging and the partially computerized *Directory,* the planning staff of the council should be retained to implement the plan.

Three Information and Referral Tasks

Reviewing this information about Baltimore's I&R Service and its recent venture into computer technology may emphasize the basic elements of the I&R service process. In the Social Security training manual we found it useful to postulate three stages in the process: (1) handling of the resources data; (2) diagnosis of the client problem; and (3) making the referral. These three stages involve three different kinds of skills: (1) data handling requires technical proficiency; (2) diagnosis requires a clinical or interviewing skill; and (3) making an appropriate referral acceptable to the client requires skill in coordination of services, and often advocacy on the client's behalf.

Most I&R services expect staff members to be able to handle all of these functions competently. The antecedent of American I&R

programs, the British Citizens' Advice Bureaux (CAB), insists on the idea that all its people are involved in all of the work (see chapter 6).

The expansion of Baltimore's I&R brought about changes over the years in the functions performed by the staff. Even before the operation of a statewide service was considered, the functions of the Baltimore office had changed subtly, as more and more agencies and community groups came to depend on the store of information, the skills and experience of staff members, and the services provided. Caseworkers in agencies consult I&R when they have exhausted their own repertoire of resources for a client. Others consult I&R on the handling of difficult problems, such as the client who threatens suicide. Groups needing statistical data call I&R to locate what they need, or to find out whether it even exists. Organizations wanting speakers to lecture about resources in certain problem areas, such as aging, child welfare, or minority problems, invite I&R staff members, perhaps the best informed persons in the community, to discuss a subject of this nature. Graduate students come to I&R to explore their seminar assignments or dissertations when community information is involved. Agencies planning new services or new locations for services consult I&R statistics. More and more, staff members have been invited to take part in conferences and institutes and share their expertise in the techniques and methods of providing information. They routinely present training programs for personnel in other organizations, such as social services, the police department, and unions.

The planning related function of I&R and the I&R staff has been only recently given recognition; the subject has been given major emphasis at National United Way conferences in recent months, probably because sources funding community projects now demand from them the means of evaluation and measuring accountability of operating agencies. The I&R services are in a unique position to provide the needed data.

These functional changes had become so pronounced that it recently became necessary to initiate a study and reevaluation of staff job descriptions and qualifications. Through a job analysis of the individual staff positions, each person's function became clearer, as well as the qualifications that are required to carry out these duties. Such an analysis also gave the administration a better basis for allocation of funds, including salary scales, and data needed for cost accounting purposes. Functional time recording was instituted while the job analysis was being done so that time allocations could be made for each of the component functions identified as part of an individual job. Complete data on this study have never been tabulated and analyzed.

The major categories of job (and time) function identified for an I&R staff worker are:

1. Handling of inquiries, including giving of information, referrals, and advocacy (examples: the caller who saw our number on a local TV show and requested referral to a nearby family counselor; the woman whose drunken husband beat her up, who was referred to us by a police officer to locate counseling, medical attention, legal action, etc.; or the family whose application for public assistance had been long delayed and needed an advocate to get things straightened out) ;

2. Outside contacts, including training, orientation, speaking, public relations presentations (examples: participation in Police Academy training program, one presentation for each graduating class; appearance on a local TV show, "Dialing for Dollars," to publicize I&R for Aging; conduct resources seminar for workshop on aging problems) ;

3. Resources development (examples: clipping items about new programs and program changes from newspapers, then tracking down full information; locating scarce resources or hard-to-find information through systematic searches of likely agencies, contact persons, directories, etc.) ;

4. Agency consultation (example: Health Department seeking data to guide placement of a new child mental health clinic; County Commission on Aging seeking advice on projects to be undertaken);

5. Personnel (I&R) training and supervision;

6. Administration;

7. One-time-only or emergency duties (examples: conducting tour for visiting Japanese architects who wanted to see housing projects for the aged; operating switchboard to maintain service on holidays; home visit to a client (very rarely done) when no other agency can provide service and an emergency exists) .

Each of the staff positions within the system carries its own job description, but there is considerable overlapping of duties and responsibilities. The positions are: Director, Assistant Director, Caseworker, Caseworker Aide, Public Information Specialist (public relations), Secretary, Receptionist, and Switchboard Operator. Two part-time positions for retirement-age persons from the Senior Aides Program were added to the staff, but are not on the council payroll. The size of the staff is apt to be determined more by the limitations of the budget than by the size of the job to be done. Statistical computations based on only one staff function, that of answering inquiries, indicate that twenty inquiries a day per caseworker represent a full workload for a seven-hour workday. Since simple questions can be handled by the receptionist or the secretary, the inquiries handled by caseworkers represent casework interviews that require significant periods of time for the initial call and for any subsequent calls, letters, etc., needed to complete the inquiry. These are counted as a single unit on a given day. Of course time must be provided for other duties, especially for resource development, to keep files current and complete. Periodic "quiet days" are necessary for each staff member to catch up on work which tends to back up in very busy periods, allowing no free time between calls. When the number of workers cannot be increased and the workload reaches or exceeds the capacity of the staff, public relations activities must be adjusted to control the number of inquiries and hold them to a manageable level. The only other alternative is the use of nonsalaried staff, volunteers, or workers from other programs to supplement regular staff.

Professional Status of the Information and Referral Worker

Many, if not most, directors of I&R services are social workers. Workers that provide the type of client service provided by Baltimore's I&R believe that they are doing social work, although not in the traditional casework sense. The formation of the Alliance of Information and Referral Services, as a component of the National Conference of Social Welfare, seems to indicate that I&R is a bona fide member of the social work profession, rating its own professional organization. The professional status of I&R as a field of social work, however, and the status of I&R workers as professionals, has not been readily accepted in many places. Salary scale, in relation to salary scales for other professional staff employed by the same councils that include I&R services, tells the story. When the Baltimore I&R staff was struggling for a salary scale equal to that of Planning, (for equal academic requirement) a survey was made of all other I&Rs attached to similar councils. The results were mixed, Some of the larger cities had established comparability for salary scales, while others paid their I&R people little more than clerical-level salaries. A number of responses to the survey indicated that a frustrating situation existed, in which the parent council recognized neither the worth of the I&R work being done nor the potential value I&R could have if it were supported and developed. Only a few councils recognized the potential planning role of I&R at that time (December, 1972).

A Social Security Training Program

In March 1972 Baltimore's I&R was asked by the Social Security Administration to prepare for them, under contract, a training manual to instruct the personnel in Social Security District and Branch offices how to provide an information and referral service (U.S. Dept. of Health, Education and Welfare, 1971, 1972). Upon completion, it was printed by SSA and distributed to the field offices directly, in two parts: *Information and Referral Service District Office Training,* and *Information and Referral Services in SSA District and Branch Office, the Information Resource File: Compilation Indexing, and Updating.*

The content of a training program for I&R is essentially the same for most communities. Agencies and services for particular types of problems, such as handicaps, retardation, or mental illness, would handle fewer general inquiries. Certain geographical locations would have specific problems not common in other areas, such as Spanish- or French-speaking populations, or large concentrations of ethnic groups having special problems characteristic of their own communities. For the most part, however, I&R inquiries fall into a predictable set of categories, and the training program was designed to cover this range of problem areas.

The basic tools for providing I&R are knowledge of the community and of its resources, and skill in interviewing. The training program begins with a session in which an invited speaker describes the structure of social welfare in the area served by the District Office. Emphasis is placed on the structure and interrelationships of governmental and voluntary organizations providing services to the community. The second session describes a resource data file and the supplementary materials a worker can use to locate information and/or resources for a particular client's needs. An expanded section on the compilation, indexing, and updating of such a resource file was separated out from the original manual as submitted and issued as a separate volume, so that the training manual was distributed in two parts.

An introduction to I&R interviewing skills was presented with three basic objectives: (1) to diagnose a client's needs, both spoken and unspoken; (2) to elicit sufficient information to refer a client to available services; and (3) to make referrals in such a way that the client is likely to utilize these services. A section on interviewing was included, covering attitudes of the interviewer, handling of sensitive topics, interviewing pitfalls, and what to do when gaps are identified in community services. To illustrate the three steps, and to demonstrate interviewing skills, a special section was included covering that frequent problem—the Social Security check that either didn't arrive, was lost, stolen, or whatever.

Seven problem areas are described in the manual: (1) Income Maintenance; Emergency Assistance; (2) Housing; (3) Health Services; Medical Assistance Program; Nursing Homes; (4) Hospital and Health Equipment; Rehabilitation Services; (5) Child and Family

Services; (6) Drug Abuse; Court System, Legal Services; (7) Alcoholism; Mental Health. While these seven areas do not cover all problems an I&R worker might encounter, the worker who has learned to cope adequately with these problems should have acquired the necessary skills and the personal resourcefulness to handle just about any kind of inquiry.

The methods used in the training program were a combination of lectures by community or agency representatives, discussion, role playing, individual assignments to explore resources, claims manual readings, etc. A film, "Tell Me Where to Turn," by the Public Affairs Committee, was suggested as a training aid, if copies were locally available.

Part II of the training manual, dealing with the resource file, described methods of building a file if none were already available in the community. Local offices were advised to seek out the files already available, such as those of existing I&R services, or files maintained by agencies such as social service departments, hospitals, and directories of community services and make use of them wherever possible. An outline described steps for building a file, places to look for information, ways to index the information, and how to keep it up-to-date. Three subject index lists of three different lengths were included for systems of different sizes that might be adapted to fit local needs. This material had been removed from the original training manual for separate distribution, since it would most likely be used by specialized personnel, rather than the Claims and Service Representatives who would ordinarily interview the client. The entire staff needed to be somewhat familiar with the content of Part II, but not in the same way as the person who would be responsible directly for the file and its maintenance.

The person sought for I&R staff positions should, ideally, be warm, concerned, and very sensitive.[1] She or he should have broad experience and mature judgment. Preferred persons are those with social work experience in several agencies, though not necessarily academic training in a school of social work. A thorough knowledge or at least ability to learn about the local community is essential. Sometimes a person who has come from another locale is more aware and more highly motivated to learn about the local community than a life-time resident. Ingenuity, creativity, and imagination are other qualities to be sought, because the worker who finds no existing resource to meet a client's need must be able to rethink the situation, work out alterna-

---

1. The reader may wish to compare these requirements with those suggested by Deahl in chapter 8. (Ed.)

tives, and invent other ways to deal with a problem. Personally, the worker needs the knowledge and awareness of self and insight that are most likely to come from either having worked in a psychiatric setting or having experienced personal psychotherapy. Workers with such a background are apparently better prepared to deal with clients in situations of emotional stress, or with their families, with less supervision than a worker without such experience. In addition, once trained a worker is expected to be able to operate with a minimum of direct supervision and to maintain professional standards of behavior and ethics as a social worker.

The formal requirement for a caseworker is for a BS or BA, plus one or more years of experience in a social welfare agency setting. A Master's degree (but not necessarily the MSW) plus experience is considered essential for the director's position. In addition, the applicant is expected to be able to conduct interviews, contact agency representatives on behalf of clients in a referral or in an advocacy role, write letters, give talks and prepare reports when required, conduct training sessions, and make public appearances before groups, on radio or television. The director and assistant director carry the more demanding and responsible of these duties, while caseworkers carry less; but the staff is essentially able, and called upon at times, to do the same things.

Applicants for positions on the I&R staff are expected to submit a professional resume which is circulated among a panel of council administrators and I&R staff. The applicant is then given a group interview by this panel whose members share their impressions afterwards. The procedure is somewhat informal, but gives panel members an opportunity to observe the way the applicant handles himself in a face-to-face encounter and under questioning not so different from that he will receive if hired for the job.

A perennial question in the field of social welfare services concerns the use of volunteers in an agency. The Baltimore I&R experience with volunteers is limited to two retirement-age persons receiving minimal compensation from a federal Senior Aides Program. It has been very encouraging.

Consideration has also been given to seeking the more traditional kind of volunteer to work in I&R. The kind of supervolunteer described in Peppi's chapter, the retired professional whose services are so expert and so expensive that they could only be obtained through his volunteering time to the program, do not seem to be very numerous in the Baltimore area. The year-old Voluntary Action Center in Baltimore reports that few volunteers are seeking the kind of work I&R would like to have done—such persons say they might as well get a job and be paid for their work. Hospitals and child-care programs in the city report a heavy turnover of their volunteers, as one after another goes into regular employment after gaining experience on a volunteer job.

Aside from the scarcity of volunteers, I&R staff has some reluctance to become involved with volunteers other than these two particular senior aides, because their workload has been so very heavy that there is no time or effort left over to devote to the necessary training and supervision. They are aware that volunteers would require considerable time and attention before their assistance could be of value to the service.

Training an I&R worker requires more than transmitting techniques or skills. Attitude is the most essential element, and sometimes the most difficult one to train. Perhaps it has to be part of the new worker's personality. To promote growth, to expand the programs of the service, there must be a heavy emphasis on attitude. There must be an openness, a free availability of service, no begrudging of service, a willingness to take the extra time, explore further, and make the extra effort. The individual worker and the staff as a unit must be willing to share the information they have—must indeed want to share it—and not operate with a defensive, guarded, or begrudging attitude. There is no shortage of information, and there is no shortage of information needs among persons or agencies using I&R services. The more help an I&R can give, the more people will turn to it for help. The information must be accurate and reliable, of course, but the attitude with which it is given is equally important. Handing out correct information about community resources is not enough. It has to be the information that will help a person who has a problem, and he has to receive it in such a way that he will make use of it and *be* helped. Relationships between the I&R service and the community agencies it serves, when built on a long experience of dependability, enable the I&R service to perform a role of advocate for clients when necessary, without losing the good will of the agencies and their confidence in the I&R as an informed and impartial third party.

I&R workers seem to get "hooked" on the work. They find it exciting, challenging, and stimulating, as well as sometimes exhausting, frustrating, and saddening. There is a pride in being one of the persons in a community who are best informed about community resources. There is immense satisfaction in being able to find help for persons in trouble, even when the only help to be given is the communication of personal understanding and concern. And there is satisfaction in being able to assist a community or governmental agency plan and develop new services and programs to serve the entire community.

I&R workers can serve their community in many ways and on many levels when their potential is fully realized.

References

Donohue, J., and Peppi, C. *The Public Information Center Project: Final Report.* Baltimore, Md.: Enoch Pratt Free Library, 1971.

Health and Welfare Council of Central Maryland. *Directory of Community Services in Maryland.* 14th ed. Baltimore, Md.: The Council, 1972.

_____. *Ten-Year Report Describing the Operation of the Information and Referral Service, Baltimore, Maryland, 1962–1971.* Baltimore, Md.: The Council, 1972.

U.S. Department of Health, Education and Welfare, Administration on Aging. *Information and Referral Services.* Working draft. A set of manuals prepared by the Institute for Inter-disciplinary Studies. Washington, D.C.: The Administration, 1971.

_____, Social Security Administration, Bureau of District Office Operations. *Information and Referral Service District Office Training.* Prepared under contract by the Health and Welfare Council of Central Maryland, Inc. Baltimore, Md.: The Bureau, 1972.

_____, _____. *Information and Referral Services in SSA District and Branch Offices, The Information Resource File: Compilation Indexing, and Updating.* Prepared under contract by the Health and Welfare Council of Central Maryland, Inc. Baltimore, Md.: The Bureau, 1972.

United Way of America. *National Standards for Information and Referral Services,* Alexandria, Va.: 1973.

Chapter 8
The Model Cities Community Information Center: The Philadelphia Experiment in Automating an Information and Referral Program

by Thomas F. Deahl

A major social problem confronting America today is the decline of its cities. In the minds of many citizens, vitality is ebbing because cities have become dangerous and unpleasant. places to live. This is due in part to increased numbers of desperate and alienated inner-city residents whose life styles hinge on survival. A survival mentality manifests itself in a variety of antisocial acts calculated to produce momentary surcease from deep personal pain. The middle classes, appalled by such self-serving and unpredictable behavior, resent their roles as victims in this new scenario and cope by escaping to safer havens. The outward migration of the middle classes is followed by business, industry, and the arts. A municipal tax base that should be growing in order to provide its citizens with the increasingly sophisticated products and services created by an advanced technology, diminishes instead, and the urban decay feeds upon itself. How this unfinished business will end is yet to be determined. One thing is certain: the price is high.

It is my thesis that this negative trend can be halted, if not reversed, and cities made livable again if the inner-city poor are provided with hope, encouragement, and opportunities to lift themselves out of the

The Model Cities Community Information Center is a demonstration project operated by the Health and Welfare Council, Inc., of Philadelphia.

Mr. Deahl is President of MICRODOC of Philadelphia. He was formerly the Director of the Model Cities Community Information Center.

oppressive environment created by institutionalized poverty. I reject the argument that people prefer dependency. Our experience in Philadelphia indicates otherwise. However, disadvantaged people cannot help themselves in overcoming genuine barriers to personal adjustment and self-sufficiency without support. The key to social rehabilitation lies in changing the attitudes of people caught in the trap of despair. The changing of attitudes depends on community responsiveness to citizen needs, and on the community being seen as responsive. Effective and timely intervention with meaningful assistance is an essential ingredient in this process. It amplifies the momentum of people who are motivated to help themselves; it can also provide the impetus for those not already so motivated.

Motivation toward self-help becomes visible when people contact community organizations for help in resolving a personal, community, or family-related problem they cannot handle alone. It is at this point of contact that the delivery system must not fail. Unfortunately, the conditions of our cities attest to the degree of such failure. There is no acceptable reason why referral steering should fail. There is no reason why, if a person contacts the wrong agency, he should not be accurately directed to one that can help. If incorrectly guided, there is a high probability—particularly with the disadvantaged—that the matter will be dropped there, and the motivation to help oneself will be lost. The attitude that "no one cares and I must bear my burden alone" is then reinforced. The community suffers because a significant portion of its citizenry has resigned itself to the view that there is no way out. It is a short step from this position to open hostility and behavior that is counterproductive to a healthy social order.

Effective community information and referral services have a vital role to play in reversing the decline of our cities by securely linking those who are motivated with appropriate community resources. It is this writer's view, however, that I&R services are not doing the job they could be doing. By and large, I&R services operate independently and do not coordinate their activities. They do not exchange valuable service information and do not report to regional planning bodies that need such service data in order to identify gaps, deficiencies, and duplication of services so that scarce community resources can be allocated rationally. They do not share training facilities and do not have standardized information and referral practice. Consequently, the quality of service varies widely.

I&R programs are handicapped by antiquated information-handling methods and by an attitude that referral work is essentially a personal act that cannot be improved except through better formal education and first-hand experience with social agencies. There is skepticism about the introduction of advanced technology into a domain in which manual methods have done a passable job for so long. With more knowledge of the advantages of technology, however, human services workers are likely to discover the values of automated information handling, and manual files and information systems are likely to give way to machine-aided referral when they do. No one denies that there are some I&R specialists who do a first-rate job of referral—i.e., they are fast, accurate, and effective. However, while a few caseworkers with good, informal networks of social service contacts can in fact render high quality referrals, the majority of them have limited contacts and perform a significantly less effective job.

As an information systems engineer, I have faith in the ability of the machine to prove beneficial in the practice of human services. I do not believe, however, that automation is a panacea. As the reader will discover from our experience at Model Cities, automation has a long way to go before it can be universally adopted. Further, it is unlikely that the computer will replace the human element in the service equation. The computer is not as complex or as subtle as the human mind. In order for us to use the technology well, we must carefully analyze the real-world process to which we wish to apply the machine's help. We have just begun to understand technically the information-giving and referral process, and have found it to be significantly different from literature-based systems. The models that have been developed for information storage and retrieval to meet patron needs in libraries are not applicable to I&R work.

Fundamentally we are asking: "What conditions must prevail before a referral can be made that has a high probability of satisfying a client's real needs?" The key lies in matching the service capabilities of agencies to the service needs of clients. For machines to facilitate the matching process, we must first structure an efficient representation of this complex activity. To do so requires a systematic analysis of the various components and their interrelationships necessary to accomplish the service objective. This is no simple task. Further, the computer in its present state-of-art cannot do the job alone. Successful matching of agencies to clients is dependent on the referral counselor's ability to define a client's real needs and to translate the needs into terms the machine can handle. The computer must be viewed as a supplemental tool. What automation *can* do is to relieve the professional from the essentially clerical tasks of file searching, file maintenance, and statistical analysis of the case service data. Thus the human services worker can be freed to pursue professional duties, such as diagnostic interviewing and counseling. It is a mistake to confuse one's ability to maintain and search a social service resource file with the professional aspects of casework.

Although the referral function has long been an integral part of social service provider operations, not until recently has "information-giving and referral" emerged as a separate service. I&R centers differ in certain important respects from care-giving agencies. It is the job of a modern I&R service to attract inquiries from those in need, dispense accurate and useful information about available community resources, locate appropriate helping agencies, facilitate appointments for service provision, and feed back to social service managers and planning bodies reliable information concerning unmet needs and the performance of the delivery system. It is not the responsibility of an I&R operation to provide professional guidance counseling and authoritative technical advice. At most, I&R services function as "first-aid stations" that are prepared to provide quality intervention until services can be obtained from agencies equipped to handle the myriad problems engendered by today's complex urban environment. In other words, an I&R service is a switching station that performs a preliminary diagnosis and either tells the inquirer where to go for help or actually assists in making contact with a person who will help. This basic function holds true whether the I&R activity is independent or is a service component of an agency that provides direct assistance.

The primary goal of the Philadelphia Model Cities Community Information Center was to develop ways to improve the social service delivery system for low-income residents,[1] concentrating in particular on the information-giving and referral aspect of this process. The specific focus was on the following:

1. How to reach those in need, including those who are motivated to seek assistance but who are uninformed about where to go, and those who are unmotivated because of alienation by the system;
2. How to speed up the linking of clients and helping services; and
3. How to ensure that needed services are in fact delivered.

Our "outreach" effort revolved around improving community awareness of what we and other community agencies had to offer. We kept our I&R service before the public through radio and television messages, newspaper advertisements, and a weekly "hotline" column in neighborhood newspapers. We trained other community workers in I&R methods and acquainted them with the services available from local providers. Our Community Education Staff spread the word through presentations to church and civic groups. We stationed a

1. The target population consisted of some 285,000 people living in North Philadelphia.

mobile unit in different parts of the Model Neighborhood and offered on-the-spot referral steering to passersby. It was our belief that the best way to reach those who had given up on the system was by word-of-mouth from friends, relatives, neighbors, and ministers—people in whom they might confide and from whom they would accept advice. Thus the more people in this latter group we could educate, the better. Sooner or later the word would reach those who paid no heed to our public messages.

The modern philosophy of social service is to provide comprehensive and coordinated assistance that results in a service plan that clients themselves have helped shape. This plan, along with necessary supports, is designed to help clients come to grips with their circumstances and to provide a firm foundation on which they may raise their life expectations. Traditionally, the client receives referral advice from social workers in the following manner: A client will telephone an advertised number—often called a "hotline"—or walk into a nearby social service office for assistance. The referral counselor interviews the client, reduces his problem to a set of specific needs, and then matches the needs against service capabilities available in the local community. The referral counselor relies on his memory and directories of one of two types. He may seek agency information from his own homemade card file or from locally published directories of social service organizations. From the file, he selects a suitable agency or set of agencies to which he can refer his client. He then gives an address and contact information to the client, who is expected to follow through with the arrangements. The counselor may, if an agency's intake procedures require, call ahead or write advising the direct service provider to expect the client.

This would appear to be a straightforward, directory-type function—i.e., a well-informed person tells a less well-informed person where to turn for needed assistance. In practice, however, it does not work well—particularly for the inner-city poor. The system breaks down at several points. The two areas on which we focused our research and development effort were the identification of suitable service providers and the completion of arrangements for client service.

Identification of Service Providers

The information files upon which the referral counselors depend are never complete, current, or sufficiently detailed enough to permit good initial matches of service capabilities and client service requirements. Nor are these files structured for rapid searching. Consequently, the referral counselor tends to rely on a limited number of broad-spectrum service organizations and a handful of specialized agencies with which he is personally familiar. This results in overuse, and thus overloading, of a few social service organizations and underuse of a great many others. We estimate that the average caseworker depends on services offered by thirty to fifty organizations in his community—a fraction of the several thousand human service providers that exist in large metropolitan areas.

If a client presents an unusual problem or set of problems, the counselor is obliged to check with colleagues for suggestions and spend a significant amount of time—often amounting to several hours— "calling around," fishing for help or verifying that old agency service descriptions are still accurate. Manually searching even an up-to-date file of some 800 to 1000 agencies is very time consuming, not only because of the nonstandard and imprecise service classification schemes in current use, but also because of widely varied and often complex service programs available that must be matched against equally complex client need profiles.

At least three different features of an agency must match with corresponding aspects of a client before a suitable referral can be made. These three features are functional services offered, absolute discriminators, and relative discriminators.

The client may present a single, straightforward problem that can be resolved by referral to an agency that specializes in a particular service. For example, during a budget dispute in the Pennsylvania State Legislature, welfare checks for thousands of recipients were delayed for three weeks. Our I&R center was swamped with requests for emergency food. Referral consisted of identifying the nearest emergency food distribution facility and communicating that information to the client.

In other cases, clients present multifaceted problems. A drug abuser may not only require rehabilitation therapy, but because he has lost his job and has been evicted from his home, he also requires assistance with job placement and housing. Our referral counselors are trained to reduce client problems to their constituent parts and to translate these into specific service needs.

The referral service objective is to provide one-stop service for the client, both at the point of referral and with the service provider. Every effort is made to locate a single agency that can handle all aspects of a client's problem. If no such agency exists or if an agency exists but is unavailable, the referral counselor is expected to establish a service schedule for the client—i. e., coordinate referral appointments with all agencies necessary to satisfy a client's multiple needs.

Virtually every agency has eligibility specifications which define who may and may not apply for assistance. These *absolute discriminators* deal with age, sex, income, residential location, education, etc. All requirements must be met before the client can receive attention. An agency may be able to provide the needed services, and a client may meet the agency's eligibility requirements yet still not be able to avail himself of the service because he cannot afford the fee, because he cannot get to the agency during office hours, because his problem is of such urgency that he cannot wait, or because the agency does not have a translator who speaks his language. These are *relative discriminators,* in the sense that if the client can overcome the obstacles, he can receive the service.

Three serious consequences flow from incomplete, insufficiently detailed, and out-of-date resource files:

1. Referral counselors spend an inordinate amount of time trying to locate suitable assistance—time that could be better spent on more professional duties.
2. Uneven use of community resources distorts the service loading and thus scarce community resources are inefficiently allocated.
3. The risk of killing the motivation to help oneself is very high and particularly serious when dealing with the inner-city poor.

Imprecise matching of client need with agency service can result in bad referrals, i.e., the agency to which a client has been referred cannot help him with his problem at all or in time or to the extent necessary to be of real value. This is likely to frustrate the client to the point where he abandons his effort to help himself. He then either resigns himself to his circumstance or turns to unacceptable social behavior.

Arrangement for Service

Another aspect of the referral process that calls for rethinking is the "completion of arrangements for client service." As pointed out earlier, in the traditional referral operation, clients are given the agency contact information and are expected to follow through the arrangements on their own. This requirement is a major obstacle to the delivery of supportive services to many inner-city poor. The interlude between presenting oneself for service and receiving an appointment can be a most unpleasant experience—one that can discourage even the most stalwart among us. To the distressed, intake processing with its attendant forms, probing personal questions, and endless waiting with no guarantee that when it is over they will receive what they came for, is a hurdle many prefer not to jump. Applications for help have ended in failure so often that they are convinced no one cares and so are naturally reluctant to follow through on a referral.

The Model Cities Community Information Center Demonstration

It was necessary to find a way to minimize the chasing around, the retelling of one's story over and over, the interminable waiting, and the uncertainty of service delivery. A partial answer, it was felt, was to improve the agency/client match to ensure that appointments were made and that a commitment to service was given.

At the Model Cities Community Information Center these referral service problems were attacked through the judicious application of modern information-handling technology, namely, the computer and the telephone. Better referrals could be made if counselors had at their disposal a comprehensive and current resource file that they could search rapidly with complex queries corresponding to the profile of the client's need. Thus we established a computer-resident data base of agency service descriptions that were accessed by means of on-line, interactive computer terminals.

To ensure that the referrals were good and that satisfactory service would be delivered, a conference telephoning system was devised that made it possible to tie the client, the referral counselor, and the social service caseworker together while we advocated in behalf of our client, if necessary, retelling his story in the technical jargon of the field.

The telephone-conference advocacy system worked; the on-line computer system did not—at least not in the way we anticipated. The successes and failures can be attributed to degree of user acceptance.

Telephone-conference advocacy. The telephone-conference advocacy system proved a useful tool in those instances in which the client appeared confused and thus unable to articulate his problem clearly. It was also used effectively when it was clear from the conversation that the client was unlikely to follow through with the referral. Success is attributed to the belief that the three-way telephone arrangement met the needs of both the clients and the provider agencies. From the client's standpoint, conference advocacy worked because he could handle the entire transaction with a single telephone call and did not have to travel hither and yon explaining his needs over and over to strangers. His confidence in the social service delivery system increased because he could hear for himself that positive assistance was being arranged by a professional who understood his problem and who, through personal intervention, demonstrated that he cared. Further, he was saved the frustrating experience of having to make an additional trip to the referred agency because he had left necessary personal records at home. These requirements are brought out in the course of the discussion and thus the client can present himself at the agency properly prepared for intake processing. The discouragement of false starts is eliminated through this technique of three-way preliminary problem review.

From the provider's point of view, dealing with a Model Cities referral was easier and less time consuming. When an MCCIC referral counselor called, the agency worker knew that he would not have to explain what his agency could and could not do. He also knew that the client had already been prescreened against an accurate agency service/eligibility profile. But in case the referral counselor had overlooked an important service requirement or misunderstood the client's presentation problem, the agency worker had the opportunity by means of the three-way hookup to clarify the matter directly with the client. Then, based on accurate knowledge of the particular situation, he could proceed either to advise the potential client that his agency could not help or give a firm service commitment.

In short, the whole referral process can be handled more positively and with much greater dispatch when referral counselors operate with accurate agency resource files and when all parties can settle arrangements by means of a telephone conference.

Technically, a three-way telephone conferencing capability requires a minimum of two outside lines, one to accept incoming client calls and one to call out to agencies. It requires a "hold" or standby capability, available on standard six-button telephone sets, and a method for coupling the two outside lines through the referral counselor's phone.

Telephone-conference advocacy by way of a three-way telephone arrangement can be adopted immediately in the information-giving and referral field. This technique can significantly improve the delivery of social services by ensuring that clients are securely installed in the intake process of an agency that has confirmed its ability and willingness to provide the needed care.

The on-line computerized information resource file. The basic agency resource file was compiled by a team of four persons on special assignment from the Free Library of Philadelphia.[2] They culled all directories they could find for agencies and programs serving the Model Cities area. They edited, verified, and classified these descriptions and then assigned the initial set of subject index terms. When we were satisfied that we had a good working file, we converted it to a computer-based system. Two years from the project's inception[3] we were on-line with an automated social service directory.[4]

2. The Free Library is also experimenting with this automated directory system. The library has placed terminals in Model Cities area branches and is evaluating the usefulness of this new kind of library service for residents of inner-city neighborhoods.

3. The Model Cities Community Information Center (MCCIC) began operation in July 1970.

4. Much credit for the continuing refinement and maintenance of this automated resource file must be given to the Data Base Section Staff of three persons headed by Ms. Marna Elliott.

The system works in the following manner: Each morning we dial our computer and activate our terminals. A question mark hovers on the screen indicating that the computer is standing by, waiting to be interrogated. If we desire current information on a known agency, we look up the agency's numeric code and enter this in our terminal keyboard. The computer fetches the latest record and displays it. If we wish to search for all agencies that provide a combination of services that match the requirements of a client whom we have standing by on the phone, we execute the following protocol:

1. We select from our subject lists those terms that best describe our client's needs and then type the alpha code equivalents of these into the terminal keyboard. (See the top half of figure 1.) The search statement "NMMH @ NMMD, CA44, AG15" translates: Find all agencies that provide maternity home service and care for unwed mothers age 15 living in zip code area 19144.

2. The computer gives us the opportunity to verify our search statement (VER:) before it begins searching. If it is correct, we push the "return" key, which signals the computer to begin matching our inquiry against the descriptors that characterize the records in the computer file.

3. When the computer has completed its file search (it takes about five seconds on a Hewlett-Packard 2000C[5]), it reports back how many agencies have been described with this combination of terms. This is called the number of "hits." If it is a large number, say ten or more, we can recast the search query in more stringent terms, that is, we can add more search qualifiers such as sex of clients served, language spoken, hours that agency is open, etc. This has the effect of making the search more precise, and thus reducing the number of records that must be examined visually.

4. The computer then asks how we want to display the results of our search. This is the meaning of "CMD?" (Command?). We have two options:

a. We can order a TAB(ular) list of agency names, addresses, phone numbers, and date the record was last updated (see bottom half of figure 1).

b. We can order the complete record display of the first agency on the list (see figure 2).

If we had ordered the Tabular List, we could have chosen any one of the items in the list for full record display by keying in the appropriate list number.

5. MCCIC purchased programming and computer services from the Instructional Computer Center, the School District of Philadelphia.

```
GET—CBIS
RUN
CBIS

?NMMH
VER :

HITS :    15
CMD ?    CLR

?NMMH@NMMD
VER :

HITS :    6
CMD ?    CLR
?NMMH@NMMD,CA44,AG15

VER :
HITS :    6
CMD ?    TAB

1 OF 6     # 753
FLORENCE CRITTENTON SERVICE OF PHILA
6325 BURBRIDGE ST PHILA, PA    19144
V18—6200     DATED :      8/73

2 OF 6     # 42
BOOTH MATERNITY HOSP.
5930 CITY LINE AVE PHILA, PA    19131
TR8—7800     DATED :   3/73

3 OF 6     # 882
CATHOLIC SOCIAL SERVICES, UNMARRIED PARENTS
222 N 17TH ST PHILA, PA    19103
587—3834     DATED :   4/73

4 OF 6     # 874
CHOICE
2027 CHESTNUT ST PHILA, PA    19103
LO7—2904     DATED :   5/73

5 OF 6   # 404
ST VINCENT'S HOSPITAL
70TH ST AND WOODLAND AVE PHILA, PA    19142
587—3834     DATED :   3/73

6 OF 6     # 402
ST JOSEPH'S CHILDREN'S AND MATERNITY HOSP
2010 ADAMS AVE SCRANTON, PA    18509
342—8379     DATED :   3/73

CLR
```

Figure 1. Computer Printout

We have had mixed results with the experiment. Our greatest success has been with file updating. Our computer file of agency descriptions is updated every four months in the following way. Every two weeks the computer service vendor delivers to us a paper printout of one-eighth of the agency records in our file. We then put the records into window envelopes designed to display the agency address. Figure 3

1 OF 6   # 753   DATED : 8/73

1   FLORENCE CRITTENTON SERVICE OF PHILA
    6325 BURBRIDGE ST
    PHILA, PA   19144   CT—238
    MRS MARY WEIST, INTAKE SUPERVISOR   V18—6200

2   MULTI SERVICE RESIDENTIAL PROGRAM FOR UNWED MOTHERS.
    SERVICES INCLUDE PRE AND POST NATAL MEDICAL CARE,
    24 HOUR NURSING CARE, EDUCATIONAL TUTORING FOR
    JUNIOR AND SENIOR HIGH GIRLS, SEWING AND ARTS AND
    CRAFTS PROGRAMS, AND FAMILY COUNSELING. PERSONAL
    COUNSELING IS OFFERED TO HELP THE MOTHER PLAN FOR
    THE FUTURE OF THE CHILD AND HERSELF. EXTENDED CARE
    IS GIVEN TO THE MOTHER AFTER BIRTH OF THE CHILD UNTIL
    ADEQUATE PLANS ARE MADE. CONTACT IS MADE WITH
    ADOPTION AND FOSTER CARE AGENCIES IF THOSE OPTIONS
    ARE THE PREFERRED CHOICE OF THE MOTHER. (MATERNITY
    HOME) ((UNWED MOTHER) (HEALTH EDUCATION, INFORMAL)
    (PRE-NATAL CARE) (CHILD CARE INSTRUCTION)

3   CA REGION
    IT CALL FOR APPOINTMENT. CLIENTS WILL BE
    IT INTERVIEWED AND APPLICATION TAKEN.
    IT ADMISSION AT ANY TIME DURING PREGNANCY.
    HR M—F, 9—5
    WT DEPENDS ON THE CASELOAD—SOMETIMES
    WT CLIENTS ARE PLACED ON A WAITING LIST AND
    WT SOMETIMES CLIENTS RECEIVE HELP
    WT IMMEDIATELY
    FE SLIDING SCALE
    IN NO RESTRICTIONS
    AG 13—24
    PH NO FACILITIES FOR DRUG DEPENDENTS OR
    PH ALCOHOLICS OR GIRLS WITH MEDICAL
    PH CONDITIONS REQUIRING CLOSE SUPERVISION
    LA NO INFORMATION
    ED NONE
    OT MUST BE ABLE TO ADJUST TO GROUP LIVING
    OT SITUATION

Figure 2.   Selected Agency Printout

shows the mail update format; note that it is different from the record display format. In addition to rearranging the record elements so that the agency address will display through the envelope window, the computer adds the name of the person who is authorized to review and correct the description. The printout, cover letter, and return envelope are mailed to the agency for review and correction. Nearly one-half of the corrected records are returned without any prodding. Another 45 percent are returned after a call to the agencies. Fewer than 8 percent refuse to cooperate. As soon as the updated records are received, our data base management section writes up change notices and forwards these to the vendor for entry into the computer file.

In other areas we have not been as successful. A major concern is

Experience

PLEASE RETURN AGENCY DESCRIPTION TO MODEL CITIES
COMMUNITY INFORMATION CENTER,
DATA SECTION
2204 N. BROAD STREET, PHILADELPHIA, PA   19132

PART 1   8/1/73

COUNTY: CESUS TRACT:238   NEIGHBORHOOD COUNCIL: 0
SPONSOR:
CONTACT: MRS MARY WEIST, INTAKE SUPERVISOR
  TEL: V18—6200
CONTACT:
  TEL:

  MISS TERESA P DOMANSKI, DIRECTOR
  FLORENCE CRITTENTON SERVICE OF PHILA
  6325 BURBRIDGE ST PHILA, PA   19144

PART II SERVICE DESCRIPTION

MULTI SERVICE RESIDENTIAL PROGRAM FOR UNWED MOTHERS.
SERVICES INCLUDE PRE AND POST NATAL MEDICAL CARE,
24 HOUR NURSING CARE, EDUCATIONAL TUTORING FOR JUNIOR
AND SENIOR HIGH GIRLS, SEWING AND ARTS AND CRAFTS
PROGRAMS, AND FAMILY COUNSELING. PERSONAL COUNSELING
IS OFFERED TO HELP THE MOTHER PLAN FOR THE FUTURE
OF THE CHILD AND HERSELF. EXTENDED CARE IS GIVEN
TO THE MOTHER AFTER BIRTH OF THE CHILD UNTIL
ADEQUATE PLANS ARE MADE. CONTACT IS MADE WITH
ADOPTION AND FOSTER CARE AGENCIES IF THOSE OPTIONS
ARE THE PREFERRED CHOICE OF THE MOTHER.
(MATERNITY HOME) (UNWED MOTHER) (HEALTH EDUCATION,
INFORMAL) (PRE-NATAL CARE) (CHILD CARE INSTRUCTION)

PART III INTAKE POLICY

CATCHMENT AREA SERVED:
  REGION
INTAKE PROCEDURES:
  CALL FOR APPOINTMENT. CLIENTS WILL BE INTERVIEWED
  AND APPLICATION TAKEN. ADMISSION AT ANY TIME DURING
  PREGNANCY.
HOURS OPEN: M—F, 9—5
WAITING TIME: DEPENDS ON THE CASELOAD—SOMETIMES
  CLIENTS ARE PLACED ON A WAITING LIST AND SOMETIMES
  CLIENTS RECEIVE HELP IMMEDIATELY
FEES AND OTHER CHARGES: SLIDING SCALE
INCOME RESTRICTIONS: NO RESTRICTION
SEX RESTRICTIONS: FEMALE ONLY
AGE RANGE SERVED: 13—24
CAN HANDLE FOLLOWING HANDICAPS:
  NO FACILITIES FOR DRUG DEPENDENTS OR ALCOHOLICS
  OR GIRLS WITH MEDICAL CONDITIONS REQUIRING
  CLOSE SUPERVISION
CAN HANDLE FOLLOWING FOREIGN LANGUAGES:
  NO INFORMATION
EDUCATIONAL LIMITATIONS: NONE
OTHER SPECIAL ELIGIBILITY REQUIREMENTS:
  MUST BE ABLE TO ADJUST TO GROUP LIVING SITUATION.

Figure 3.   Mail Update Printout

that the system is seldom used by our referral counselors. In an evaluation of the process, we discovered that the referral counselors were using the computer to search the file about once every other day, or one out of forty cases. The computerized directory system was not being used for several reasons:

1. Problems called in from our clientele—the inner-city poor—fell into about twenty recurring categories. Our staff had memorized the community resources that were available to help and thus mentally selected the agencies for referral. They might need to look up only current phone numbers, which could be done much faster by referring to their 3-by-5-card files.

2. Search input protocol on the computer was too slow. Looking up the appropriate index terms and their codes and inputting these and other eligibility factors might take a couple of minutes.

3. The results of the search was displayed too slowly. Our terminals, video displays, and hardcopy terminal printer initially were set to display at the normal teletype rate of ten characters per second. This meant it would take a minute or two to display each of several records. The staff simply did not want to make their clients wait on the phone for up to ten minutes while they interrogated the computer-based resource file. And, as noted earlier, in thirty-nine out of forty cases they were familiar with suitable resources and didn't feel it necessary to make a client wait.

4. Searches were imprecise. This problem stemmed from our inadequate indexing vocabulary. Under broad subject headings, too many agencies, and, in some cases, the wrong type of agency would be retrieved by the computer. The fault lay not with the computer but with the vague and unstructured terminology with which we were obliged to work.

The input and display rate problems can be solved. The subject search terms and eligibility factors can be stored in the computer and called up for review during the search statement formulation stage. A less costly approach would be to display these "index terms" in any one of several different types of desk top stands. (Our search instructions and query vocabulary are currently listed on sheets in a looseleaf notebook.) The display rate of search output with appropriate computer hardware and software support can be speeded up to 100 or even 200 characters per second, with the result that complete agency records can present themselves in two to three seconds. Computer hardware and software (programming) are equal to any task we can conceive in the information and referral field. What is not ready is the intellectual ware—the words we use to describe both the varied and complex services offered by agencies and the needs of clients. If this problem is not solved, the power of the computer cannot be properly exploited.

If the computer has failed in this initial demonstration to prove its value in referral operations, one may ask "Why bother to go on?" We concluded that the computer would prove useful if we were serving a broader socioeconomic clientele distributed over a wider geographic area. The range of problems and available relevant resources would be too many for even the most experienced referral counselor to keep in mind. And he certainly would find it impossible to keep current a personal resource file in excess of 100 agencies. We are convinced that a computerized resource file would be used if it were simple to operate and if the search results were responsive to the counselor's needs. From the administrator's point of view, adopting a computer-based directory of community resources is no problem if the costs can be justified against the benefits received.

Before the social welfare field can benefit from automation of their agency resource files, two major problems must be solved. The first problem is the *classification and indexing vocabulary* used to characterize agency services. In manual directory systems, the index to the file contents is usually either an alphabetical subject list or a classified list in which related index terms are grouped under broader subject headings. Such finding aids are of limited value because they are often created by people who use the language differently than do the users. While cross-referencing an agency's service under different but similar terms alleviates the problems of term standardization, this technique is severely limited by space constraints in published directories.

People in the information systems field have developed two tools for solving this problem. One is postcorrelated searching, in which the computer takes any combination of very specific subject terms fed into it and retrieves agencies described by that combination. The other tool is the thesaurus. It functions something like *Roget's Thesaurus* but with a difference. The modern thesaurus is a means for organizing and standardizing the working vocabulary of an entire field. It was developed in response to requirements dictated by machine-aided information retrieval. By controlling the indexing vocabulary used both to index a record and to search for it, the thesaurus helps all parties to use the same language. Once they are using the same language, the power of the computer can be brought in to augment the search process.

A thesaurus is a list of all possible subject terms that anybody in a given field might want to use to find a document in a given file. Only a portion of these terms are regarded as "acceptable indexing terms," but whatever term one starts with, the thesaurus will lead to

SLUMS 490
NT Urban Slums
BT Depressed Areas
(Geographic)
RT Cultural Disadvantagement
Ghettos
Inner City
Slum Conditions
Slum Environment
Slum Schools
Urban Environment
Urban Renewal Agencies

SLUM SCHOOLS 470

BT Schools
RT Slums
SMALL CLASSES 280
BT Classes (Groups Of Students)
RT Class Size

Small Engine Mechanics
use AUTO MECHANICS
Vocational Adjustment

SOCIAL AGENCIES 370

BT Social Organizations
Welfare Agencies
RT Agency Role
Social Services
Social Work
Social Workers

SOCIAL ATTITUDES 040

NT Discriminatory Attitudes
(Social)

BT Attitudes
RT Activism
Bias
Interpersonal Competence
Northern Attitudes
Political Attitudes
Political Socialization
Public Opinion
Social Action
Social Change
Social Characteristics
Social Influences
Social Relations
Social Values
Sociology

SOCIAL CLASS 490

NT Lower Class
Middle Class
Upper Class
BT Groups
RT Culture Conflict
Social Background
Social Dialects
Social Integration
Social Relations
Social Status
Social Structure
Status
Subculture

Social Class Differences
use SOCIAL DIFFERENCES
Social Class Integration

Figure 4. Excerpt from a Thesaurus Page

terms by which items in the collection have been indexed. This is also true for a list of subject headings, but a thesaurus has a richer variety of relations among the terms and a deeper hierarchical organization, while the terms in a subject-heading list are usually connected only by "see" or "see also" bonds. For example, in figure 4, BT, NT, and RT stand for relations such as "broader term," "narrower term," and "related term."

Unlike a priori classification schemes such as UWASIS,[6] a thesaurus is built up out of the meaningful terms used in day-to-day practice.

6. UWASIS (United Way of America Services Identification System), Alexandria, Va., 1972. This is the only really controlled vocabulary in the social welfare field and it is not good enough because the terms are too broad. The ERIC thesaurus, on the other hand, is too limited.

Many of the terms are used only as access points to acceptable "descriptors"—i.e., terms that have been rigorously defined and arrayed in order of their specificity. The broader terms in the hierarchical ranking become the natural candidates for service classification terms and may be used in service accounting and statistical reporting schemes.

Lack of precise definition is thwarting the creation of a thesaurus in the social welfare field. The terminology in this area is characterized as a "soft" vocabulary; that is, the terms are vague, ambiguous, and overlapping. Practitioners use the same words but mean different things, or use different words to designate the same thing. It is futile to attempt to automate information systems in a field with a soft vocabulary. A computer will seek records that match exactly the terms of the search statement—it has no way of responding to the fact that indexer and searcher intended to signify different ideas by their use of the same terms. Thus, if the classification and indexing vocabulary is soft and uncontrolled, machine-aided file searches will yield a large number of irrelevant and useless agency references. It might also fail to yield some that would be useful. Until a comprehensive and controlled human service vocabulary is established, machine-aided file search systems will remain inefficient and unacceptable on a national scale. Thesauri are used extensively in the fields of engineering, physical sciences, medicine, and education. The social welfare field needs such an aid also. However, a thesaurus is not put together overnight by three or four people sitting around a conference table—certainly not one that will meet national acceptance. Input is required from all allied social service groups. A representative working committee of twelve to fifteen people plus lexicographic consultants must be assembled. They must be furnished with term lists, special dictionaries, and glossaries. Sorting, selecting, defining, and hierarchically arranging this terminological authority will take from one to two years and could cost as much as one-half million dollars. Further, since language is constantly changing, a national clearinghouse must be established which processes suggested term changes, additions, and deletions on a continuing basis, and issues an updated thesaurus every two or three years.

The second major technical and administrative problem relates to *cost*. Over and above a host of strictly technical problems, one must consider the cost factor in using a computer in a directory application. Computer hardware and associated programming tasks are becoming less and less expensive, relative to a given task. Perhaps by the 1980s we shall all be using computers in one way or another in our daily lives. Today, however, cost is still a factor to be carefully considered. In an automated information directory system, we are concerned with the costs of computer and telecommunications hardware, programming, and data-base maintenance, in addition to system administration and operation. Few agencies can afford to operate an in-house system for their exclusive use. However, if costs are shared among many users, the charge per search can be reduced to a reasonable amount. The concept proposed here is that of a social service information utility, analogous to an electric power utility.

There are two basic ways of distributing the costs of an automated information system. Costs for accessing a centralized data base can be shared among users by (1) indirect access through telephone inquiries to a regional information center where intermediaries conduct the search for the caller, and (2) direct access to the resource file through on-site terminal facilities.

Much experimentation and cost-benefit analysis remains to be done before firm conclusions can be drawn as to which is the best way to configure a computer system in order to supply accurate, up-to-date information on available services to workers in a referral environment. In this writer's view, direct access through on-site terminal facilities is the approach most likely to be accepted by users. If the quality of referrals is to be enhanced through the directory look-up function, users will almost certainly want to search the file themselves and not go through an intermediary. Further, there is evidence that the precision of agency/client matching will diminish if a referral counselor is obliged to filter his search through an information center operator. The presence of a "middle man" increases the probability that important information will be lost in the translation. Moreover, when the search results are displayed, only the operator will be able to read the detailed descriptions. It would not be practical for the information center operator to read them to the referral counselor over the phone. Thus the person responsible for the quality of the referral would have to rely on both the search formulations and recommendations of a remote file searcher.

Decentralized and direct access, on the other hand, in which agencies or even workers themselves have their own terminals, permits counselors closest to the clients to precisely shape the searches and make final referral decisions based on their own firsthand review of complete descriptions of service alternatives and options. Direct file access through local terminals, however, is more expensive. It seems unlikely, in terms of the present state-of-the-art of multiple on-line terminal access systems (computer time-sharing), that computerized resource files can be made available for much less than $800 per month per terminal.

Before agency administrators can justify the introduction of computerized directory services, two things will have to happen. It will be necessary to prove that the machine-aided referral technique will make a significant difference in the quality and quantity of services rendered, and the cost of this new information appliance will have to be greatly reduced. In terms of current trends, it is reasonable to assume that within the next five years both objectives will be met and that by the mid-1980s, no major social service agency in cities of more than 200,000 population will need to be without an automated directory of local human services.

Chapter 9
Crisis Information Services to Youth

by Carolyn Forsman

A new kind of social service, the Crisis Intervention Center, is under development to meet the needs of troubled youth. Such centers, which provide counseling, as well as information and referral services, have emerged within the past six years in hundreds of urban, suburban, and rural areas.

The crisis centers call themselves by such names as Hotline Switchboard; Free Clinic; Rapline; Help Line; No Heat Line; Y.E.L.L.; Rescue; H.I.P. (Help Is Possible); Somebody Cares; We Care, Inc.; Listening Post; Night Line; Drug Aid; Y.E.S. (Youth Emergency Service); Community Youth Line; and Your Information Unlimited.

The crisis center was developed as an alternative to traditional community mental health and medical services. Because I&R are integral to the operation of hotlines, switchboards, and free clinics, they can also be looked at as an alternative to traditional library services for young adults.

As with any new phenomenon, the basic terminology is often neither clear, concise, nor consistent. However, agreement seems to be growing that the term "crisis intervention" includes three fairly distinct types of crisis services: hotlines, free clinics, and switchboards. A *hotline* is an emergency, anonymous telephone service for young people in crisis; it provides a listening ear, and offers referral to agencies and professional backup when necessary. A *switchboard* is primarily a telephone I&R service, as well as a message center. Unlike a hotline, it may also have a walk-in or message-drop facility. A *free clinic* is basically a walk-in center that provides direct medical services. It also has facilities for individual or group counseling in both medical and nonmedical problems, such as birth control and, until recently, the draft.

An earlier version of this chapter appeared as an article, "Crisis Information Services to Youth: A Lesson for Libraries," in *Library Journal,* March 15, 1972.

Ms. Forsman is Chief, Telephone Reference, Washington. D.C., Public Library.

An example might better explain the relationships and differences between these facilities in a community. A teen-ager thinks she is pregnant. If she calls the switchboard, she will be referred to the local free clinic for a pregnancy test. At the clinic, in addition to the free test, she may choose to receive counsel on birth-control methods, on possible solutions to her immediate situation, and/or on her relationship with the father.

If she calls the hotline instead of the switchboard, the person answering, without asking the identity of the caller, will ask a few questions to determine if she might indeed be pregnant, and also refer her to the free clinic for a test. The listener will not advise her to have an abortion, or to marry the suspected father, or otherwise tell her what to do. Instead he or she will, in a series of questions and replies, help the caller discover the options for herself. The hotline will more likely be used for this type of problem, since hotlines emphasize and specialize in interpersonal and individual psychological needs. Switchboards tend to satisfy more concrete needs, such as food, housing, transportation, and information on political and leisure activities. If a call to the hotline requests a place to "crash" for the night and the caller is over 18, he more than likely will be referred to the switchboard. If he is a minor who has run away, the listener will encourage the youth to question his action in terms of himself and his family.

In certain crises the person is not in any condition to be referred to another agency, no matter how logical it may seem. Persons experiencing a "bad trip" on drugs, contemplating suicide, or going through another life-threatening situation, who call in a state of panic, are handled by whichever of the three services they happen to call. Hotlines, free clinics, and switchboards do not advocate or encourage illegal behavior, including the harboring of runaways without the parent's permission or the use of drugs.

Switchboards

Switchboards and free clinics arose out of the counterculture of white alienated youth. The first switchboard began in the summer of 1967 in San Francisco to serve the Haight-Ashbury community as a message and referral service. Its prototype was the old "central" switchboard in American communities, which not only connected telephones, but also was a source of solutions to human problems. The new switchboard started out primarily as a crisis and problem center (the hotline's present function), but soon expanded into a community resource center. The switchboard, with the help of its community, created a "human resource file," a list of people willing to teach and share their skills and knowledge with others. Its aim is to help people control their own lives by providing them information so they can make their own decisions. Other files developed to further this goal show the extent of a switchboard's services: "jobs," "housing," "transportation," "buy and sell," "music," "theater," "education," and "messages."

A switchboard is usually reached by telephone (San Francisco had 150,000 calls in its first two-and-a-half years). Its number may be found in a local alternative newspaper listing of frequently called telephone numbers. Some have a walk-in service, where visitors can read bulletin boards for notices on survival, politics, and youth culture activities, or leave and pick up messages. The message service is also used by parents of runaways as a possible point of contact. It is the policy of the crisis centers to respect the youth's privacy and confidentiality.

Switchboard workers are volunteers from the community who try to make decisions in a democratic manner. When there is a coordinator, he or she has no more rights than the volunteers. Often the staff lives together as a collective. Switchboards are funded by donations from the community, including local ministries. The manual of the San Francisco Switchboard details the philosophy, services, and policies of one of the oldest and most stable information services to the youth community (Haight-Ashbury Switchboard, 1973).

Free Clinics

The first free clinic opened in Los Angeles in November 1967 as a drug treatment center for the "free" community. The philosophy of the free clinic movement is to treat the whole person; as such, it was natural to extend its services to include counseling on birth control, abortions, diet and nutrition, and drugs, as well as on such non-medical areas as the draft and the law. Counseling is performed by community volunteers, professional and nonprofessional.

A client who enters the clinic is assigned a "facilitator" or "advocate" who is responsible for seeing that the youth's needs are met by a doctor and/or counselor. The facilitator is there to determine the person's needs, to put him at ease, to refer him to the right service(s) and to follow up after treatment.

Free clinics are supported by donations, foundations, and federal dollars. The last are sought reluctantly because of the restrictions often attached. As with switchboards, decision making is communal or by a board of directors composed of volunteers, the few full-time staff on subsistance salaries, and members from the community.

Free clinics are loosely organized into a National Free Clinic Council, which facilitates communication through national meetings and a newsletter (*NFCC Newsletter*).

Hotlines

Community volunteers, a nonbureaucratic organization, sensitivity to community needs, and an ability to adapt and expand services in response to these needs are significant features of hotlines, as well as switchboards and free clinics.

While the free clinics originated in response to the drug problem, hotlines have evolved from suicide prevention centers in the community mental health movement. In 1958, the Los Angeles Suicide Prevention Center opened its telephones and doors to answer the "Cry for Help" that was described by E. S. Shneidman, its founder, in the book by the same name (Farberow and Shneidman, 1965). Experience and research have indicated that most persons responding were not contemplating suicide but were in a crisis situation, at a point of extreme stress in which a decision had to be made, while the persons felt immobilized and unable to cope and were liable to behave in a self-destructive manner. This situation is common in adolescence, itself a "crisis of status discontinuity" socially, psychologically, and physiologically (Sebald, 1969). In response to the need, the Los Angeles Children's Hospital began its Hotline for Youth in April 1968. Hotline quickly became a personal, anonymous, emergency telephone service, a "port of call for angry, frightened, and frustrated young people" (Bell, 1970).

Interdisciplinary Approach

Although crisis intervention began in the medical community, it soon aroused the interest and cooperation of professionals from the fields of psychology, psychiatry, therapy, health education, social work, pastoral counseling, nursing, and even law, anthropolgy, biostatistics, and logic. This multidisciplinary participation, in turn, encouraged the expansion of services provided by the switchboards, free clinics, and hotlines.

Confidentiality

Implicit in the provision of crisis intervention services is an atmosphere of trust—one hotline is even named "Trust." To engender trust, a potential source of financial support will be refused if it threatens the center's credibility. Basic to trust is confidentiality. The relationship between caller and listener on the hotline, between patient and counselor at the free clinic, and between client and staff at the switchboard is confidential, regardless of the client's age. Respect for the confidential nature of the client-crisis center relationship when the client is a minor is a unique feature of crisis centers. The position of the centers is: "We are responsible to the youths who come in, not to their parents." Hotlines, in particular, can guarantee confidentiality to both the caller and the listener by means of the anonymity the telephone provides. In fact, the location of a hotline is often kept a secret to protect both parties. Should a parent inquire as to whether and why his child has used the hotline, the listener can honestly reply that he doesn't know and can explain the hotline's purpose.

Alternatives

Crisis services for youth are consistent in their nonjudgmental approach. Hotlines do not advocate drugs, but neither do they preach their evils. Free clinics are not proabortion, but neither will they moralize to an unwed parent. Switchboards do not encourage runaways, but neither do they turn them in. The services do not judge the persons, nor do they recommend one solution, but instead they try to evaluate and recommend the best resource from the range of alternative solutions, whether it be a person, agency, book, or pamphlet.

For example, during a telephone encounter, an unwed pregnant teen-ager would learn that abortion and adoption are among her alternatives. The listener would not judge her predicament, nor ask her how she could have been so cruel to her parents, etc. If the caller should consider adoption, she would be given a list of recommended adoption agencies and homes for unwed mothers. In contrast, if the same young woman had asked a librarian, she might very well have received a casual remark, or even a short sermon, about the *badness* of her condition. Then the librarian might have handed her an outdated health and welfare directory for her to evaluate herself. Or if a young man were contemplating shooting heroin or smoking marihuana and let the librarian know this, it would not be surprising if he were told about the evils of drugs in general. But the librarian would not feel responsible for misinformation in any book or pamphlet the youth might find by himself and would probably not feel confident to recommend one title over another. A hotline or free clinic worker would discuss with him the possible consequences of drug use and would be prepared to recommend a particular book that had been evaluated as containing accurate information in a nonsensational way.

Hotlines do not advise, but they do more than listen. The aims of a crisis line are to provide constructive alternatives to a problem and to help the caller examine the situation from all angles, making use of his own resources to the fullest extent possible. If it is necessary to go beyond this, the volunteer listener will consult a file of human resources in relevant fields and "patch-in" to the telephone line a lawyer, doctor, psychiatrist, or clergyman who has volunteered to be on call as a professional adviser. Alternatives might also be sought from the community resource file for the caller himself to contact later. Crisis centers hope to alleviate the immediate crisis, but also consider it important to prepare the caller to deal with future crises and become a better problem solver. The repeat caller to a hotline, indicating a growing dependency upon the service, is not encouraged.

Support

Hotlines are operated primarily by volunteer youth. In the mental health services community, aides were used initially because of the shortage of professional manpower. Experience proved them to be more than an inexpensive, second-best substitute. In fact, their knowledge of the community and their similarity to the clientele were qualities that the professional could not substitute for with skills, and they became recognized members of the mental health team.

Though the structure and organization of hotlines are more varied than that of switchboards and free clinics, even the most traditional—those organized by mental health and religious associations—have a youth advisory board and employ teen-agers and college students as volunteers.

Other hotlines are sometimes part of a city youth agency, a university counseling center, or are nonprofit corporations. Support comes from their parent organizations (if any), as well as from civic groups, personal donations, benefits, and foundation and federal grants. In any case, their budgets are miniscule compared to those of health or information services in their communities.

Problems

An analysis of the problems that are brought to these centers is possible because of the detailed records kept of each contact, whether by telephone or in person. A data log sheet will include age, sex, marital status, and first name; the degree of crisis; the attitude and approach of the listener; whether the problem was resolved by referral, professional advice, or went unresolved; and where the caller heard about the service.

Though at this time no systematic analysis exists comparing one center to another, a general picture does emerge from inspection of the records of several crisis centers. Most calls involve interpersonal relationships: mainly boy/girl, peer, or family conflicts. Problems arising from an internal mental state, especially loneliness and depression, are the second largest category. Suicidal calls are listed separately and are relatively few in number, though they are the most serious and have the greatest impact on volunteers. Medical problems, including drug information, drug overdose, tripping, pregnancy, venereal disease, and other sex problems, rank third. Only about 10 percent of the calls are drug related. Questions about the legal status, rights, and obligations of youth, including the draft, runaways, parental support, and marriage, make up the next significant block. School-oriented problems occur less frequently, but enough to be a category. Only a small percentage of problems involves employment or housing.

Crisis centers do not give medical, legal, or other advice. Volunteers do not engage in the practice of medicine or law without a license, but they are, nonetheless, able to serve youth in many sensitive areas that have legal and medical implications, especially runaway, sex and drug information. The possibility of legal suits, raised by Kahn (1966), Levitan and Pavey (1970), and Brockopp and Oughterson (1972) on hypothetical and empirical grounds, was dismissed by all. Public and school libraries have feared to tread in these very sensitive areas, without good reason.

Crank calls, including put-ons and obscene calls, are generally treated seriously. The rationale is that the caller has a problem but is afraid to reveal it, perhaps even to himself.

On every hotline, female callers predominate over males, the ratio extending from two to one to as much as five to one. But boys, when they call, have more specific problems than girls, who comprise almost all of the "lonely" callers. The average caller is about sixteen, though older at college crisis centers. In one county, 16 percent of the callers were twelve or under.

Many hotlines receive over 2,000 calls a month. In the Washington, D.C., area alone, over fifty hotlines, switchboards, and free clinics were identified as providing listening, counseling, and information or referral service to young adults. This is not an unusually large number for a metropolitan area. The combination of many centers, each with a potentially large volume, indicates the possible, if not the actual, impact of these services upon other information and referral services.

ADVOCACY

Crisis centers not only intervene in individual immediate crises (the "bandage" function), but also work to prevent future crises in a community. With the data collected on user problems and with the follow-up and feedback provided on referrals, the centers function as a social indicator of the needs and gaps in community service. Perhaps the hours or regulations of an agency inhibit or prohibit its use by potential clientele, or there may be no agency at all that is concerned, or a local ordinance on minors' rights may need changing. With data in hand and a constituency of community groups and professionals behind it, the crisis center can be powerful in persuading appropriate bodies to alter services or regulations. Alfred Kahn (1966) calls this "program and policy advocacy" in describing the range of services a neighborhood information center could provide.

REFERRAL FILES

A referral system of community agencies and professionals is an essential element of any crisis center, whether hotline, switchboard, or free clinic. One measure of the effectiveness of the center is how well a problem can be matched to referrals. Before an agency is used, as much information as possible is collected about it, including the identification of a particular contact person, so that a client is told whom to see and not just where to go. Sometimes an agency is checked out by means of a fake call for its services.

Crisis centers rely on users to improve their files. Volunteers are guided to ask the client for feedback on how helpful the referral was. If the center is unable to provide him the information needed, he might be asked to call back and make the files more complete with other resources he had discovered. This mutual learning process also takes place between the center and the agencies themselves. The crisis center influences and educates professionals and agencies in more effective ways to handle the problems of young people, while the professionals and agencies provide training and expertise to the center. Both user and agency feedback to the center provide material for the continual updating of the file's "vital" information. The data sheets also encourage the search for, and development of, new referral resources.

ACCESS

Since crises can occur at any time and by their nature require rapid intervention, hotlines and other crisis centers try to be open twenty-four hours, seven days a week. When this is not feasible, they close in daytime hours during the week, since emotional emergencies tend to occur most often at night and on weekends.

It is not enough to be open; a service must be made known to its target audience through every effective medium. These include calling cards distributed at schools, stickers in phone booths and on cars, public service announcements on TV and local radio rock stations, stories in the local paper, listings in the alternative press, and posters in neighborhood stores. In these imaginative ways, crisis centers try to reach troubled youth, while parents are informed by a center's Speakers Bureau, PTAs, and periodic written reports to the community. Ironically, the one point of access that has been a stumbling block is the telephone directory and operator. Some directories require an address in order to be listed, and those hotlines that demand anonymity have been refused a listing. In addition, telephone companies have yet to agree on how to list these centers in the Yellow Pages (Fisher, 1972).

TRAINING

The philosophy, services, and techniques of crisis intervention are initially conveyed to volunteers through a short training period of not more than a dozen sessions, in which role-playing, sensitivity groups, outside experts, and real crisis situations are used. Before an individual can help others, it is necessary that he understand himself and makes himself sensitive to the real, but unstated and hidden, needs of people seeking help, and so the volunteer is placed in situations which reveal his own biases and hang-ups. Authorities on problem areas provide the information to answer these needs. Additionally, the volunteer receives instruction in the content, organization, and updating of the referral files. The data sheets suggest training consistent with the user population and its problems. Telephone techniques in particular are explained, demonstrated, and practiced through role-playing and actual supervised calls.

The initial training period, during which some volunteers are asked to drop out or do so by choice, is followed by weekly or monthly meetings to discuss problems, unanswered needs, and internal policies. Though written material plays a minor role initially, most crisis centers develop a training manual for future reference. The manual describes the goals and services and emphasizes the importance of follow-through, feedback, and update, so that services and resources will reflect community needs.

NETWORK

An informal network connects the over 750 crisis centers in the United States and Canada. The total number is increasing rapidly, despite the high death rate for new centers. *The Exchange* has established its responsibility for the production of the *National Directory of Hotlines and Youth Crisis Centers* (Beitler, 1973). At the first International Hotline Conference, regional divisions were organized. The network also consists of smaller metropolitan area councils, such as in Baltimore, and national research centers, most of which publish newsletters or journals and hold conferences and workshops. But there is a great resistance to any strong network with regulatory powers. A proposal for national standards and accreditation was defeated in 1971, but the minimum criteria suggested—twenty-four-hour access, continuous training, justification of need for a service, and formal

141

evaluation to include feedback—accurately reflect their importance to the crisis center philosophy.

A ROLE FOR LIBRARIES?

In summary, a crisis intervention center is an easily accessible storefront or telephone community facility, in which counseling, advocacy, information, and referral services feed into a larger human services network. Using paraprofessionals from the community who are peers of the clientele, and professional advisers when needed, the centers provide stopgap crisis services until more comprehensive and preventative services are found.

When viewed this way, the crisis service can be seen to parallel storefront library "outreach" programs. With librarians today searching for new and innovative ways to reach the nonuser, they can ask themselves: First, can they learn anything about changes in services, hours, personnel and training, and public relations from a similar but nontraditional service? Second, several public libraries have gone into the information and referral business themselves, and so it is not entirely academic to ask if and how libraries, both school and public, might become a part of this network and cooperate with crisis centers as equals. The library could assume the function of program or group advocacy; even if it is not an advocate for individuals, it could make available to appropriate groups or organizations its accumulation of "unanswered questions" to substantiate and justify changes in community services.

Third, can librarians serve their public indirectly by providing information and back-up services to the staff of the local hotline, switchboard, and free clinic that is consciously serving community groups? Several crisis centers have indicated the desire to establish a resource library in their facilities, made up of handbooks, pamphlets, periodicals, and directories, for reference by both staff and clientele. The staff of one newsletter, the *Confederation*, mailed a questionnaire to centers asking for recommended materials for such a basic collection. Materials so identified could be considered for inclusion in a library's collection; perhaps the library could provide them on indefinite loan to its local crisis center.

Fourth, how can librarians apply the information that crisis centers are collecting about the needs of troubled youth in their own communities to traditional library services, for example, in areas such as book selection and programming? Librarians must reckon with the number of hotline callers aged 12 or under. What implications are there for the present boundary in libraries between children and young adult or adult services at 13 or 14 years, or for the programs and materials in the children's room? Should the territorial boundaries in both libraries and library associations be redrawn to include 11- and 12-year-olds in young adult services? Should junior novels be written, reviewed, and selected with the 10- to 14- rather than the 12- to 16-year-old in mind? Can public and school librarians honestly compare the crisis centers' policy of confidentiality with the library's policy on access to circulation records? How often are they guilty of telephoning a parent even before a teenager's or child's use of materials on, say, sex or drugs?

Young adult librarians have always taken pride in their ability to change with the times, to be sensitive to their clientele's needs and to be innovative in services and programs. Perhaps they can learn from the crisis intervention center new ways to serve the young adult in his complete range of information needs.

Crisis centers—in their philosophy, organization, services, training methods, publicity, and insight into youth's problems—contrast sharply and usually favorably with library service for young adults. They suggest possible new roles and directions for libraries and librarians.

"Every community needs a police department, a public school system, a mental health clinic, a welfare agency, a fire department, . . . and a suicide and crisis intervention service . . ." (McGee, 1970). Is the library ready to assume its place among these community helping systems?

References

Beitler, K., ed. *National Directory of Hotline and Youth Crisis Centers.* Minneapolis, Minn.: The Exchange, 311 Cedar Avenue South, 55404, 1973.

Bell, J. "Take Your Troubles to the Hotline." *Seventeen,* 1970, *29,* 242–43.

Brockopp, G., and Oughterson, E. D. "Legal and Procedural Aspects of Telephone Emergency Services," *Crisis Intervention,* 1972, *4,* 15–25.

Farberow, N. L., and Shneidman, E. S., eds. *The Cry for Help.* New York: McGraw-Hill, 1965.

Fisher, S. A. "Publicity and Its Relation to Telephone Emergency Services." *Crisis Intervention,* 1972, *4,* 99–104.

Haight-Ashbury Switchboard. *San Francisco Switchboard Screening and Training Procedures Manual.* San Francisco: The Switchboard, 1797 Haight Street, 94117. 1973.

Kahn, A. J. *Neighborhood Information Centers.* New York: Columbia University School of Social Work, 1966; Brooklyn, N.Y.: University Book Service, 1971.

Levitan, D., and Pavey, J. "Proposal for a University of Maryland Crisis Intervention Center," Mimeographed. College Park, Maryland: University of Maryland, 1970.

McGee, R. K. "Towards a New Image for Suicide and Crisis Services." *Crisis Intervention* 1970, *2,* 63.

NFCC Newsletter. San Francisco: National Free Clinic Council, 1304 Haight Street, 94117.

Sebald, H. *Adolescence: A Sociological Analysis.* New York: Appleton, 1969.

Part III

Research and Analysis toward Understanding Information Needs and Processes

Much remains to be learned about citizen information systems. Research is needed to provide the required knowledge and understanding. The concepts and techniques of investigation draw upon not only the information sciences, but on the behavioral and social sciences as well. In particular, human communication and organizational research and urban/regional studies are needed to deal with the larger environments in which the systems are to operate.

The first chapter in Part III is an analysis of the citizen information system concept, showing the applicability of mathematics and computer science. It stresses the distinction between what makes people use an information system and what makes it valuable. It provides a conceptualization that may be useful for further theoretical (e.g., mathematical) and experimental research. It also offers some insights that may help designers of field studies and novel experimental systems.

In chapter 12, Thomas Childers gives a critique of the effectiveness of measures conventionally applied to information services and suggests improved techniques. He assumes that the purpose of providing a client with information is to change his behavior. He says "the behavior of the client should be altered in some way as a result of his contact, direct or indirect, with the service." However, behavior

144

modification requires that someone specify the direction of change. In therapy the client usually specifies the goal, and the therapist helps him to articulate and specify it to the point of being able to attain it by instrumental conditioning reinforcement techniques. An example is overcoming a phobia. In the operation of an information service, one cannot assume either (1) that the client recognizes a need for a change in his own behavior or (2) that the direction of a change is ever made explicit.

Perhaps Childers's assumption should be modified as follows: The purpose of an information service to a member of the community is to provide him with more *options* for what he can do than he would have thought of without the service, *plus* the *wisdom* to make a "good" choice among these options. Information alone is necessary but not sufficient for options and wisdom. Education, attitudes, wealth, and power all help too. But the disadvantaged sometimes have considerably more wisdom than their more advantaged counterparts; they simply lack the options. Information about options that are not actually available to them can only aggravate the sense of frustration and bitterness that comes with the realization of gaps between what is and what could be.

The unavoidable companion of impact or benefit measurement is cost measurement. In chapter 11, Wilson and Barth present the case for deliberate, and sometimes formal, analysis of costs in relation to benefits, giving a very down-to-earth description of things that need to be assessed and techniques available for that task. Though advocating as careful an analysis as is justified for a given problem, they argue that much can be accomplished with an informal, common sense approach, and they discuss the critical questions that a manager should ask and answer prior to making a decision. The chapter contains useful warnings that touch upon cost-benefit and cost-effectiveness analysis. The section on "cost-effectiveness analysis" does not describe the cycle that is usually understood by that term in the management science or economics literature; this has recently been extended to the analysis of information systems in human service organizations (Cohen, 1975).

It is helpful to compare the approach of Wilson and Barth with Deahl's remarks on evaluation. Deahl stresses user acceptance of technological and organizational innovations in evaluating an I&R system. His concern is primarily with how well *his* system serves the client and secondarily with what kind of system best serves the client. This approach is shared by many technologists. Wilson and Barth suggest that entrepreneurs, for whom technology is but a means to an end, ask which of several alternative services would bring the greatest benefit to a given clientele. Their viewpoint is that of an entrepreneur, whereas Deahl's is that of a technologist, and they might extend their position to ask not only what service could the entrepreneur provide to a given clientele, but what clientele would he most like to serve. Concern with blacks, the poor, and the elderly may imply a lower benefit-cost ratio than would be implied by concern to serve the needs of managers in banks, insurance companies, doctors, lawyers. In other words, benefit-cost considerations alone would not justify information systems meeting needs of inner-city residents or disadvantaged segments of society; ethical and moral considerations justify those better.

When the authors remind us that users will utilize an information service only when doing so costs them less than not using it, they are appealing to a principle that information scientists refer to as "Mooers' Law." The cost to the user in using a system is seldom taken into account: it is critical. It plays a large role in what Deahl calls user acceptance.

The use of market mechanisms, such as raising prices when supply is short and demand high, though widely understood and used in other services, would be an innovation in information services. Many people have for too long viewed information as a free benefit. Moreover, as Boulding points out, information may not be beneficial at all, but harmful—a cost; it is knowledge that people need, rather than information (Boulding et al., 1972; Kochen, 1974).

How much a person is willing to pay for a service is a reasonable indicator of the service's value. It is, however, critical to distinguish carefully among prices, costs, and disutility. Prices relate to markets. Costs are determined by technologies, markets for labor, and raw materials and efficiency. Disutility relates to the user's preference judgment among alternative goods and services.

Wilson's discussions of marketing raises numerous ideas and questions of research interest. Of most importance is his drawing attention to this aspect of management science as vital for the investigation of information services. An idea that should be added to those discussed by Wilson is that after the initial advertisements for an information service, utilization of the grapevine or informal community communication net is perhaps the most important marketing device.

In chapter 13 Havelock, like Long, suggests specific hypotheses for empirical testing. The design and conduct of such tests is an important and difficult challenge. The methods used and results found by Brenda Dervin are indicative of what is being done. So is the exploratory fact-finding survey by project *Search* (Cauffman et al., 1972). This survey describes the characteristics of 321 existing Health Information and Referral Services in Los Angeles as being predominantly unified within a larger organizational structure. Sixty-one percent of them had neither an advisory board nor a governing council; 61 percent were privately owned, not-for-profit corporations; all had regular daytime hours except one, which had a twenty-four-hour answering service; 94 percent provided year-round services; 89 percent provided specialized services; and 55 percent did not keep written records of service activities.

The average number of monthly referrals varied from 2 to 14,000. Fifty-five percent did not perform referral follow-up. None filed their information by computer methods. Of 276 respondent organizations, 14 used only volunteers, while the others used paid staff plus occasional volunteers. The average service organization has 3.4 full-time equivalent employees, 53 percent of them in social services, with one nonprofessional for every three professionals.

The Los Angeles survey corroborated the findings of an earlier similar survey (Bloksberg and Caso, 1967), that a typical health I&R service is part of an integrated organizational structure, has a social worker as an administrator, has neither governing council nor advisory board, is privately owned, provides specialized services, does not perform follow-up, and uses paid staff. The findings of the Los Angeles survey, that there are no major differences among existing services in Los Angeles county, was used as an argument for the feasibility of a computer-based county system to link them. What is perhaps novel, from a methodological viewpoint, is the applicability of survey research techniques to this kind of problem area. The data uncovered by such surveys also suggests important research problems not always provided for by conventional analytic methods.

The four chapters in Part III, together, give the impression of a new research area in its infancy making modest progress. That is probably a representative and accurate assessment of research in this field. The problems are difficult because they are hard to transform into well-defined, researchable problem statements. Their contemporary importance might be expected to be proportional to the resources society is willing to invest in their study, even though more determination and a well-organized, well-funded program to solve the problems does not guarantee success. Adequate support is necessary but not sufficient.

The chapter by Havelock provides some tentative ideas toward understanding the processes by which knowledge is transferred from where it is to those who need it. These ideas are based on observations of how research findings are disseminated and used by organizations in the federal government, but they can serve as useful hypotheses for other human service organizations as well. His investigation and synthesis of what has been written about the diffusion and utilization of research and development results led Havelock to propose this way of looking at problems. The "resourcer" of figure 2 in Havelock's paper can be conceived as a chain or network, in which an I&R center stands as an intermediary. The I&R center's role is at the front end of need processing. An I&R center contributes slightly to need arousal, by advertising its existence, by having word spread of its effectiveness with specific problems, by interacting with clients. It does a great deal of need definition and analysis. It does not do nearly as much of the other five functions in figure 3 (page 206) as it could and should. Here is a very great, as yet untapped, potential of the I&R centers to make highly significant contributions.

References

Bloksberg, L. M., and Caso, E. K. *Survey of Information and Referral Services.* Final report. Waltham, Mass.: Brandeis University, 1967.

Boulding, K.; Davis, C. H.; Jones, W.; Kochen, M.; and Olsen, R. "On the Economics of Information." Summary of proceedings of a panel discussion. *Journal of the American Society of Information Science,* 1972, *23,* 281–83.

Cauffman, J. G.; Lloyd, J. S.; Lyons, M. L.; Lynch, N. T.; and Cortese, P. A. *A Survey of Health Information and Referral Services Within Los Angeles County.* Los Angeles, Calif.: University of Southern California. Report to DHEW–PH–110–68–17, 1972.

Cohen, M. "Steps in Planning an Information System." In "Information Systems for Servicing People," by M. Cohen, L. Ferman, M. Kochen, and M. Peterson. Unpublished manuscript (1975).

Kochen, M. *Principles of Information Retrieval.* New York: Melville/Wiley, 1974.

Chapter 10
What Makes a Citizen Information System Used and Useful

by Manfred Kochen

When a family moves into a community, it is usually not too long before one of its members needs a family doctor. If the family is not tuned in to the grapevine, obtaining useful recommendations may prove to be difficult. It seems plausible to suppose, therefore, that an average family would pay for the use of a good referral system to help them find a good doctor when one is needed. It may, in fact, pay enough to offset the cost. Testing this hypothesis would require setting up an experimental system of the kind described in BenDor's chapter. A less satisfactory but workable way of testing it would be to devise an interview instrument to estimate demand in response to a system that respondents are asked to imagine.

An information system to help citizens with such needs is really beneficial if it has two properties. First, the citizens must really use it. They must not only pay for it, but give it high priority over the alternative sources of information that might meet their needs. They must use it because they have found it responsive in the past; the information it provides and the means of its delivery have been and are acceptable to the users. They have found, and continue to find, its use reinforcing.

Second, to say that a citizen information system is really beneficial

Parts of this chapter draw on material found in "Directory Design for Networks in I&R Centers," *Library Quarterly,* 1972, *42,* which also appears in D. R. Swanson and A. Brookstein, eds., *Operations Research: Implications for Libraries.* Chicago: University of Chicago Press, 1972. This was done with the permission of the publisher.

Dr. Kochen is Professor of Information Science and of Urban/Regional Planning and Research Mathematician, University of Michigan, Ann Arbor, Mich.

Thanks are extended to Dr. Flora Wallace for her substantive and stylistic help in preparing this chapter, as well as to Dr. Dagobert Soergel for a careful, constructively critical review of an earlier version.

means that it provides authoritative information. In the above example, the citizen is actually referred to the best possible doctor who can give him a timely appointment. The system can be relied on to be correct, even if the user does not realize it. After all, he uses the system because it embodies an expertise superior to his own.

An information system may be used, then, but not be useful; it may also be useful, but not used. It may even be neither useful nor used. It is ideal if it is *both* used and useful.

A system designed to help Johnny with his high school mathematics must be one that is actually fun to use. A computer-managed course or remedial session over cable television, for instance, should motivate him to switch from a commercial channel offering an entertaining TV program to the educational channel. Yet, in the attempt to compete with the commercial channel, the mathematics material may be presented in such a way that, although it is amusing, it is incorrect or represents an incomplete understanding of the subject matter on the part of the program producer—and, therefore, is not useful. On the other hand, a program designed by a competent mathematician may not reach a single person in the audience if it does not have in addition some of the artistic qualities that draw and hold attention and interest and provide motivation. What is presented must be both correct and authoritative, as well as acceptable and enjoyable.

Suppose that a citizen needs help with a major decision, such as choosing a college, a career, or one of several jobs that he has been offered. The user must not only trust and be able to rely on any advice or counsel provided by the system, but this advice should in fact be the best available, especially since he may not actually be able to judge its value until some months or years after he has made his decision. The system designer, on the other hand, should be able to judge the quality of his information on the basis of data, collected over a period of years, that reports the system's rate of success. He can also rely on peer evaluations of the competence of the sources that supply information into the system's data base.

By exhorting citizens to settle for no less than the best available, designers are setting up a goal, one that may not be actually attainable. Designers may offer only incremental improvements, but awareness of this goal helps citizens judge if the incremental steps are favorable.

In this chapter I have attempted to conceptualize more clearly the distinction between *valued* or *used,* as indicated by the user's acts of choice and use, and *valuable* or *useful,* as revealed by the prevention, solution, or partial alleviation of the user's problems.

In the following three sections I have (1) analyzed the needs for citizen information systems in terms of these two determinants of quality; (2) described some of the kinds of resources and information systems that might match such needs; (3) surveyed some of the key analytic techniques that are available; and (4) suggested directions for further research, development, and design.

The main thrust of this chapter is, then, to indicate methods for identifying, analyzing, and creating new combinations of information resources that will provide the best available match with the needs. This requires the identification of some of the basic independent variables that characterize information systems, some of the basic dependent variables, notably those having to do with a system's use and usefulness, and, finally, the relations between the independent and dependent variables. I will also indicate some of the constraints on these independent variables, suggest some hypotheses to be tested experimentally or in the field, and derive the implications from the hypotheses that suggest steps for further research or improved design.

Analysis of Citizen Information Needs

The most obvious way to measure a citizen information system's extent of use is to count the growth in the number of frequent users. A more refined, and possibly more sensitive, measure is the number of users who, having used the system for the first time, come back to it a second time. Crickman, in chapter 15, points out how such a measure could, in addition, be interpreted to indicate how poorly, rather than how well, such an information system is serving the community. If a citizen information system is expected to help people to both cope with and prevent problems, there should be a decrease in the number of problems they need outside help in solving, and this should manifest itself by a decrease in their use of the system.

However, the need for services, like the need for goods, is one that recurs. Also, potential users are constantly confronted by a variety of needs which they do not as yet realize can be met by the information system. It is plausible to assume that the number and *variety* of such hidden needs is constantly increasing as our society becomes more complex. A citizen information system, therefore, can help its users by assisting them in recognizing its potential to help in all areas. Moreover, a user does not have to be in a chronic state of recognized need to use an information system. Most people, in fact, are unaware of the large number of opportunities for betterment available at all times. An information system provides a means for exploring these many and diverse opportunities. Dervin has noted that professional and nonprofit agencies tend to be used, to a large extent, by the elite. Crickman further points out that the wealthy are also more likely to suffer from information-input overload than the poor. For a citizen information system to be successful, then, it must be used by those at the lower end of the socioeconomic spectrum, as well as by the affluent and powerful.

Thus, measuring the effectiveness of a system by the number of users per se is plausible. Empirical data on the case load handled by information and referral centers are now being collected, constituting another reason for choosing the growth in number of frequent users, or the number of citizens who use the system repeatedly, as a response variable, subject to changes over time.

It is possible, by means of a mathematical model, to predict how the number of frequent users will vary as a function of time. This depends on the conditional probability that the user switches from using the system with a frequency of a stated number of requests per month to a frequency of one use per month more, one use per month less, or the same number of uses per month, given his current frequency of use. The resulting model is a Markoff Chain. Its analysis leads to a diffusion equation, which predicts that the number of users will vary with time and frequency in a way that is analogous to how a solute or a drop of ink spreads through a solvent such as water over time and space. The models have been refined to take into account the spreading of information about the system; if it has been of help to some users, not only will the likelihood of their return increase, but the expected number of other citizens who become first-time users will also increase, because the satisfied users have spoken about the usefuless of the system to others (Kochen, 1972a).

An alternative mathematical model utilizes the equations that govern the spread of epidemics. Here it is assumed that the number of citizens who become new, first-time users is proportional to both the number of citizens who are already users and the number of citizens who are potential users but have not yet tried the system. This model may be more appropriate because some citizens are "immune" to the use of information systems, especially if the systems are computer based.

In refining both of these two mathematical approaches, it is possible to introduce variables that characterize the effect of the system's responsiveness and acceptability to its users. This includes such physical vairables as the proximity[1] of the nearest imput terminal to a citizen's location and its availability when he needs it. Also important are: the response time of the system, measured from the first expression of a citizen's need to the first feedback response from the system; the number of such feedback passes that enable him to converse easily

1. Proximity would be measured in hours or dollars (based on an hourly rate), rather than miles. Ten miles for a young person with a car may be closer than 1,000 feet for an elderly person who must walk.

with the system; and the flexibility and naturalness of the language in which his interaction with the system takes place.

Beyond these physical variables are numerous psychological variables that represent barriers or inhibitors to the use of an information system, resistances that cannot as yet be stated with sufficient precision to introduce appropriate variables into the mathematical model. Even without the introducion of such psychological considerations, the mathematical models which are sufficiently sophisticated to take into account most of the physical considerations are already so complex that they cannot be analyzed without the help of computers to provide insights. There are, however, computer programs for analyzing more sophisticated models (Kochen, 1971).

The value of introducing and analyzing mathematical models goes beyond the increased precision and depth of the conceptualization that this provides. The formulation of a mathematical model also forces its creator to select the variables he considers most central, and to state explicitly the assumptions he considers plausible. By deducing the implications of these assumptions, he obtains considerable insight into the effect of alternative methods for meeting citizen information needs. The most important products of such analytical activity are perhaps the novel ideas for improving the services that otherwise would not have been considered by the system designers. In other words, a sharper and deeper conceptualization of the nature of citizen information needs is often accompanied by new ideas for meeting them; the goals and delivery services of the information system should be articulated as a response to the stated citizen information needs.

A citizen probably will not even bother to use an information system if he believes that his needs are not understood, when he feels that the agent in the citizen information system is listening from a different frame of reference or cognitive map. This may make it very difficult, if not impossible, for a single information system to serve many different citizens, characterized by vastly different cognitive maps of, and visceral reactions to, their worlds.

Perhaps, though, a greater proportion of potential users share cognitive maps that are approximately the same than are radically different. If so, a user community for a single information system could be determined. Before this is done, however, it is important to have some idea about the distribution of cognitive maps and visceral reactions over the entire population. Gossip grapevines or peer-kin networks, which Dervin mentions in chapter 2, and cultural and social conditioning all contribute to defining the shared world views which make up individual and collective cognitive maps.

For a citizen information system to meet a user's needs, then, it is necessary for the system to pay attention to and understand the user's felt needs as expressed, and to feed back appropriate aid and advice. At the same time, the user must pay attention to and accept the aid or advice offered by the system. Such acceptance by the user is necessary but not sufficient—the aid and advice must actually be useful. That is, it must be relevant, significant, valid, clear, and novel to the user.

To be useful, advice and aid must be *relevant*. Some known or "proven" relationship must exist between advice given and problem solution. Criteria for judging relevance are more clear cut for some needs than for others. It is easier for the information system to respond with an appropriate remedy for acute poisoning than to identify and articulate the qualifications that make for mutual satisfaction in a job, a marriage, a career, or for most of the important real-life situations.

The *significance* of information provided by a citizen information system depends greatly on the need which it is to help meet. Data about a company being considered by an investor differs vastly from the kind of data that helps an employer judge a job applicant, and the place where the applicant was born may be less significant than his date of birth. The user may not know how to sift significant from insignificant information when given two equally relevant items of information. Thus an employer, presented with the records of two applicants who both qualify for his opening, may not be certain whether he should consider the more pleasant personality of one as more significant than the greater experience of the other. The information systems counselor—e.g., the manager of a personnel or executive talent scouting service—has the benefit of hindsight. He remembers cases in which his client was satisfied, and he can attribute this to having properly assessed the significance of certain data elements. If an information source consistently produces information of high significance, that information, as well as that source, can be so marked.

Similar observations can be made about the *validity* or authenticity of information. Incorrect information can increase rather than lessen the client's needs. In the case of scientific information, there is little controversy about the criteria for judging validity. A mathematical theorem is either true, false, or undecidable. The proof of such an assertion is either correct or incorrect. The situation is different when, among the qualifications of an applicant for a job, there is a statement that "he gets along well with others." The validity of this statement may vary greatly with the judge. In that case, however, information about the qualifications and the consistency of the judge would be valuable additional information.

The elements of information that are collected and transformed into feedback messages from the system may be facts or data already known to the client in some form; to become useful "information," some *new* interpretation, some new meaning must be given the data by the I&R system. In this respect, "useful" is to "used" as "novel" is to "seemingly new or shiny," or simply to "stated as though new." The system must strive to reduce the variance between its understanding and that of the user.

The user's perceptual images are shaped by past experiences; aid and advice as offered very often do not fit within the user's value system, and therefore may not be valued as useful choices (Taylor, 1960); and they may not fit different clients' levels and styles of linguistic and cognitive competence. A message sent by the system may be translated into a grammatical response at an entirely different dispositional level, as the user translates the message through his own linguistic competencies, attitudes, values, and sets. Wilbur Schramm (1969) has noted that in predicting the communication effects of a message, it is "much more likely to succeed if it fits the patterns of understanding, attitudes, values and goals that a receiver has; or at least if it starts with this pattern and tries to reshape it slightly." It is important that the expectations of the client be fulfilled, exceeding neither his ability to comprehend nor his attention span. It is vital, then, that incoming information about needs be represented within the system so that it can be translated into linguistic responses of various kinds and styles. As a client interacts linguistically with the system, the system should acquire data about his response potential so as to adjust its output to continuously improve the match between that output and the client's cognitive, linguistic, and value-orientation requirements.

Five qualities, therefore, account for a system's use: (1) relevancy/salience (the / can be read: "as operationalized by"): (2) significance/imposingness; (3) validity/authoritativeness; (4) clarity/simplicity; and (5) novelty/impression-of-newness. Each of these can be measured operationally by observing the behavior of people in responding to messages having these properties. For example, will people concerned with food stamps select a particular message medium from an array if it is audio rather than video, loud rather than soft, stresses the phrase "food stamps" or "food" above others? The properties and attributes of usefulness, on the other hand, are specified by variables that depend on both the content of the message and the client's needs. The properties that make a system used also depend on the client's need, but more on the form than on the content of the message (McLuhan, 1970).

For some needs usefulness is far more important than usability. When a person is lost at sea and has been without food for days, the properties that would normally make food desirable or used by him—e.g., relevance of the food to his taste at the moment, how it is prepared, whether it is familiar, edible, etc.—become secondary considerations; whether it is useful as food is of primary concern. The need for making a selection from a menu in a restaurant, on the other hand, is best met by an informative menu, in which the desirability of various items on the menu is more important than their nutritive value. We can try to characterize any need by two weights. The first is the weight assigned by a client to the usefulness of the most appropriate response. The second is the weight given by a judge to the likelihood that a client will actually use a most appropriate response. If two weights are numbers on a seven-point semantic-differential scale, we could take the ratio of these two weights and try to order the information needs of the client along this scale.

Analysis of Citizen Information Systems

In this chapter "citizen information system" refers to an I&R center, a hotline, a twenty-four-hour telephone answering service, or any of the phenomena referred to as public information centers, some of which are described in this book. The idea is not new. Newspapers have long served the information needs of citizens with letters to the editor, "Dear Abby" columns, and, more recently, "courses by newspapers" (Lewis, 1973). The role of the Bintel Brief, a problem-solving column in a Yiddish newspaper, in assimilating the great immigration waves at the end of the last century has been amply documented (Metzker, 1971).

The great proliferation and expansion of the services of I&R centers is new. Libraries have experienced a significant expansion of funding for neighborhood information centers in various cities. The Social Security Administration has made it mandatory for all its offices to provide I&R services. The United Way has set up a national work/study committee in this area and published a manual for national standards and for operating an I&R center.

I will not attempt to give a comprehensive or even representative list of citizen information systems, because that list would be obsolete by the time this book is published, or certainly within a year after that date. I will try to sketch in gross outline three typical citizen information system concepts likely to be of importance in the near future. Any particular system may use a mix of these different concepts.

One of the most natural, ancient, widely used, and well-known kind of citizen information system is the "gossip grapevine," which is the central theme of Crickman's chapter and to which Dervin refers as the "peer-kin network." A community in which this informal network of personal acquaintances functions well may not need many other information resources, such as I&R centers. If each person has 100 acquaintances, and if each of these have 100 acquaintances of their own and so on, a person can reach 10,000 others by asking a friend to contact a friend, and a million others by going to one more remove. This assumes, however, that people do not move in circles, an assumption that is most unrealistic. Groups of people are stratified, and two engineers are more likely to know one another than are an engineer and a poet. The average number of removes for any two American engineers to form an acquaintance chain is much less than the average number of intermediaries in the acquaintance chain connecting two randomly chosen Americans.

Doctors obtain patients primarily through recommendations, which come not only from colleagues but from other patients and perhaps from the acquaintance chains of patients and doctors as well. The same is true of lawyers and other people in similar service professions. The information transmitted by an acquaintance is valuable or useful to the extent that the acquaintance originating the message is considered to be reliable, trustworthy, and competent.

Two well-known types of errors may be made by the recipient of the information: that of commission, or following advice of a source erroneously judged to be competent; or that of omission, or failing to use recommendations because the source is erroneously judged to be incompetent. The first kind of error causes people to use information that is neither valid nor useful and, as we have noted, can increase rather than lessen the client's needs—it may even be harmful. The second kind of error causes them to miss beneficial feedback from the system because the information is considered to be neither valid nor useful. The danger in the use of an acquaintance network is that errors of the first kind may be propagated and amplified. Of course, it also has a great deal of error-correction potential. Errors of the second kind tend to greatly diminish the extent to which the acquaintance network is used, but this is where the role of professionals is most important.

Consider now a second kind of citizen information system and its resources. I have called this type a network of "referential consultants" (Kochen, 1973). Such a network *resembles* the acquaintance network or gossip grapevine. The difference is that each referential consultant is an expert in some specialty. As such, each expert can field questions from a client or a colleague. He may respond to any question directly, or he may refer the question to a colleague whom he judges to know more about the matter than he knows himself.

For our purpose, each referential consultant can be characterized by three probabilities. First, that he knows the answer to a randomly selected question, in the sense that his response will meet the needs of the client. The second is the probability that he will refer the question to a particular colleague in the network when he does *not* know the answer that would satisfy the need of the client. The third is the probability that he will answer the client's question when, in fact, he does know the answer that will satisfy the client's need.

With the help of some plausible assumptions, it is possible to show that a network of such consultants can have greater utility than the smartest consultant standing alone. As an example, consider a net of five consultants. The first is smartest and can answer 80 percent of the questions coming his way. The other four can only answer directly 3 percent of the questions addressed to them by clients or other consultants. The probability of nonreferral when a consultant knows the answer is taken to be .9. The probability of nonreferral, or answering when he does not know the answer, is taken to be .1.

If the first referential consultant stands alone, he will respond adequately with a probability of .9 x .8, which is .72, but he will respond inadequately with probability .1 x .2, or .02. If the utility to the client of a satisfactory response is V units of benefit, and if the client's disutility of an unacceptable answer is C such units, then the net utility to the client is $.72v - .02C$ units. The client gets no response at all with probability .26.

Suppose now that the smartest referential consultant does not stand alone but is the first recipient of each request. If he does not have the answer for the client, he refers the question to the next referential consultant, who refers it, if need be, to the third, who passes it to the fourth, who passes it to the fifth. The fifth one may consider the fourth to be more knowledgeable than he in the area of inquiry and therefore returns the question to him. We can calculate that the net utility of this network to the client is $.734V - .104C$, as compared with $.720V - .020C$ for the first consultant by himself. The network's utility exceeds that of the smartest one alone when $.023V - .084C > 0$. This happens if the ratio of V/C exceeds 3.7. Here is a situation where a wrong answer causes little damage and a correct answer helps a great deal. This might be the case in a contest or in betting on a nonchance game with great odds. The result is that five heads, one genius supported by four pseudoexperts or semiexperts, are better than one head (or genius).

This conclusion is supported even more strongly if we make the model a bit more realistic in the following sense. Suppose that at least four of the five referential consultants are specialists in four different fields. The consultant who is first to receive a client's question, if he decides to refer it, classifies it into one of the four special fields and refers it to the consultant who is a specialist in that field. There is now a probability that he misclassifies the question. The probability that the consultant who is specialized in that field answers the question to the point where it satisfies the client's needs is much greater than the 3 percent we had assumed previously. That is, the probability of a semiexpert being able to answer a client's question satisfactorily is greater if the question was referred to him by another consultant than if it came directly from the client. Furthermore, if the first consultant had misclassified it, the second consultant to whom it was referred can now correct this error and refer it to the appropriate colleague.

This more realistic and refined model is also more difficult to analyze mathematically. It leads to yet another line of inquiry and analysis which is very fundamental in the design of citizen information systems, that of the structure of directories to aid referential consultants in deciding on how to best field a question. Questions are characterized not only by subject field but by level of difficulty.

Each referential consultant has his own directory which, for the sake of discussion, is in the form of a table. Each row in the table denotes a class of questions. Each column in the table denotes an information resource that might supply an answer to the question. The class of information resources includes other referential consultants to whom the question may be referred, documents that may be retrieved and consulted by the consultant who is fielding the question, computer-accessible data bases for the consultant's use, or other sources of help, such as professional agencies or citizens in the community who are not part of the formal system or network of referential consultants.

Each cell in an individual table, which is characterized by a row (i.e., question class) and a column (i.e., particular resource), contains the referential consultant's judgment categorized into the following four information items:

Information item 1—personal notes recorded by the consultant which indicate to him the degree to which he can rely on getting an acceptable answer to help the client from a resource corresponding to a question class. It is, of course, essential to insure the privacy of such data. These personal impressions may be the result of synthesis by the consultant of responses from many clients he has served. The consultant's reliability judgment is assumed to include the validity of a response to the question in the class.

Information item 2—the consultant's judgment of the likely benefit that a response from the resource is likely to have in meeting the client's needs. This includes his judgment (*a*) of relevance and significance of the information likely to be provided by that resource for the question in the given class, and (*b*) of whether that resource, if he uses it, will provide him with information he did not already hold in his own memory. Resources used by the consultant are intended, after all, to amplify his own memory, to serve as an auxiliary external extension to his memory.

Information item 3—the cost to him of fielding the request directly by accessing and using the resource for a question in a given class. This includes his judgment of (*a*) how difficult it is or how long it takes to start an interaction with that resource, and (*b*) how much effort will be involved on his part in interacting with the responses of the resource. His estimated costs will be high if the resource provides responses that assume a linguistic sophistication and knowledge that is above the consultant's head. If that level is below his, judgment of benefits will be lower.

Information item 4—the cost in using the resource; this time, however, it is his estimate of the cost to him of acting as middleman to help the client indirectly by *referring* his question to that resource.

For the purpose of analysis, it is possible to generate such a table for each referential consultant by means of a computer program that will simulate the behavior of a network of referential consultants who use such directories. The computer program is now used to trace the fate of a sample of client requests through the network of referential consultants. That is, each request is assumed to be fielded by some initial recipient of the request. The recipient can either try to use the resources available to him to respond to the request directly, or he can refer it to another referential consultant who, in his judgment, is more qualified to answer that question. There is the possibility that the request may become trapped in a bureaucratic nonending cycle. The various error probabilities are built into such a model. The computer program then is used to derive, for a sample of incoming client requests, the distribution of time, cost to the system of referential consultants, and benefit of the final response to the client.

This leads to another line of analysis that stresses the client's costs and benefits. The client's judgment of the extent to which the response from the network of referential consultants meets his real need might be quite different from that of any of the referential consultants. None of these participants may possess an "objective" way of measuring the extent to which the client's need has been met. Presumably, however, the most expert consultant in the network should be in a better position to judge the extent to which the system's response has met the client's need; otherwise, it would hardly have paid for the client to use the services of the network.

With regard to the cost to the client, the simple assumption would be that the total cost to the network of fielding his request is passed on to the client, together with some fee to cover the cost of maintaining the network. Presumably the benefit to the client exceeds that of the cost to him or else he would not be using the service. Actual cost, however, is determined by many factors, such as the salaries of the referential consultants. This, in turn, depends on the demand and supply of their labor.

There are, in addition, other costs to the client that depend on the extent to which the network is centralized or decentralized. A decentralized network consists of an adequate number of consultants, sufficiently dispersed over an area, sufficiently specialized and coordinated into an organization so that the mean time or effort a client spends to obtain satisfactory service is minimal. However, a decentralized network, in which there may be more consultants than there are in a centralized network, is more costly. There is therefore some point beyond which further decentralization is counterproductive. Again, analytical techniques have been developed to model and estimate the optimal degree of decentralization in this sense (Kochen and Deutsch, 1969, 1973, 1974).

The most important consideration to bear in mind when discussing various resources designed to meet citizen information needs is that the average citizen is a generalist, not a specialist. It should not be assumed that he knows precisely what kind of information he needs. He should not be assumed capable of articulating his needs with the precision and accuracy called for, and expected by, many of the information retrieval systems aimed at helping scientists in their search for scientific or technical information.

To illustrate this point, consider the frantic cry for help by a mother who calls Poison Control Center to report that her baby has just swallowed a black liquid and is in convulsions. It would be unrealistic for the respondent at the other end of the phone to try to get from this client the information required to help him categorize this need or request into the kind of subject headings or index terms employed by indexers or classifiers when creating an index to antidotes. Despite the emotionally laden communication difficulties, he must try to obtain such useful data about the poison as will enable him to enter a directory. The entry points to that directory must offer sufficient sensitivity and flexibility to accommodate a wide variety of users who will ask an equally wide variety of questions. It must provide the recipient of the call for help with relevant questions to pose to the anxious client at the other end of the phone. The directory should have built into it the following important features.

First, it should allow its user to zoom in rapidly from an overall perspective of the problem in its context to a more detailed but circumscribed aspect of the problem. At the high level of zooming, he sees the forest rather than the trees. As he zooms in on a particular area of the intellectual forest, the details become clearer and clearer and he can decide on which grove or section of the forest to train his next observation. It is most important that he be able to see the entire forest and the smaller section of the forest which he is viewing in more detail *at the same time.* He then probes into one or another special area until he finds the one that appears worth looking at in more detail. Zooming into that section and repeating the process until he pinpoints the subregion that appears to be most appropriate, he examines it at the level of detail that is just right for the problem in question. All this activity must occur very rapidly, while the client is still on the phone. That is what we have called "zoomability."

Second, the forest must be so organized as to present the consultant/viewer with a cognitive map, a usable overall picture that shows how the various parts within fit together. We use the analogy of the map to indicate that it must be possible for the searcher to see these relations in parallel, not one at a time.

The third, and perhaps most important, feature of an information resource in dealing with such problems is a device to trigger shifts in point of view. Too often a consultant is locked into a particular point of view, a definite way of representing the problem to himself. What he believes to be true about other forests—perhaps all forests—is what he automatically believes to be true about this forest. His perceptual set is such that he can define the problem only as he has defined it in the past. He is so engrossed with his way of looking at the problem that he can not see it in any other way. The probability of a relevant/salient/appropriate response to the immediate problems of this particular forest and these particular trees is significantly reduced.

Therefore, a desirable property for an information resource is that it trigger or jog shifts of representation in its staff when rigid perceptual sets distort incoming and outgoing messages. The system must provide some means of freeing the consultant from his "believing is seeing" approach to client problems, a means that will result in adequate guidelines for defining problems and formulating more appropriate responses. Many information referral systems are meeting this need through encouraging continuing education and participation in group work. Thus they seek to explore the use of new stimuli that will trigger shifts of representation of images of forests and trees—of clients and their problems and new solution formulations.

A third typical citizen information system concept, rapidly gaining importance, should also be mentioned in this section. This concept involves the development of technologies that enable the citizen to converse directly with the "system." Rather than approaching the nearest referential consultant or other professional server, who will respond or refer the request to others within *his* network, the client is directed to one of a vastly larger set of entry points than the community of professionals alone. This resembles once again the gossip grapevine, or the informal social network with its potential of linking anyone to nearly anyone else. The differences are: (1) the network is enriched; (2) its use is systematized; and (3) its potential is thereby not only increased but more fully realized.

The technology of current interest in this connection is that of two-way cable television. The following ideas and hypotheses are taken from a proposal for experiments on citizen involvement in community problem solving using this kind of information resource. This proposal was developed jointly by Donald Pelz, who is Professor of Social Psychology at the University of Michigan and Director of the Center for Research on the Utilization of Knowledge, and the author.

In designing the proposed experiments, we assume a developed capability for electronic response to permit more or less instantaneous voting by the public for alternative options, and the almost instantaneous tabulation and presentation of these votes during the course of a given television program. The idea of interactive, on-line voting has been discussed before (Sheridan, 1971; Stevens, 1971; Parker, 1972) but controlled experiments of the kind proposed here are just now being seriously considered.

The general premise underlying these experiments is that providing an opportunity for individuals or groups to voice their opinions on community issues, and to have these opinions explicitly considered by decision-making bodies within the community, will lead to an increased sense of efficacy and also an increased level of actual participation in the community decision-making process, such as through voting.

In this experiment an effort will be made to involve residents in a number of neighborhoods throughout the city in polarized debate on a current issue. For example, we might take a current example from Ann Arbor, Michigan: should local sewage treatment facilities be expanded within the city, or alternatively should sewage treatment for several communities and cities be incorporated into a larger regional plan. The two opposing organizations are invited to prepare a series of video-taped neighborhood debates regarding this issue. These debates could take place in the home of some member of a local organization or be staged by a high school English class assigned to prepare the debate. People may need to decide whether a given percentage of improvement in sewage treatment is worth a certain cost to them; if a trade-off among various technical arrangements is called for, it must be presented to them in such a way that they can decide with a level of knowledge and understanding that is no greater than they are willing to acquire, and no less than is required.

We assume that the city is divided into definable neighborhoods, which might correspond to voting precincts. A certain number of these neighborhoods have been selected by a probability sampling method to insure that the sample of precincts is representative of the entire city. Each of the organizations is invited to designate a spokesperson who will meet with a panel of residents selected from a given precinct.

For illustration, say that about a dozen neighborhoods have been selected. Within each of the selected neighborhoods a one-hour panel discussion is held in which the spokespersons for the two viewpoints present their arguments and the neighborhood residents are given a chance to raise questions and voice opinions and objections.

During a given time period of (approximately) two weeks, the different sessions are aired. Some might be repeated in response to indications of preference obtained by the two-way cable system.

At the beginning of each session a preliminary show of sentiment on the issue is requested by means of the two-way response technique, and the same technique is used at the middle and again at the end of each session, with responses displayed to the viewing audience. Of courses people other than cable television owners may become aware of this experiment, and use telephones, the mail, and face-to-face contacts in parallel with the two-way cable response medium. Indeed, such experiments could be staged without cable television altogether, but television has the advantage of amplifying the effect and reach of debate. To reach 100 citizens, a candidate would have to meet with five groups of 20 people each face to face. With television he could meet with one group, and the other 80 who view that one could interact with him over the two-way medium.

A general premise underlying this type of program is that residents in a given neighborhood will be particularly interested in seeing the issue discussed when they know that some people within their own neighborhood—possibly acquaintances—will be participating in the discussion.

Hypothesis 1. Assume that if electronic votes are taken, then it is possible to identify the location of each respondent by neighborhood. The hypothesis to be tested is that a higher level of response will be registered from viewers who live in the neighborhood that is being represented in a given session. A related analysis becomes possible if the issue being discussed is one that will subsequently appear on a ballot for voting in the city. It is then possible to test two more hypotheses:

Hypothesis 2. In neighborhoods that are represented in the televised debate sessions, there will be a higher turnout (a higher proportion of the electorate voting on the given issue).

Hypothesis 3. Regardless of whether a given neighborhood (or precinct) was represented by having some of its members participate in the televised debate, those precincts in which there was a greater proportion of electronic response to the televised debate at any point will be the precincts in which there is a proportionally higher turnout in the actual vote.

In reference to the last hypothesis, it is of course true that tendency to respond to the televised debate may be indicative of a generally higher level of responsiveness on public issues, which in turn will lead to higher turnout, regardless of the televised debate. It will therefore be necessary to use a mode of analysis that compensates with statistical controls for the prevailing level of turnout in previous elections. The hypothesis would then examine whether the level of electronic response induced by the televised debates had exceeded what would be expected from voting turnout in prior elections.

The three kinds of information resources discussed in this section offer an abundance of opportunities for social experimentation and innovation that may help improve the quality of the average person's daily life by coupling him more effectively with existing knowledge, understanding, and wisdom.

Conclusion

In this section, I have briefly sketched where we stand with regard to matching the resources described in the last section with the needs described at the beginning of the chapter; I have considered a few of the open problems requiring research and analysis, and I have summarized both the main analytic techniques that might be used for dealing with these problems, and experimental techniques likely to be useful in that task.

The informal communication network that we have previously called the gossip grapevine has been studied both empirically and analytically. The referential-consulting networks I have discussed have not as yet been set up. Communities of professionals have, of course, maintained such networks in an informal way as long as there have been professions. To my knowledge, these have not been studied. Information and referral centers, on the other hand, have been. The chapter by Deahl describes current operations and analyses of an I&R center which was established by Ball (1971) and analyzed by the author (Kochen, 1972a). It is that analysis that led to the diffusion model described in the second section of this chapter. The third kind of information resource mentioned in the last section—two-way cable television—is just now gaining impetus (Parker and Dunn, 1972; Leonard et al., 1971; Lomont, 1973).

Altogether, then, a fair amount of practical experience in the use of technologies (communicable and teachable ways of solving problems) has been accumulated to date. The techniques of operations research, mathematical analysis, and computer programs that simulate the function of a network of referential consultants for an I&R center make it possible to compare several proposed variants of such systems with regard to benefit-cost ratios much more precisely than given by the above judgments. These are valuable first steps toward the creation of a more rational, scientific basis for designing systems, badly needed at this time because of the large-scale movements toward setting up a whole variety of such services. These movements are often staffed by energetic, very talented, and dedicated workers. But they would be greatly helped by two resources: the availability of a sound underlying discipline, and a set of goals likely to produce some consensus toward which the major thrust of these movements could be directed in a natural, spontaneous manner. The primary message of this chapter, then, is to suggest that some progress has been made toward developing the needed underlying discipline, and that it is both feasible and desirable to build vigorously upon that start.

One of the key problems requiring analysis and resolution is that of specifying the social, economic, and political conditions under which any of the systems that we have discussed so far could both remain viable and continue to effectively meet the needs of citizens. It is not sufficient to say that simply because there is citizen demand for a certain information service, and because that information service adequately meets these needs at a cost the users can afford and consider justified, such a service will be set up and remain self-supporting or profitable. It takes some significant initial capitalization, competent management, special marketing skills, and considerable knowledge of how to provide and deliver the needed service most effectively.

Among the special problems which must be solved if a referential consultant is to provide a useful service are: (1) designing a good directory; (2) pooling such directories and resource files; (3) identifying the users most likely to benefit; (4) selecting a procedure for reaching them with information about the system; and (5) characterizing the distribution of cognitive maps and visceral perceptions of information needs of potential users to optimize the system's response to those needs.

A substantial amount of research is required for these extremely difficult problems. The first step is to formulate them with much greater clarity and precision so that they can be subjected to operational analysis. This requires a much deeper and sharper conceptualization of the key variables, which can be divided into three broad classes. The first, which are analogous to independent variables in a controlled laboratory experiment, are those that characterize the usability and usefulness of the various information resources or any mix of these that may constitute a particular information system. The second class contains intervening variables. These are the behaviors which are likely to appear in response to the independent variables. The third class consists of dependent variables. These are behavioral responses, or performance measures of users or clients to the services provided by information systems. These are behaviors that are expected to vary in relation to the intervening variables, or possibly directly in relation to the independent variables.

The second step is to formulate constraints on the possible values that the independent variables may take. These constraints can take the form of relations among the independent variables. The constraints limit the number of options among the information resources that are available to a system designer, as well as the combinations or mixes of information resources that are possible.

The third step is to postulate some relationships between the independent variables and the dependent variables. These are now stated in the form of hypotheses to be tested experimentally under controlled conditions, or empirically under field conditions. Examples of such hypotheses were given at the end of the last section.

The relations postulated between the independent and the dependent variables that appear plausible and do not require empirical testing might simply be assumed to be true. From these postulated relations and those hypotheses that have been empirically verified, interesting and nonobvious deductions are now made. Some of these implications are deduced with the help of mathematical analysis, as illustrated in the last section for predicting the growth in case load for an I&R center. Other implications are derived with the help of computer programs. This was illustrated in the last section in the analysis of directories in networks of referential consultants.

For empirically testing the previously mentioned hypotheses, there are a variety of experimental and survey analysis techniques. The best procedure would be to set up real-world experimental systems, such as the CRIS system described in chapter 16. When such a system is first introduced, it is occasionally possible, though difficult, to create conditions that are sufficiently controlled so that valid statistical inferences can be made about accepting or rejecting a hypothesis. The difficulty arises from the attempt to provide a useful service to clients with real needs, at the same time that the requirements of an experimental design are being met. For example, in attempting to evaluate the effect of cable television programs upon voting behavior of citizens, the "experimental" group would be paid to watch a certain channel on cable television, and a control group would be paid not to watch that channel. This is a reasonable technique to assure a good experimental design. There is little guarantee, however, that the conclusions reached from such an experiment can be generalized or transferred to a situation where television viewers are not paid to watch or not to watch.

Another technique that is scientifically desirable, if it can be implemented in the cases I have discussed, is a controlled laboratory experiment. To try to identify the psychological barriers to the use of computerized data bases in a citizen information system, it is desirable to specify hypotheses involving one variable at a time. It might, for instance, be hypothesized that a citizen is reluctant to contribute to the updating of a data base if he does not access and search it fairly frequently. The best way to test such a hypothesis is, again, to set up an experimental group that is allowed both updating and access, and a controlled group that is denied one or the other. This presupposes the availability of a completed data base and an updating and retrieval system. On the other hand, it cannot, of course, be completed because it is constantly being updated by the inputs of citizens. Hence, a variety of compromises must be worked out.

The availability of cable television with an electronic two-way response will greatly facilitate the collection of data for experiments of the kind I have just described. Unfortunately, such programs on cable television will reach only about three percent of the general population. When a way is found to utilize the existing telephone network with an input-output device that is audio-coupled to the phone hand set, far more people will be reached. It is, of course, necessary to make such an input-output device sufficiently ubiquitous by making its price low enough to enable almost anyone to purchase it. The capability required would be little more than a cathode-ray tube display and a keyboard input. The amount of information transmitted to and from such terminals must be sufficiently small so as not to overload the channels of the telephone network and its switching capacities.

The last technique to be mentioned as an alternative for testing such hypotheses is the use of an interviewing instrument to determine attitudes and feelings. The attitudes of citizens would be directed toward a simulated information system. An interviewer would present a citizen with a question of the form: "If you had available a system which works as I am about to describe, how would you feel about . . .?" Designing such an instrument would involve the problem of making it sufficiently sensitive to elicit the subtle shades and nuances in the user's feelings from day to day, and from one individual to another.

In this chapter, I have tried to show the need for, and possibility of, research in information science toward a better theoretical and empirical basis for the analysis and design of citizen information systems. While such research has not yet advanced to the stage were it can offer soundly based recommendations to system managers, it has reached a point where the most desirable directions for further research are beginning to emerge. It is to be hoped that researchers in the information sciences will be stimulated to further the basic and applied research that is needed and feasible, and that managers, sponsors, and the potential users of citizen information systems will provide the necessary support.

References

Ball, J. "Model Cities Community Information Center." Mimeographed. 2204 N. Broad St., Philadelphia, Penna., 1971.

Kochen, M. "Switching Centers for Inquiry Referral." In *Procedural Conference on Interlibrary Communication Networks,* edited by J. Becker. Chicago: American Library Association, 1971.

_____. "Directory Design for Networks of Information and Referral Centers." *The Library Quarterly,* 1972a, *42.* Also in *Operations Research: Implications for Libraries,* edited by D. R. Swanson and A. Bookstein. Chicago: University of Chicago Press, 1972a, pp. 59–83.

_____. "WISE: A World Information Synthesis and Encyclopedia." *Journal of Documentation,* 1972b, *28,* 322–43.

_____. "Referential Consulting Networks." In *Towards A Theory of Librarianship; Festschrift in Honor of J. Shera,* edited by C. Rawski. Metuchen, N.J.: Scarecrow Press, 1973, pp. 187–220.

_____.*Integrative Mechanisms in Literature Growth.* Westport, Conn.: Greenwood, 1974a.

_____. *Principles of Information Retrieval.* New York: Melville/Wiley/Becker-Hayes, 1974b.

Kochen, M., and Deutsch, K. W. "Toward A Rational Theory of Decentralization: Implications of a Mathematical Approach." *American Political Science Review,* 1969, *63,* 734–49.

_____. "Decentralization by Function and Location." *Management Science,* 1973, *19,* 841–56.

_____. "A Note on Hierarchy and Coordination: An Aspect of Decentralization." *Management Science,* June 1974, *20.*

Leonard, E., et al. "MINERVA: A Participatory Technology System." *Science and Public Affairs, Bulletin of the Atomic Scientists,* 1971, *27,* 4–12.

Lewis, C. A. "Courses by Newspaper." University of California, Extension Service, San Diego. P.O. Box 109, LaJolla, California, 92037, 1973.

Lomont, V. C. "Computer-Based Communications Media and Citizens Participation." Paper presented at the NATO Advanced Study Institute in Information Sciences, Aberystwyth, Wales, 1973.

McLuhan, M. and Fiore, Q. *The Medium Is the Message.* New York: Bantam, 1970.

Metzker, I. *A Bintel Brief.* New York: Doubleday, 1971.

Parker, E. "On-line Polling and Voting." In *Planning Community Information Utilities,* edited by H. Sackman and B. Boehm. Montvale, N.J.: AFIPS Press, 1972, pp. 93–109.

Parker, E., and Dunn, D. A. "Information Technology: Its Social Potential." *Science,* 1972, *176,* 1392–99.

Schramm, W. "How Communication Works." In *Dimensions of Communication,* edited by L. Richardson. New York: Appleton-Century-Crofts, 1969, pp. 3–25.

Sheridan, T. "Citizen Feedback: New Technology for Social Choice." *Technology Review*, 1971, *74*, 46–51.

Stevens, C. "Citizen Feedback: The Need and the Response." *Technology Review*, 1971, *74*, 38–45.

Taylor, D. W. "Toward An Information Processing Theory of Motivation." In *Nebraska Symposium on Motivation, 1960*, edited by R. Jones. Lincoln, Neb.: University of Nebraska Press, 1960, pp. 51–79.

Thies, B. H. *Newsletter of the National Alliance of I&R Systems.* I&R Services of Los Angeles County, Inc., 621 S. Virgil Avenue, Los Angeles, California 90005.

Chapter 11

*Cost Analysis for Community
Information Services*

by John H. Wilson, Jr., and Joan W. Barth

In establishing a community information service center, planners
should take into account several major economic factors. User benefits, pricing and marketing, costs of operation, funding and budgeting,
and program budgeting are all important items to be thought through
carefully before a center is established, in order to minimize the chance
of failure. This chapter focuses on a cost-analysis approach to the
problems involved in creating a new community organization.

User Benefits

Planners of a proposed center should first of all determine that a
need exists in the community for the kinds of services envisioned for
the center. In the initial planning stages, they should undertake to
assess needs by exploring such questions as: Who will the user be?
What will he want to know? What should the center try to supply to
the user? What will it be worth to the user? Will the user's real needs
be met by the proposed program? Will the information given be used
by the client? What specific benefits do the backers of the service
envision? By thinking through answers to such questions, a thorough
analysis of benefits can be made. Clearly, information services should
be furnished only when the benefits provided to the community equal
or exceed the cost to the community.

Negative utility. In addition to ferreting out positive benefits, a
proposed program should also be examined in terms of its negative
aspects. Is the program structured so that a user can be assured that

Mr. Wilson is Information Systems Specialist, Division of Biomedical and
Environmental Research, Energy Research and Development Administration. Ms.
Barth is Assistant Editor, Mental Health Research Institute, University of Michigan.

the cost of his time and effort will not exceed the benefits he is likely to receive? For example, if a client is given accurate—but wrong—information in answer to his particular problem, he will spend his time futilely in contacting inappropriate agencies or receiving information unrelated to his problem. Weaknesses in programs resulting in a worsening of problems can be thought of in terms of negative net utility.

Interagency benefits. It is likely that in any community in which an information service is contemplated there already exist several formal information activities that are being carried on by working subgroups of federal, state, or local agencies. Since various community information services are likely to form at least an informal network, the value of the new activity within this network must be considered. Early exploration of how the proposed service can meld its activities with those of currently existing organizations is recommended. Cooperative efforts might allow an agency now supplying a particular service to relinquish it to the new center, perhaps relieving the agency of an activity that is not central to its role. Services now performed by several agencies might be consolidated and carried out more efficiently by the proposed organization. An approach should be taken that emphasizes benefits to existing agencies as well as to the community at large.[1]

Long-range benefits. In justifying the need for a new community service organization, as well as in undertaking a long-range plan, long-range benefits must be examined. Such benefits are often closely tied to the question of funding. Local, state, or federal agencies supplying all or part of the funds constrain a program, since they will specify benefits and client populations permitted by their overall mission. There are also certain services they cannot support because of administrative fiat or because of limitations in their enabling legislation. In relation to funding, the benefit question becomes: What funds are potential backers willing to expend to satisfy what needs of what type of users?

Pricing and Marketing

Charging policy. In addition to benefits, pricing and marketing are important factors of a exploration program. Should clients be charged fees for services? If help is free, it might not be regarded as being valuable. Charging for service also has a weeding-out effect by discouraging the casual inquirer, and by helping to control the workload. Prospective clients will become paying customers if products and services are competitive or if there is no other source of help. If a

---

1. The two are not necessarily the same. (Ed.)

decision is made to charge the client, the amount of the fee must then be determined. Since fees that would cover all costs would probably be so astronomical as to drive away clients, sliding fee scales should be considered. Costs can also be imposed on such items as published materials that the agency must purchase for distribution, thus discouraging waste. One avenue of obtaining operating money would be to assess a one-time charge, similar to a membership fee. Such a charge has the disadvantage, however, of forcing the client to pay before he can determine the value of the service to him.

There are certain types of services for which one can expect to charge full costs. For example, a local company might ask the center to perform services for its employees. Since company staff time will be saved and since the service may be tax deductible for the company, the organization would probably be willing to pay for what the center can provide. Revenue so raised can help defray costs of other activities that are less self-supporting. One way to underwrite the cost of a new program is to provide services that carry a high probability of attracting customers who are willing to pay. Once a base of operations has been established, the agency can then expand into activities less likely to pay for themselves, assuming, of course, that motivation to do so has not meanwhile been lost.

Marketing. Following consideration of ongoing financing, planners should explore ways to market their product. Prospective clients must be informed that information services are available to them and in addition must be encouraged to use such services. Initial announcements about the center can be made in newspapers and on television and radio, care being taken to place stories in those media whose audiences encompass possible clients. Equal concern should be given to making certain that the information printed is factually correct, so that prospective clients will not be misled about the kinds of services offered. Proper timing of announcements is important; they should not appear too early, since readers forget opening dates that are too far in the future. Free time for spot announcements on television and radio is usually available to community organizations, and participation in local talk shows can often be arranged. Community organizations such as schools, service clubs, and unions can be solicited to make explanations to their members. It is not very productive to use direct mailings—purchasing the lists may be expensive and the response is often minimal.

Marketing efforts should not stop with initial announcements, even though satisfied clients will carry on advertising by word of mouth. The same media that were effective initially are likely to continue to be so; follow-up articles should appear in the original sources, reporting on progress that the center is making. It is usually not feasible to undertake hard marketing studies that involve hundreds of interviews, because low-budget operations such as community information centers have neither the staff nor the funds to carry out such research. However, for a larger unit, such as a big city, county, or a state that is considering establishment of several centers, marketing studies are needed to determine whether the proposed services will indeed "sell." In these instances, it might even be best to survey those who work with clients—teachers, caseworkers, association officers—rather than the people who are expected ultimately to benefit from the system.

Costs of Operation

Cost-effectiveness analyses. Once goals have been decided and stated explicitly, cost-effectiveness analyses should be made. They need not be elaborate. Rough estimates of the comparative costs of various ways to achieve the goals may suffice. Outlined below are items that should be explored.

One of the first factors to consider in cost-effectiveness analysis is site location. Even though it may be considered unlikely that passersby will come to constitute the majority of the clientele, a convenient, well-trafficked site is desirable. A center that is hard to get to may go unused. However, provision of rent-free or low-cost quarters may force location at a particular place. Longer-range planning should take into account what will happen if free quarters are reclaimed by the donor or if the rent is raised on low-cost quarters. Considering the cost of moving, it might be less costly in the long run not to accept a free location if it is for a limited period of occupancy. If alternative sites are available, the site that needs the least remodeling may, for that reason, be most desirable.

Following the architectural principle that form should follow function, the kinds of services and products to be provided determine the way the operation is organized, and this in turn affects costs. For example, counseling services would require different staffing and work-flow plans than material distribution services or referral services. Small, reasonably soundproof rooms must be provided for counseling sessions. Current case records must be handled with circumspection, not being left in the open work area, and it must be remembered that cumulative files are even more sensitive. It will be necessary to provide locked cabinets to assure client confidentiality. For brochure distribution, comparatively large storage space may be needed. Referral services provided mainly by phone will, of course, result in large costs, especially if special equipment is required.

Two types of record keeping must be considered. Documentation or summaries of services provided will be needed in assessing the value of the services and in seeking funding. Record keeping costs money.

Yet, running a community information center without records is nearly equivalent to not being organized at all. In addition, money records must be maintained in acceptable form for accounting purposes. The books must be set up by an informed person and should be audited at least yearly. Poorly kept records can be a major deterrent to a potential funder who might want to know how much time is spent with clients or the monthly cash flow.

Functional statements and staffing plans may seem academic if the center is a three-man operation. But what is to be done by whom must be decided for any organization other than a one-man operation. Putting off work allocation decisions can result in inefficiency. The center may be able to dispense with a secretary, a telephone answerer, etc. It may be able to substitute forms for many letters. If most telephone calls are for the referral service, the referral specialist can answer the phone. On the other hand, if there is enough clerical and handyman activity to keep one person busy, then it is inefficient to have higher-level, more expensive people doing such work. Such "trivial" questions as who is to do the sweeping, mopping, dusting, and emptying of ashtrays, or who is to remove from the publication storage area the torn, mutilated, outdated forms, brochures, and instruction booklets may affect critically the success of day-to-day operations. Professional volunteers may be available for higher-level activities, but it will be necessary to hire housekeeping help.

The way in which information is packaged is closely related to the cost-effectiveness of any operation. The same information can be packaged in many ways: books, pamphlets, reports, newsletters, letters, memos, telephone conversations, interviews, computer printouts, documentary films, exhibits, videotapes, audiotapes, and microfilms. Interviews are expensive in their demands on skilled manpower. Documentary films are expensive to make but may be rented cheaply or may even be free. Letters are probably more expensive than telephone calls. If clients need pieces of paper on which to carry away information, they can be provided with preprinted forms which should be run in as large quantities as are cheapest to print and for which there is adequate storage space. If the printed forms can be made self-explanatory, so much the better with respect to cost of center manpower.

Postage can be a major expense if a great quantity of material is being mailed out, especially if it is sent first class. Care should be taken to send printed matter at optimal rates. To save postage, clients may sometimes be asked to come to the center to pick up material, at least when there are reasons for wishing to establish face-to-face contact.

In the event that the proposed service is to be located in an already existing organization, cost-effectiveness analysis may be somewhat different. Staffing and space problems are better known in advance and overall costs are usually less, especially if the host organization is self-supporting. Possible alternative ways of meeting goals are more limited than if the operation is started from scratch.

Cost accounting. Standard methods of cost accounting should be mentioned. The first step is to list the overall expenditures of the organization, grouped into logical categories. While the specific line entries will vary somewhat from organization to organization, the individual expenditure items will generally organize into three groups: (1) salaries, (2) materials, and (3) indirect costs or overhead, including fringe benefits. Next, it is necessary to assign a fair portion of the expenditures for each of these categories to the activities performed. This is the total cost associated with given products or services. Finally, dividing the cost for each product by the number of products yields the desired unit costs.

Costing for information. For information systems costing, five tags are recommended: project, product, account, organization, and function. The project tag identifies a major or significant set of the activities being costed. The product tag refers to a subset of a project, usually a coherent activity or set of activities contributing to a specific goal or output. Rare indeed is the information system where the inputs have a consistent one-to-one relationship with the outputs. Since information systems are almost universally subject to varying workloads, the most effective approach to costing seems to be unit costing. However, the lack of a one-to-one relationship between inputs and outputs makes it necessary to select for unit costing relatively small elements which constitute building blocks from which final costs for an output can be "assembled." Proper selection of building blocks for unit costing can provide precise, useful cost information without significantly impairing the flexibility needed to respond to changes in the volume and nature of the workload.

The building blocks for information system costing can be categorized as follows:

Inputs: Activities that contribute to the building or maintenance of the information store.

Outputs: Activities that draw on the information store to produce information products for users.

Collateral services: Activities not necessarily dependent upon the created information store, e.g., document dissemination in either microform or hard copy, user records, and the like.

Specials: Activities that are ad hoc in nature or that support the system itself.

Burdens: Activities that are essential to and support the system as a whole, e.g., management activities.

Accounts are the classes by which costs must be collected for the purpose of maintaining an organization's financial records, providing control and identification for audits. Typically, they are in five broad classes: direct labor, direct materials, supplies, other direct costs, and indirect costs. Almost invariably, these are further subdivided into more specific subsets with varying levels of detail, depending upon the organization and circumstances.

For any except the smallest organizations, some kind of organizational structure is necessary. Even if a small information center or library is a part of a larger organization and obtains services from other elements, it will find organizational tags useful in validating or reviewing costs.

Function, which is applied to direct labor only, identifies what the individual is doing to the item being costed. While it is not common in most cost systems, it has been found to be extremely valuable in tracking costs of information systems, particularly small ones where a single individual may perform several functions.

Fixed-budget approach. The fixed-budget approach is a technique for comparing operations for cost-effectiveness under various assumed budgets. Potential annual fundings from possible sources are listed, along with services that can be provided for these amounts. After establishing the limits of each of several modes of operation, the best alternatives can be found by suboptimization. This is done by permuting suboperations to see what their effects are on other suboperations. It pays to be hard-headed about costs and services that can be provided for given amounts. Ways of achieving more for less money will become evident, and a consensus will likely develop about what can be provided for each alternative.

Even if assumptions of funding are purely speculative to begin with, by the time cost-effectiveness discussions have gone several rounds a plan will have been developed that can be presented to potential funders to show them what they will get for their money.

Cost-effectiveness of interagency cooperation. The question of free assistance from other community agencies should be looked at in costing terms. If a community information center has no money at all, there is, of course, no cost-effectiveness problem. Even when money first begins to be available, work allocation decisions will probably be made so that assistance provided by others, since it is free, will continue to be used. No matter how much money is available, supplying services that other agencies are already providing is a waste of community resources.[2] However, assistance may come at too high a price. For example, a state welfare office may take referrals but demand more paperwork than the center can afford to provide. It is in these instances of assistance that costing should be explored.

Staffing. Brief job descriptions are quite valuable in cost-effectiveness analysis, in the actual hiring of staff, and in keeping tabs on how assignments are working out as the operation gathers momentum.

In planning a staff, the question of using volunteers will most likely arise. Volunteers can be expensive. If there is no money to supply backbone services, it will become necessary to use volunteers, but it should be remembered there is always the cost of space, materials, and supervisory time. Often volunteers cause extreme scheduling difficulties and, worse yet, may not show up when the center's calendar conflicts with their own calendar. Volunteers will seldom be professionals or trained in the skills needed, although they may be highly educated and intelligent, and they may be less inclined to follow supervisory direction than paid employees would be. Consequently, costs for salaries must be balanced against hidden costs for volunteers. Women or men with requisite professional backgrounds who are not working full time because of family responsibilities, and who may be hired for half days at respectable rates, can be expected to be more dependable and more amenable to supervision than volunteers.

Operation within an established organization. Cost-effectiveness considerations can be expected to favor establishing the community information service within an ongoing organization. Operating as a unit in a public library, for example, has obvious cost advantages. Initially, the community information center may be nothing more than a desk in the lobby of the main branch of the library. It may expand to a desk at each of the branches; it may expand to a facility of its own, having branch status, or to being the specialty of one branch library. In addition to costing less, operating within an existing library may even help the library get additional funds. School, college, and university libraries may also serve as cost-effective bases of operation.

Funding

The question of funding is, of course, central to the establishment of an information center. The problem becomes one of determining sources of funds. Only diligent searching will uncover funds available in a particular locality. Possible ways of getting information include contacting federal and state agencies listed in the telephone book that have nearby offices, writing to the local congressman and to

2. There is, of course, the benefit of choice that a citizen obtains when he can turn from an agency with which he is dissatisfied to a competitor. (Ed.)

both senators from the state, and finding out if there is an office in the state government that assists people in obtaining federal moneys.

Multiple funding, money pouring in from several federal or state sources, may seem highly desirable. Such a situation has the advantage that if one sponsor defaults, services do not have to stop. But there are many disadvantages to multiple sources of funds. For example, the different agencies may require their own accounting systems, their own ways of presenting budgets and making reports, and individual payment cycles. Such variations add to the cost of running a center.

There are agencies with regional missions that may respond to the establishment of multiple-site information centers. Starting three centers at the same time may be easier because parties representing each site must be concrete about goals, organization, and staffing, particularly when the intent from the outset is to approach a specific agency known to have money available for this type of regional project.

Longer-range funding. Longer-range funding from politically oriented sources is maddeningly difficult anywhere in the United States. A project may operate throughout its lifetime on a year-to-year basis. Special appropriations for multiyear projects would appear to be one answer. However, even when passed by legislatures, funds may be impounded by presidents or governors. It may be safer and easier to include provision for funding an information center as part of a bill to aid public school or academic libraries than to seek funding by an independent appropriation.

Program Budgeting

When a small manufacturer goes to the bank to borrow money for a new product line, he goes with facts and figures. He has them not only for this year but for the next year, and the next—for as long as the loan is to run. So, too, should the planners of a community information center approach potential funders, ready to present their facts and figures for several years in advance. Planners should work out a program budget that projects over several years what they hope to achieve, program by program.

For the community information center that initially has one counselor, one literature specialist, and one referral specialist, the goal in three years is not necessarily to have two of each. Nor will its purpose be to improve its counseling program, its publication dissemination program, its referral program. These are not programs; they are functions established to carry out the program. A program statement might read something like this:

To establish a center to inform senior citizens of the Borough of Exeter about the federal and state services available to them, and to assist them in obtaining those services to which they are entitled. Further, to train and encourage senior citizens to assist in and within three years assume management of the center.

There are three programs referred to in the statement: establishing services related to federal information, establishing services related to state information, and training senior citizens to take over the center. Milestones to be achieved by the end of the three years should be plotted for each of the three programs. With a clear goal, with a projected cutoff date, with milestones stepped off—assuming money is available—the planners of this center will likely be more successful in establishing it than if they wrote up their program in vague statements.

Most federal and state agencies require preparation of a program budget before granting funds. Operations change as they go through life cycles; a program budget provides the guidelines for directing that change toward the goals to be achieved, the subprograms to be successfully completed. Phased operations should be related to a phased financial plan. The program budget should state explicitly the percentage of resources to be allocated to each service at each stage, as well as what must be done to complete each stage on time and within projected costs.

Bibliography

Little has been written that is specifically related to the economic aspects of community information centers. Listed below are items of possible pertinency from systems analysis and program budgeting applied to libraries.

Blaug, M. *An Introduction to the Economics of Education*. Baltimore, Md.: Penguin Books, 1970.

Bromberg, E. *Simplified PPBS for the Librarian*. Paper prepared for Dollar Decision Pre-Conference Institute, Library Administration Division of the American Library Association, Dallas, Texas (ED–047–751), June 1971.

Brophy, P.; Buckland, M. K.; Ford, G.; Hindle, A.; and Mackenzie, A. G. *A Library Management Game: A Report on a Research Project*. University of Lancaster Library Occasional Papers, No. 7. Lancaster, England: University of Lancaster Library, 1972.

Brutcher, C., et al. "Cost Accounting for the Library." *Library Resources and Technical Services*, 1964, *8*, 413–31.

Buckland, M. K., and Hindle, A. "The Case for Library Management Games." *Journal of Education for Librarianship*, 1971, *12*, 92–103.

Childers, T., and Krevitt, B. "Municipal Funding of Library Services." *American Libraries*, 1962, *3*, 53–57.

Committee on Scientific and Technical Information (COSATI). *The Management of Information Centers*. Proceedings of a forum sponsored by the COSATI Panel on Information Analysis Centers, May 1971.

Crum, N. J. "Cost-Benefit and Cost-Effectiveness Analysis: A Bibliography of Applications in the Civilian Economy." Santa Barbara, Calif.: General Electric, TEMPO. Report 69 TMP 30 (ED–047–715), April 1969.

Dasgupta, P.; Sen, A.; and Marglin, S. *Guidelines for Project Evaluation*. United Nations Industrial Development Organization, Project Formulation and Evaluation Series, No. 2. New York: United Nations (ID/SER.H/2), 1972.

Donbito, P. A. *Annotated Bibliography on Systems Costs Analysis*. Santa Monica, Calif.: Rand Corporation, March 1967.

Dorfman, R. ed. *Measuring Benefits of Government Investments*. Presented at a Conference of Experts, November 1963. Washington, D.C.: Brookings Institution, n.d.

Evans, E.; Borko, H.; and Ferguson, P. "Review of Criteria Used to Measure Library Effectiveness." *Bulletin of the Medical Library Association*, 1972, *60*, 102–10. Also published in *California Librarian*, 1972, *33*, 72–83.

Fazar, W. "Program Planning and Budgeting Theory: Improved Library Effectiveness by Use of the Planning-Programming-Budgeting System." *Special Libraries*, 1969, *60*, 423–33.

"Federalism Report/Revenue Sharing Bill Authorizes Sweeping Innovation in Federal Aid System." *National Journal*, 1972, *4*, 1553–66.

Goddard, H. C. "An Economic Analysis of Library Benefits." *Library Quarterly*, 1971, *41*, 244–55.

Hearle, E. F. R. "Designing Urban Information Systems." *Nation's Cities*, April 1970, 16–19.

Jones, A. "Criteria for the Evaluation of Public Library Services." *Journal of Librarianship*, 1970, *2*, 228–45.

Kountz, J. *Library Cost Analysis: A Recipe*. Orange County Public Library, California. (Request from the author.)

Krettek, G., and Cooke, E. D. "Federal Legislation for Libraries During 1971." In the *Bowker Annual of Library and Book Trade Information*. New York: R. R. Bowker, 1972, pp. 207–13.

Lutz, R. P. "Costing Information Services," *Bulletin of the Medical Library Association*, 1971, *59*, 254–61.

Mackenzie, A. G., and Buckland, M. K. "Operational Research." In *British Librarianship and Information Science 1966–1970*, edited by H. A. Whatley. London, England: The Library Association, 1972, pp. 224–31.

Marron, H. "On Costing Information Services." In *Proceedings of the American Society for Information Science 32nd Annual Meeting, Vol. 6*. Westport, Conn.: Greenwood Publishing Corp., 1969, pp. 515–20.

Newhouse, J. P., and Alexander, A. J. *An Economic Analysis of Public Library Service*. Santa Monica, Calif.: Rand Corporation, (R–848–BH), 1972.

Novick, D., ed. *Program Budgeting: Program Analysis and the Federal Budget* 2nd ed. New York: Holt, Rinehart & Winston, 1969.

Nussbaum, H. *Operations Research Applied to Libraries*. Detroit, Mich.: Wayne State University, Department of Library Science (ED–045–121), 1968.

Pfister, R. L., and Milliman, J. W. *Economic Aspects of Library Service in Indiana*. Indiana Library Studies, Report No. 7, Bloomington, Ind.: Indiana University, 1970.

Price, D. S. *Collecting and Reporting Real Costs of Information Systems*. Washington, D.C.: American Society for Information Science, 1971.

Schultz, J. S. "Program Budgeting and Work Measurement for Law Libraries." *Law Library Journal*, 1970, *63*, 353–62.

State and Local Federal Assistance Act of 1972, Public Law 92–512, October 1972.

Stocker, F. D. *Financing Public Libraries in Ohio.* Columbus, Ohio: Ohio State University, Center for Business (ED–048–892) , 1971.

Tudor, D. *Planning-Programming-Budgeting-Systems* (Exchange Bibliography 183) . Monticello, Ill.: Council of Planning Librarians, 1971.

Veazie, W. H., Jr., and Connolly, T. F. *The Marketing of Information Analysis Center Products and Services.* Washington, D.C.: Educational Resources Information Center, Clearinghouse on Library and Information Sciences (ED–050–772) , 1971.

Yocum, J. C., and Stocker, F. D. *The Development of Franklin County Public Libraries, 1980.* Columbus, Ohio: Ohio State University, Center for Business and Economic Research (ED–044–160) , 1970.

Young, H. A. "Performance and Program Budgeting: An Annotated Bibliography." *American Library Association Bulletin,* 1967, *61,* 63–67.

Chapter 12
Community Referral Services:
Impact Measures

by Thomas Childers

Social services are assumed to have an impact on the people they are designed to serve—their target groups. Describing this impact in hard terms is a problem that has frustrated social agents for a long time. This article focuses on a relatively young social service: the referral center, a center designed to direct a person in need to the agency or person that will satisfy the need. First, some of the general problems of measuring the impact of social programs will be identified, followed by suggestions for some general approaches to measuring the impact of a referral center.

Evaluation

The many approaches to evaluation can be laid out on a spectrum, most easily described by defining its extremes. At one end are evaluations that are wholly *intuitive*. Here, the "data" used in the evaluation are collected accidentally, chanced upon in the course of personal experience with the phenomena, and filtered through personal attitudes, beliefs, biases, etc. In a social service these may include a client's expressed need or unsolicited reaction to a service transaction— gathered perhaps unwittingly, stored and processed unconsciously, and eventually used in evaluating the service. The evaluation may ultimately be an impression of client "needs" or a feeling of success or failure in serving. The systematic collection of data has not occurred, and the resulting evaluation itself may never rise to conscious thought. Such data, absorbed and processed without a plan, run a high risk of presenting a distorted picture. Resulting evaluations likewise run a high risk of being wrong.

Dr. Childers is Associate Professor, Graduate School of Library Science, Drexel University.

At the other end of the spectrum are evaluations based on *systematically collected data*. These are data gathered by design. We would expect them to represent the "real" world accurately—not just the limited portion of the real world that directly reaches our senses. (Suchman, 1967, in his important work on the evaluation of social services, offers a similar distinction. The ends of his spectrum are labeled "evaluation" and "evaluative research.") Systematically generated data are more reliable and lead to better judgments than intuitively generated data.

In addition to philosophical arguments, there is at least one practical reason that compels the systematic collection of data, one that adds some urgency to the search for nonintuitive, or systematic, data in the area of social services. This reason is that such data are needed in obtaining support. Competition for the public dollar has increased in recent years, and public policy makers are being pressed to make better decisions. As a result, they have been demanding more and more hard facts illustrating the impact of social services, so that they can evaluate the various public programs. Evaluations based on hard data can lead to sound decisions on how public dollars should be spent on public programs.

Evidence of a trend toward greater accountability abounds. It can be found in the widespread attempts at program budgeting, cost-effectiveness analysis, systems analysis, the context-input-process-product model, and other techniques of accounting for dollars spent in terms of actual or anticipated impact. As public services are held more accountable for their "impact" or "effectiveness," they will be compelled to generate data systematically. There will be greater urgency for data that bear closely on their impact or effectiveness.

MEASUREMENT AND MEASUREMENT PROBLEMS

What is meaningful? The systematic generation of data implies *measurement*. Measurement means that the phenomenon must be transformed into units, and the units counted in some way. That is, the phenomenon must be quantified. It is the primary focus here, since we are concerned with improving the data bases upon which evaluations are founded.

Yet quantification alone is not enough. Some factors related to social service have been systematically counted; the means for some kinds of measurement does exit. For instance, in the field of libraries and information service, counting has been occurring on a nationwide basis for nearly 100 years. Still, the available measures of impact are widely considered inadequate—meaningless, unreliable, misleading.

Quantification per se is not enough; the nature of the quantification must be improved. This means moving away from simple counts of input data (books purchased, dollars spent, staff size, collection size, etc.) to data that carry more meaning in terms of service output, impact, or effectiveness. For the library field, some effort in this direction has been witnessed in recent years.

There has been some discussion and development of measures centering in one degree or another around service impact on the target group (Beasley, 1964; Morse, 1968; Raffel and Shishko, 1969; Trueswell, 1966). Hamburg has recently completed a systems analysis of public and academic library output statistics (Hamburg et al., 1972). For the past seven years or so, some concentrated effort at the Graduate School of Library Service, Rutgers University, has turned out several doctoral theses and faculty research reports in which new measures of service impact were explored. A large scale effort to identify and polish new measures of public library effectiveness was recently completed at Rutgers (DeProspo et al., 1973).

If service is seen as an unending cycle, a number of points on which to focus measurement can be noted (see figure 1).

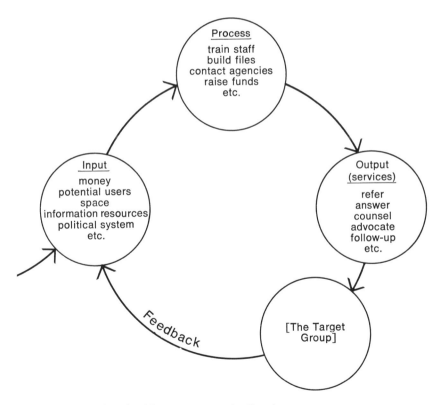

Figure 1.   Points for Measurement of a Service

In the social services, probably the most obstinate point of measurement is where the target group and the service meet. Impact, effectiveness, potential impact, or quality of the service as viewed from the client's vantage are difficult things to measure. Most frequently services are measured in terms of their *inputs* and *processes,* often simply because such measures are there for the taking, or because the data seem to accumulate with no real effort.

Dollars spent, professional staff per 100,000 population, and square feet of the service outlet are ordinary kinds of input measures. Number of agencies contacted, file cards produced, and time spent updating files are common process measures. *Output* is most easily (and therefore, often) measured in terms of the transactions that occur between the service staff and the user group. The transactions may be classed according to any number of topics, such as information, referral, counseling; housing, job, child care, etc.; amount of time spent with the client; or others.

These measures have at least one thing in common: they do not provide any obviously meaningful statements on the impact of the service. They do not view the service through the client's eyes, nor—with the exception of subject classifications like housing, job, etc.—do they relate it to the community and its needs.

A study in the field of information and referral, emphasizing service for aging people (Long et al., 1971), concludes that the types of statistical data most often gathered by I&R centers are:

1. Agency to which client was referred.
2. How client contacted the agency.
3. Did client contact agency to which he was referred?
4. Client characteristics ("i.e., sex, age, occupation, address, living arrangements, income level").
5. Type of service requested; for example, information, referral, counseling.
6. Source of client's knowledge of I&R center.
7. Persons contacting the center by phone.
8. Activity performed by the center before referring.

Note that almost all, whether input, process, or output, are discrete and simple data that carry virtually no implications for impact, quality, or effectiveness. (The third, and possibly the sixth, might be construed as impact-oriented.)

One of the elements in the process of measurement is to identify meaningful measures. Ordinarily, these will be measures of impact or effectiveness, usually occurring at or after the point where service and client come into contact.

What is the organization trying to do? A search for measures of a phenomenon that carry meaning related to impact must be undertaken. At the same time, in order to be quantified, the phenomenon must be transformed into observable units.

An obvious way to identify meaningful units of a social service is to look at the desired result of that service. If the desired result of a service is fewer undernourished children, it would be more reasonable to take that as a measure of impact than to collect data on, say, the number of dollars spent nourishing children, or the number of children per household in the target area. While these latter measures may have a bearing on some decision-making in the nourishment program, they are relatively distant from the desired result of the service, and thus, standing alone, they say little about impact.

The service objectives could simply be taken as measures of impact but evaluation is not quite that easy. Goals, objectives, and plans abound in the social services. A little examination, however, indicates that great numbers of them are nonspecific. They are seldom guides to action. Instead, they often appear in the form of a *creed* such as "the individual should realize his full potential," or a *mission* such as "eliminate illiteracy" and "inform the voter" (Granger, 1964). While creeds and missions perform certain functions critical to the survival of organizations, these goals lack the specificity that would provide clear-cut prescriptions for action and, thus, for measurement. They leave many questions unanswered—for example: How much? How well? How often? or just How? And to the extent that the goal's call to action is ambiguous, the means of measuring the action will be ambiguous.

It must be obvious that there are fewer ambiguities in evaluating the achievement of "one personal information transaction per capita per year" than in "keep the community informed." The first not only indicates a fairly concrete service to be delivered, but also simultaneously points to a simple, though crude, measure of success: counting the number of personal information transactions and dividing by the number in the target group. The measure is inherent in the specific objective.

In a general paper specific objectives for all referral services cannot be listed. Theoretically, there will be as many different sets of objectives as there are services. Refining creeds and missions into more specific objectives will depend on the context in each particular situation. Falling into two broad classes—client needs and service constraints—the factors to be considered in the context might be:

Client needs:
1. Social and demographic characteristics of the client group: education, income, standard of living, family size, welfare statistics, unemployment, etc.;

2. Communications characteristics: media input, media consumption, informal communications channels (e.g., churches, clubs street corners, employers), community activities, etc.

Service constraints:
1. Available sources of "needed" information;
2. Available wherewithal: space, funds, people;
3. Milieu: local community and larger political situations.

Measuring impact without specific impact objectives is virtually impossible. It is vital to understand the importance of precise and unambiguous objectives in the processes of measuring and evaluating.

Limits of service measures. If measurement is to occur, there must be a *way* of measuring. Of course we cannot measure everything we would like to measure. Like everything else, measurement is a trade off between what *should* be done and what *can* be done.

A method of measurement represents the point at which the ability to measure intersects with one point of the phenomenon under investigation. Like the proverbial elephant and the seven blind men, many social phenomena cannot be observed in a simple, direct way. Each of the blind men approaches the elephant obliquely and draws conclusions based on gross assumptions, observing only small parts of the elephant. While one such observer may accurately describe a specific part, he may not do so in proper relation to the total context. In the same way, each of the existing measures of a social phenomenon is limited.

A strong case can be made for saying that the easier, more obvious measures of a phenomenon are usually the most deceptive. The elements that are most susceptible to being observed tend to yield data that only crudely represent the "elephant," offering an incomplete or distorted picture. So the Gross National Product, a handy measure of America's economic progress, has been recently challenged as a meaningful measure, because it does not distinguish the *constructive* flow of wealth from the *nonconstructive* flow (Bell, 1969). Turning again to the information world: library evaluators have long admitted the inadequacy of "materials circulated" as a measure of impact. While the data are very easy to collect, they provide an extremely limited view of library use. A prodigious number of relevant factors remain undescribed, among them use of material within the library, nonlibrary (e.g., social) use of the library facilities, and the number of persons per circulation who have contact with material. Beyond that, and more related to impact, is the significance of this service for the individual and for the community.

The weaknesses that exist in virtually every social measure are compelling arguments for the use of several measures that all converge on the same phenomenon. (This pincer-like approach to measurement has been called "multiple operationism" by Webb et al., 1966.) Rather than attempting to invent a single measure that accurately describes the total phenomenon (probably impossible at the present time, at any rate), it is probably more profitable to use a number of existing measures that add up to a fairly complete picture. An understanding of the impact of a social service is advanced to a degree by individual measures such as the client's expressed satisfaction, or the numbers of clients treated successfully, or the nature of the treatments. Yet it is probably only by utilizing several (or all) of these measures and others as well that we can expect to approach any kind of total understanding of service impact.

An important element in evaluating service impact, then, is to establish a *program* of measures that will converge in some meaningful way on the impact of the service. Some of the standard and easy measures will be employed. More exotic and possibly expensive measures will have to be developed as well, perhaps by selective borrowing from other fields or by sheer invention. It will be difficult to establish valid measures of service impact without resorting to elaborate and costly experimental and quasi-experimental research designs employing one or more control groups. (*See* Suchman, 1967, for a discussion of such design.) In most service operations, it must be assumed that budgets will not permit rigorous evaluative research, and lesser measures must serve. Some rules of thumb may add confidence to thrifty measures: where possible, take measures in such a way that comparisons can result—comparisons either over time or over space. Compare the referral center with other service agencies. For example, a client's expressed satisfaction with center service has more impact meaning when it is compared with satisfaction expressed at another time (so as to indicate improvement or deterioration of center service) or with satisfaction expressed with another agency.

APPLICATIONS

There are several ways to approach the measurement of referral services. Of course, the specifics of the service and of its objectives will vary from situation to situation, and the measures will vary, too. The purpose here is to display a number of possibilities for evaluating a referral service from the point of view of the target group, in the context of the community or the individual. What follows is by no means exhaustive. It is intended to make it easier to ponder a number of measures and to develop measurement programs, depending on the particulars in each given situation, that may ultimately paint a fairly complete picture of impact.

The general setting will be a free service, called a referral center, designed to help the average or "nonspecialist" adult citizen satisfy his daily needs in contemporary urban society, through referral to appropriate agencies and individuals. This referral center is a community-wide, community-based service with responsibility for pointing the client toward, or putting him in contact with, a particular information agency, social service agency, crisis intervention agency, or other helping group or individual appropriate to the client's need. The referral center deals in nothing but referral and related counseling. No other product or service is dispensed. The referral center primarily resembles a directory or file of addresses of agencies and private individuals to be accessed selectively for the client. The file might include: legal aid societies, mental health clinics, mayor's information offices, clergy, welfare rights councils, local homemakers, teachers, child care centers, local broadcasters, publishers, community businessmen, tenants' councils, club presidents, state employment offices, and federal housing officials, among others.

For additional context we can sketch out an omnibus mission of the referral center:

> Maximize the meaningful personal information transactions between (a) members of the community (i.e., the target group) and (b) the formal and informal helping agents and agencies.

The articulation of more concrete objectives will depend upon the particular situation. Although the topic is treated in a general way in this discussion, it should be reiterated that the formulation of concrete, specific objectives is fundamental to the development of actual methods of evaluation.

Several measures that might be related to the impact of a referral center are listed below. Impact measures do not dwell on inputs to, or processes within, the referral center. Instead, the measures describe the activities of the center as they relate to the community at large, to other agencies within the community, or to the individual.

The file and its potential. Unless client interaction with the file is considered, measures of resource files in isolation can only be treated as indications of service readiness or *potential*. However, it is possible to develop measures that speak of readiness in terms of the center's actual environment (the community). These will be more meaningful than most measures of potential, such as staff hired or dollars spent. Below are three measurement possibilities centering around measures of potential rather than of actual impact. If observed carefully and in conjunction with impact measures, in time they could be useful as predictors of impact, thereby offering detours around expensive community-wide impact studies.

First, many studies indicate that a community's informal leaders enjoy higher than average access to information and are high volume users of information (Parker, 1966; Troldahl, 1965). Similarly, the human information resources are apparently among the most used for many purposes (Greenberg, Bowes, and Dervin, 1970; Dervin and Greenberg, 1972). In the initial file-building it would be logical to tap the community's leaders in developing a list of credible and high-yield information sources. After that, a periodic survey of the leaders can measure the degree to which the center's file lags in its currency, while pointing out gaps in the file. However, because of the biases that will develop in surveying any small closed group time after time, the reliability of this measurement must be viewed critically. Applied carefully, it can result in some limited data related to the quality or potential impact of the referral center file as compared to the human "file" in the community.

Second, it should be assumed that information agencies other than the referral center, and service agencies operating in the community respond in some way to the needs of the community's citizens. Taken as a whole, the files of those agencies could provide a yardstick against which the center's file can be matched. Measured over time, the degree to which the center's resource file matches or exceeds the other community-based files will be a partial indication of the quality of the file. Territorial problems reside in this measure, though. Each agency will have a natural tendency to protect its own file from outsiders, particularly outsiders who are even vaguely felt to be competitors. Free access to other files will depend on a widespread attitude of co-operation and openness.

Finally, the desire for currency and accuracy is inherent in the updating of the center's files. Assuming that the most current or accurate file has the greatest potential impact on the client group, the nature of updating may be a valuable indicator of potential. Files may be updated by two methods. Depending on the method, the measure will have greater or less reliability. The file can be updated (1) systematically, by canvassing the file entries by phone, mail, or in person at regular intervals, or (2) spontaneously, as contact with the file entries in the natural course of referral center business reveals new information.

The simple frequency with which a file is updated is a measure. However, the paradox described earlier is still at work: while the data can be collected easily, the measure is an extremely indirect one, and its relationship to potential impact largely remains to be inferred.

This kind of measure needs to be improved so that it can express something more meaningful. Formulas that explore the relationships among important service factors can be devised. Formulas go beyond simple raw counts of, say, number of file entries undergoing an update check in a given period (U), or number of file entries actually corrected (updated) in the period (C), or the total number of responses from the file during the period (R). Formulas have the advantage of allowing the description of the interaction of all three of these factors. Using the variables and symbols above, an uncomplicated formula can be built, for example:

$$\frac{C}{U} \cdot R$$

This formula will provide a rough indication of the number of likely incorrect service responses from the agency files.

File/client interface. To the extent that File A is more useful to a client than File B, we would expect to find significant differences in the relevance and/or recall of the two files. "File A" and "File "B" can be the same file observed at different points in time, or they can be the files of two distinct community agencies that are being compared. So, the measures below can be applied to a single file *through time* in order to compare one operating period with another, or they can be applied *through space* to several files, say, a welfare agency and the referral center, in order to compare the community's information-related agencies.

The primary scales considered here are (1) the degree to which pieces of information such as agency names and addresses, legal referrals, or welfare counseling advice, given to the client in response to his inquiry, are useful to him (relevance) and (2) the degree to which *all* potentially useful pieces of information are made available to him (recall). Relevance and recall can be approached in several ways. Among them:

1. The client's expressed satisfaction on receipt of the information or referral, through interview or questionnaire on the spot.

2. The client's expressed satisfaction after a specified time period has elapsed. (A follow-up questionnaire or interview after, say, two weeks' lapse would give the client an opportunity to have tested the quality of the referral center's service. Having a chance to follow through on the center's response to his query would allow the client to formulate more valid opinions on the quality of the referral. The follow-up can take several forms. It would be most revealing, though expensive, to interview a sample of clients in their homes. Telephone interviews would be cheaper; postcard questionnaires would be still cheaper, but the data collected would be necessarily limited and nonresponse to the questionnaire would probably be quite high.)

3. The referral center professional's reaction to the relevance or recall of the file and its accessing facilities. This is necessarily a

less client-centered approach. It is of questionable validity when speaking of impact or potential impact.

A report produced for the American Rehabilitation Foundation (Long et al., 1971) suggests that to the extent that an I&R service is hitting its target—the hitherto unserved—referrals will not be redundant. That is, a client will not be referred to a service agency that he had already approached. Over time, and from agency to gency, figures on the degree to which referrals are nonredundant for each client can be taken as a comparative measure of the impact of the center.

In addition, many social services are based on the assumption that members of the target group should behave differently as a result of the service. So, interaction with the center should result in improving, through referral information, the client's ability to act, to solve problems. This improvement has several aspects, among them:

1. Speed of moving from the problem to a source of information that will aid in its solution;
2. The quality of problem-solving;
3. The amount of information on which problem-solving is based (Dervin and Greenberg, 1972) ;
4. The number of sources from which information is sought for purposes of problem-solving (Troldahl et al., 1965);
5. Amelioration of patterns of living, such as upward social movement, improvement in standard of living, increased power or leadership in the community, wiser spending, etc.

It is possible to design a controlled study of file users and nonusers in matched pairs—matched for education, community leadership, income, occupation, race, age, etc.—and watch their social mobility, geographic mobility, economic indicators, community leadership, "sense of helplessness," and other factors. However, it would be expensive. The design would have to be fairly complex, and data would need to be collected over a long period of time.

Other methods may be somewhat less rigorous, but may allow considerable probing of the target group or of actual clients. One of these is the panel approach to interviewing. Johnson and Ward (1972) go into some detail on the usefulness of a community-based panel as a source of information about social and environmental change in the community. Although the "data" from such a panel would be less consistent than data from a questionnaire, in all likelihood it would permit more insights into the impact of social services.

An alternative method is the Delphi technique of questioning. It was originally developed as a way to tap the opinions of experts in a sort of incognito seminar. The intent is to keep the "seminar attendants" at a distance from each other, so that the interaction of their personalities would not dilute their opinions. Delphi consists of several rounds of questionnaires. The whole sample receives a questionnaire that is very open-ended; the responses are used to develop a second questionnaire; responses from the second help make up the third; and so on. Eventually a pattern of consensus can be drawn from the respondents. Delphi has typically been used to gather opinions on the future of a limited field by experts in that field. However, it could be applied to community leaders in order to discover widely held opinions about the state of the community, its rate of change, the effectiveness of its services (including the referral center), and the short and long term futures.

If the expense and time involved in these methods are unacceptable, and that will be the case in the average situation, sights must be lowered. Measures that have less obvious meaning in terms of impact must be reverted to, because they entail data that are more easily collected. Here the less direct measures of effectiveness, measures from which the agency's degree of success might be inferred, must be turned to.

To the extent that it responds well to a client's needs, the referral center can be expected to experience (1) repeated use of the service by the same individual, and (2) expanding demands on the service (Kochen, 1972). There will be continual probing—especially by regular users—into the fringe areas of the referral center's service parameters. Data for this measure would include the subject area of client inquiry, frequency of inquiries by a given client, and success of response by the center. It may entail some brief interviewing, or analysis of verbatim recordings of client interviews, in order to determine real demands underlying client inquiries.

Another way to measure service quality and implied impact is to test the delivery of services. One technique has been explored by Orr and his colleagues (Orr et al., 1968a,b,c). It consists of collecting a variety of client requests from nonsample libraries. The requests are then fed into the sample libraries, and data are collected as to whether or not they have been filled and, if so, how much time it took. This constitutes a test of the library's capacity to deliver service.

Ordinarily, this kind of test has been applied in the traditional testing atmosphere. The person knows he is being tested. To some extent, what is actually being tested is the person's performance in a testing situation—which invariably is artificial in one way or another—and not his performance on the real job. To overcome this typical kind of limitation, hidden testing can be employed. Proxies are hired to approach the center with bona fide demands; the process of negotiation and the ultimate response to the demands are then evaluated in terms of "satisfactoriness."

The major advantage of hidden testing is that considerable detailed data can be gathered on the process *and* on the output, from the client's point of view. Analysis of the simulated client/service interface can then proceed along a number of dimensions, for instance: staff characteristics, such as receptivity, persistence, and negotiation of the inquiry; lapsed time; adequacy of response; follow-through; and, public policy as opposed to operating policy. (For an example of hidden testing of an informal service, *see* Childers, 1972.) This particular kind of measure has a major pitfall, which is its effect on the center's operators, who may feel extremely threatened under the conditions of being tested in a hidden way (assuming that they would in some way discover the testing). Unobtrusive techniques must be applied with great care for the human elements.

COMMUNITY-WIDE EFFECTIVENESS

To the extent that the target group is "hit," we will find characteristics of it evenly represented among the actual clients. Simply compare critical characteristics of the clients and target group. Over representation or under representation can be used as a parameter of impact.

While formal (say, center-generated) means of publicity may be important in launching a new service, informal means, such as word-of-mouth publicity by ways of friends, neighbors, relatives, or employers will quickly become the major channels for advertising the service and its programs (Rieke and Junker, 1968). It can be hypothesized that even if a service is not used directly by an individual, the informal communication network will make the service visible to him as long as the service is important to some others in the community (Palmore, 1967). A few methods can be used to ascertain the extent of community-wide visibility:

Community survey consisting primarily of open-ended questions. Ask respondents to give the correct name of the service, describe its general nature, enumerate its specific programs, list their entitlements from the service, and name other characteristics of the service, such as funding sources, governance, or history.

Sheppard reports on a technique of determining the saliency of a social service (Sheppard and Belitsky, 1966). The technique plays an open-ended question against a "yes-no" question. Suppose 30 percent of the sample mention the State Employment Agency in their responses to "Where do you get job leads?" Another question asks "Do you check with the State Employment Agency?" Suppose 80 percent respond with a "yes." The saliency of the agency is then assessed at 50 percent. Admittedly this is an artificial measure. However, it is an interesting attempt to describe an agency's prominence as a function of its effectiveness.

Purposive sample of community leaders. It could be hypothesized on the basis of existing literature that the first and greatest impact of a new referral center is on the established leaders of the community (Williams, 1968). Sampling only community leaders would result in greater survey economy and possibly more sensitive data. It is possible to combine a purposive sample of community leaders with a general community survey, and to weight the responses from community leaders by an arbitrary factor of, possibly, two, to account for the value of these persons in the two-step flow of community information.

Content analysis of the media. Simple counts could be made of the frequency with which the referral center, as compared with other social services, appears in the various media, both published and broadcast, local and city-wide. The expense of this approach may not be worth the amount of data it yields. On the other hand, it is an unobtrusive method of tabulating community-wide visibility.

Attitude measurement. In social measurement, the measuring of attitude is less certain than measuring use or awareness. For instance, does the expression of a negative attitude toward an abortion referral service indicate low impact in the community? On the other hand, what does the expression of a positive attitude toward an institution suggest? Studies of attitude tend to be extremely time consuming, and may yield data of questionable validity. This is not to say that knowing the attitudes of the target groups would be of no value in making decisions, but it does suggest that evaluation money might be put to better use. The more concrete measures of effectiveness should be favored, particularly when the referral center is a relative newcomer on the measurement scene.

Survey of agents and agencies. If the center is effective, the serving agents and agencies (both formal and informal) to whom referral is or might be made can be expected to feel the impact. Surveys of the agents and agencies by way of in-person or telephone interviews, or by questionnaire could provide a variety of pertinent data, such as:

1. Awareness of the referral center and its programs. (*See* the community survey suggested above.)

2. Awareness of other serving agents and agencies. This would be based on the premise that one of the center's important subgoals, if only a by-product of its major role, is to foster interagency and interagent communication.

3. Changes in inquiries and client group, such as an infusion of

new, previously unserved clients, proportionately fewer unentitled inquirers and erroneous inquiries, and increased pressure from the clients for their respective entitlements. These data should evidence the effectiveness of the referral center in its role of mediator, counselor, and referrer, and the consequent increasing savvy of the target group.

Conclusions

Attempts at measuring service impact can be costly and frustrating. Ingenuity is needed to establish measures that say something meaningful about impact, and at the same time avoid the great costs and disruption to service of elaborate research designs. In addition, however, certain rules of thumb can make the measures more meaningful:

1. The measures should be oriented to output rather than to input or processes, and as close to the point of service impact as possible.
2. The measures should be based on stated impact objectives.
3. Rather than a single measure, a program of measures should be adopted in order to paint a more complete picture of service impact.
4. Measures should be taken in such a way that comparisons within a service or between services are permitted.

I&R centers are in their infancy. They are still at the stage of establishing their identity, answering questions such as "What am I?" and "How do I operate?" It would be most profitable to ask at the same time, "How do I describe my impact?" Individual efforts at impact measures will advance the state of the art to some degree. A more promising approach is a coordinated effort for collecting, almost indiscriminately, a great variety of data at selected I&R centers around the country. From these data tentative impact indicators could be developed and applied to a number of centers, after which the indicators would be revised, retested, revised again, and reported to the service community at large.

A coordinated approach will require a substantial financial commitment on a national level. Yet its benefits to measuring the impact of I&R centers of all kinds could be expected to be a real saving, in terms of the outcome. Isolated efforts may improve the state of the measuring art; but the most reliable and cost-effective approach would be to launch a large scale study to develop impact measures of I&R centers. Until such a study is performed, however, the need for carefully applied individual efforts will persist. The demand for meaningful impact measures will not wait. As long as public money is limited, public policy makers will continue to insist upon ways of evaluating the worth of social services.

References

Beasley, K. E. *A Statistical Reporting System for Local Public Libraries.* University Park, Penna.: Institute of Public Administration, The Pennsylvania State University, 1964.

Bell, D. "The Idea of a Social Report." *Public Interest,* 1969, *15,* 72–84.

Childers, T. "Managing the Quality of Reference/Information Service." *Library Quarterly,* 1972, *42,* 212–17.

De Prospo, E. R.; Altman, E.; and Beasley, K. E. *Performance Measures for Public Libraries.* Chicago: American Library Association, Public Library Association, 1973.

Dervin, B., and Greenberg, B. S. *The Communication Environment of the Urban Poor.* East Lansing, Mich.: Department of Communication, Michigan State University, 1972.

Granger, C. H. "The Hierarchy of Objectives," *Harvard Business Review,* 1964, *42,* 63–74.

Greenberg, B. S.; Bowes, J.; and Dervin, B. *Communication and Related Behaviors of a Sample of Cleveland Black Adults.* East Lansing, Mich.: Department of Communication, Michigan State University, 1970.

Hamburg, M., et al. *Library Planning and Decision-Making Systems.* Washington, D.C.: Department of Health, Education and Welfare, Office of Education, Bureau of Libraries and Educational Technology, 1972.

Johnson, N., and Ward, E. "Citizen Information Systems: Using Technology to Extend the Dialogue Between Citizens and Their Government." *Management Science,* 1972, *19,* 21–34.

Kochen, M. "Directory Design for Networks of Information and Referral Centers." *The Library Quarterly,* 1972, *42,* 59–83. Also in *Operations Research: Implications for Libraries,* edited by D. R. Swanson and A. Bookstein. Chicago: University of Chicago Press, 1972.

Long, N., et al. *Information and Referral Centers: A Functional Analysis.* Minneapolis, Minn.: American Rehabilitation Foundation, Institute for Interdisciplinary Studies, 1971.

Morse, P. M. *Library Effectiveness: A Systems Approach.* Cambridge, Mass.: M.I.T. Press, 1968.

Orr, R. H., et al. "Development of Methodologic Tools for Planning and Managing Library Services: I. Project Goals and Approach." *Bulletin of the Medical Library Association,* 1968a, *56,* 235–40.

————. "Development of Methodologic Tools for Planning and Managing Library Services: II. Measuring a Library's Capability for Providing Documents." *Bulletin of the Medical Library Association,* 1968b, *56,* 241–67.

————. "Development of Methodologic Tools for Planning and Managing Library Services: III. Standardized Inventories of Library Services." *Bulletin of the Medical Library Association,* 1968c, *56,* 380–403.

Palmore, J. "The Chicago Snowball: A Study of the Flow and Diffusion of Family Planning Information." In *Sociological Contributions to Family Planning Research,* edited by D. J. Bogue. Chicago: Community and Family Study Center, University of Chicago, 1967, pp. 272–363.

Parker, E. B., et al. *Patterns of Adult Information Seeking.* Stanford, Calif.: Institute for Communication Research, Stanford University, 1966.

Raffel, J. A., and Shishko, R. *Systematic Analysis of University Libraries: An Application of Cost-Benefit to the M.I.T. Libraries.* Cambridge, Mass.: M.I.T. Press, 1969.

Rieke, L. V., and Junker, J. M. *Evaluation of Legal Services for the Poor. Final Research Report.* Seattle: Social Change Evaluation Project, University of Washington, 1968.

Sheppard, H. L., and Belitsky, A. H. *The Job Hunt: Job-Seeking Behavior of Unemployed Workers in a Local Economy.* Baltimore, Md.: Johns Hopkins Press, 1966.

Suchman, E. A. *Evaluation Research: Principles and Practice in Public Service and Social Action Programs.* New York: Russell Sage Foundation, 1967.

Troldahl, V. C. "Public Affairs Information-Seeking from Expert Institutionalized Sources." *Journalism Quarterly,* 1965, *42,* 403–12.

Trueswell, R. W. "Determining the Optimal Number of Volumes for a Library's Core Collection," *Libri,* 1966, *16,* 49–60.

Webb, E. J., et al. *Unobtrusive Measures: Nonreactive Research in the Social Sciences.* Chicago: Rand McNally, 1966.

Williams, J. D. "Communications with the Inner City." *Communities in Action,* 1968, *3,* 7–10.

Chapter 13
Research Utilization

by Ronald G. Havelock

Emergence of a Federal Concern for Research Utilization

A large majority of all research and development activity in the United States is directly supported by the federal government. This support is provided on the explicit assumption that research and development (R&D) benefits society directly by meeting recognized national needs. This belief in the social utility of R&D sustained an enormous growth in R&D support during the 1960s, especially in the social service agencies of government. Now, however, the assumption is coming under increasing challenge by policy makers. Growing concern and emphasis is being placed on making the researcher "accountable" and making the research "useful." As noted by a former secretary of Health, Education, and Welfare in a recent policy statement (Richardson, 1972), "Too much of this money [for R&D] has gone into poorly conceived projects, too few of the results have been vigorously assessed and our means of disseminating the worthwhile results have been too feeble."

A growing body of research and theory is helping us to understand how knowledge is diffused and utilized in the social system. Major literature reviews by Everett Rogers and Floyd Shoemaker (1971), Edward Glaser and Goodwin Watson (NIMH, 1972), and me (and others, 1969), not only demonstrate an impressive empirical base, but also provide useful frameworks or models which suggest that a clear and comprehensive understanding of these phenomena is possible.

Some of the problems of social R&D are undoubtedly "quality" problems, i.e., the work that is done is poorly conceived and poorly executed, so that nothing even *potentially* useful results. However,

Dr. Havelock is Program Director of the Center for Research on the Utilization of Scientific Knowledge (CRUSK), Institute for Social Research, University of Michigan.

quality in the usual sense is not the only important question to ask about an R&D program. We are becoming increasingly aware of the fact that "goodness" by itself does not guarantee utilization. For this reason, several federal agencies have set up special units concerned with the diffusion and utilization (D&U) of the research sponsored by the agency. Many of these D&U units have developed elaborate strategies of demonstration and network building, specialized coordinator roles, and the like, on the assumption that such specialized mechanisms will accelerate the flow of knowledge.

Some of those agencies have also supported applied research and evaluation studies on their own dissemination efforts in the hope of arriving at more effective strategies. For example, the National Aeronautics and Space Administration has commissioned studies to evaluate its Technology Utilization Program (Arthur D. Little, 1965; Denver Research Institute, 1967), and the Office of Naval Research has sponsored a study of the transfer and utilization of the behavioral research it has paid for over a number of years (Mackie and Christensen, 1967). Such studies generally arrive at dismal conclusions indicating the inadequacy of various mediating and translating mechanisms and the absence of human elements—"warm terminals"—to negotiate the questions of potential users. In reviewing such studies, one often develops an additional suspicion that the research or development work that is being "diffused" is simply not relevant or useful to anyone.

A few projects have also been undertaken to design and execute diffusion field "experiments" in which particular "good" or "excellent" projects are demonstrated and promoted in various ways (e.g., Fairweather, 1971; Glaser, 1971; Glaser et al., 1966; Richard, 1965). Such studies have had mixed results but have been helpful in pointing out the range of diffusion approaches that can be used and studied and that can be effective when used in combination on various types of target audiences.

Recognizing the need for a more serious and systematic look at the utilization of social science research, the Center for Research on the Utilization of Scientific Knowledge, Institute for Social Research, the University of Michigan, is now studying the information flow and exchange resulting from research grants and contracts in four federal agencies. One of these is in the Department of Labor—the Division of Program Utilization, Manpower Administration. The other three, all in the Department of Health, Education, and Welfare are the National Center for Education Communication, Office of Education; the Research Utilization Division, Social and Rehabilitation Service; and the Mental Health Services Development Branch, National Institute of Mental Health.

From interviews with the staffs of these agencies concerning past and current research utilization philosophy and strategy, and from extensive previous review of research in this area (Havelock et al., 1969), we arrived at the descriptive conceptualization that forms the substance of this chapter.

The Ideal Framework: A Problem-Solving Dialogue between the Research and Development Community and the Needy Society

We assume that the government supports social research and development to provide solutions to society's social needs, and that resource utilization is, therefore, a part of a problem-solving dialogue between researchers and the rest of society. Figure 1 depicts this model in simplest form.

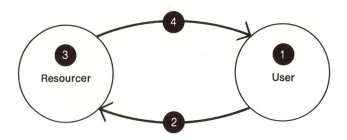

Figure 1.   The Problem-Solving Dialogue

The "user," (1), is some person or group in society which requires something from an organization capable of delivering solutions or instrumental knowledge. In order to acquire this, it reaches out into the environment (2) to find some person or group capable of delivering needed solutions or services. If such solutions or services are available or can be created, then they have to be delivered to the user (4).

We next assume that six kinds of functions are necessary if the R&D community and the client groups in one need domain are to work together as one problem-solving system. We start with the user as the one who has the need, feels the "pain," and tries to help himself. He articulates and communicates that need to the resourcer, who transforms this into a problem amenable to R&D by a series of functions we call "need processing." The latter generates or builds solutions, processes these solutions, and transmits them back to users. These six kinds of processes are not necessarily sequential and they overlap.

Sometimes, it is possible to bring together certain researchers to work on specific user problems at close range with genuine and immediate dialogue with the users themselves. This approach is sometimes called "action research." In the present context it is called "microsystem building," because those involved form a complete resource-user problem-solving system unto themselves, working on a specific user-defined problem. There are many variants on this theme, but the common idea behind them in bringing specific users and researchers together to collaborate and perhaps learn a bit about each other in the process; this mutual learning may make them more receptive to each other's inputs in the future.

A final set of functions applies to the total process of problem solving at a much broader level, encompassing all the knowledge and resources that might be available in a given area of need. This "macro-system building" would include such activities as mapping and monitoring the system as a whole, identifying gaps in research or in service delivery, building up an awareness of the system among its members, establishing linking mechanisms (such as new roles or media or new organizations), and attempting to improve the functioning of the system and the interrelatedness of all elements through various forms of governance.

Some summary comments on the relevance of this model can be made on the basis of our work to date. Most encouraging was the fact that the six-stage model seemed to fit each of these very different agencies reasonably well, so that we could see what they were doing and so that they, too, could see themselves in a larger context through this device. Needless to say, no one does a really good job at all six functions, but some do quite well in different areas. Before the middle 1960s there was very little stress on either dissemination or utilization as such. Rather there was an assumption, still prevalent, that research itself was what was important; simply to get quality research done in broadly relevant areas was enough of a role for government to take, and in the mental health scene, at least, this philosophy led to a rather large, distinguished, and very diverse research program. The communication and use of what was generated was left pretty much to the channels that were already well established in psychology and psychiatry. However, in the early and middle 1960s there were some moves toward making better use of research by some means or other, and in this period the specific units we are studying had their beginnings. In the Manpower Administration and in the Office of Education in particular, the early emphasis was on dissemination or "getting it out," a very simplistic version of what we label as "solution processing." The trend since 1965, however, has been steadily toward an expansion of the solution processing to include all manner of transformations of research information for different media, and targeted to different audiences. There has also been a noticeable shift from dissemination to "utilization" and to a more broadly systemic problem-solving view of the whole process. Of the four agencies we have studied, the NIMH unit is still the most solidly research centered and academically oriented. In contrast, the Office of Education is the most heavily focused on the solution processing and diffusion aspect, devoting most of its 8 million dollar annual budget to information storage, analysis, packaging, and dissemination. The Manpower utilization unit specializes in microsystem building, and both the Office of Education and Social and Rehabilitation Service units have devoted much of their energies to macrosystem building. The need-processing function is seen by most of the federal utilization people as somebody else's job; with the exception of the Manpower group, they do not have any important influence on what research gets done and do not act as much of a two-way feedback mechanism with the research community. We were not at all dismayed at this. Indeed, need processing is usually seen as a political and policy-making process not related to utilization directly, even though it is crucial to what happens in utilization. Including it is important as a reminder that such functions must exist and be performed well if the total system is to work effectively.

In the next few pages, each of the six functions will be analyzed separately, comparing the performance at each agency we studied with a hypothetical ideal level of functioning.

1. User Self-Servicing

We proposed that the ideal user-consumer has to have many self-helping skills, both in order to solve problems internally and independently and also to make effective use of resources in the social environment. These skills include a sensitivity to his own needs, an ability to make a reasonably accurate diagnosis, knowing when, where, and how to seek outside help, and knowing what to do with that help when he gets it. If he is part of a group, the user must also have skills in building consensus around needs and diagnostic perceptions.

None of the four utilization units we studied focused primary attention on user self-servicing. On the other hand, all stressed problem solving as the right way to look at knowledge utilization, and several have developed manuals and training programs for extension agents and consultants based on the process helping notion (NIMH, 1972; Havelock, 1973; Muthard et al., 1971).

2. Need Processing

"Need processing" denotes the various activities required to communicate user needs to resource persons and systems. Some of these are suggested in figure 2. Of course, 2.1–2.4 are part of self-servicing also, and 2.8 is already part of solution-building as well. None of the four agencies studied had a major role to play in need processing, although these functions are important for dissemination and utilization.

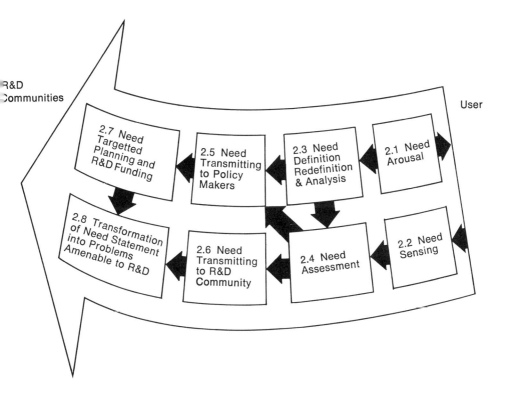

Figure 2. Need Processing Functions

The existence of needs must be transmitted to policy makers, even though they may have already created solution-building instruments, because they must continually engage in reality testing, in checking whether they continue to be responsive to real needs.

3. Solution Building

The third major segment of the macro problem-solving system is part of the R&D process. A number of these are shown in figure 3. Three processes are singled out for special mention because they are especially relevant in the present context of knowledge flow in a national problem-solving system.

Function 3.1, "relevance pressure," is increasingly evident in all fields of science, but especially the social sciences and in government-supported programs.

Function 3.2, "pressure toward utilization," is also gradually becoming a fact of life for the scientific community. No longer is it enough to publish in a scholarly journal (with one's scientific colleagues as

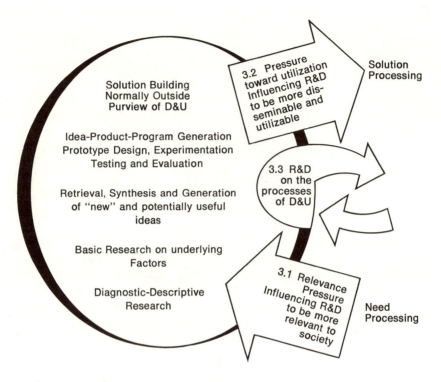

Figure 3. Solution Building Functions

the sole audience). The scientist is asked, and is usually motivated, to publish more popular versions of his work, to consult with government policy makers more frequently, to feed back results to respondents, to put on demonstrations, and to conduct conferences at which practitioners and policy makers are an important part of the audience. All of the agencies we studied used various types of coercion and persuasion to get their research grantees to do something about utilization.

4. Solution Processing

Many steps are required to move a valid solution idea into implementation in a user system. The words "dissemination" or "diffusion" are often used to denote this transfer process, but they are clearly inadequate to suggest the full range of activities usually involved. We would prefer the term "solution processing," to indicate the fact that R&D knowledge requires many types of transformation, as well as transmission, just to reach users in the first place, and once arrived it cannot be utilized unless the user is able to adapt and integrate such "outside" material to fit an inside need.

A solution processing agency must have three overriding concerns:

first to transform R&D knowledge so as to maximize its value to the various audiences defined as "relevant"; second, to transmit this knowledge to and through the social system so as to reach the largest number of persons within these relevant audiences; and third, to insure that such transformation and transmission be to the self-perceived benefit of those audiences and the people served by the agency. Put more succinctly, the agency must transform knowledge, transmit knowledge, and help people to use the knowledge.

All four units have struggled mightily to integrate and transform the research that they get so that it will be useful to a variety of audiences; they also work on ways to disseminate to these audiences; and they do at least something to help users adopt, adapt, or integrate the findings in their own situations. By far the most ambitious program for accomplishing all three of these solution processing functions has been undertaken by the Office of Education. The cornerstone of their system is ERIC, the Educational Resources Information Center, begun in 1965. ERIC is, first of all, a vast repository for education-related documents, all of which are abstracted, stored on microfiche, and cross-indexed. Documents entering the system come from nineteen clearing-houses specializing in different subject areas spread across the country, with most located on university campuses or with professional associations. These centers do the abstracting and cataloging, and they produce bibliographies, state-of-the-art papers, newsletters, and a variety of targeted written products within their respective specialties.

In many respects ERIC is a model system equipped to do all of the print-based archival, integrative, and transformation functions necessary to give users complete access to the storehouse of knowledge in a major social problem area. Indeed, there have been some discussions in each of the other agencies about "buying in" to the ERIC system, increasing its coverage to a larger range of social problem areas, and perhaps ultimately *all* areas.

In general, the largest defect of the system to date has been the lack of emphasis on user needs and user information-seeking habits. No extensive studies have been made of ERIC users and user behavior, but it is generally recognized that 95 percent of the potential audience is not reached or directly influenced by the ERIC system at all.

Prior to the time that such communication functions were transferred to the new National Institute of Education, plans had been laid by the National Center for Educational Communication to fill the gap with an extension agent system, based in state education agencies. Each team of agents would have a home base with a library staff and a complete ERIC file; they would travel to school districts in their area, inquiring about user needs and problems, and supplying information, print materials, and microfiche as they deemed them appropriate and relevant to these users. A pilot program along these lines has been initiated in three states with some degree of success. Evaluations of the program (Sieber, Louis, and Metzger, 1972) seem to indicate that these extension agents can be effective catalysts for change because they are not *selling* particular products or programs or even a set of values, but are providing information input more or less as neutral resource linkers. Users are not urged to adopt any particular item.

None of the other agencies studied have anything quite equivalent to either the ERIC system or the Extension System. NIMH does contain a National Clearinghouse for Mental Health Information. However, this clearinghouse does not actually provide documents to users and has no outreach capability.

NIMH is decentralized and laissez-faire in philosophy and practice, and it relies heavily on the professions and the scholars to do whatever they see fit by way of disseminating information, applying it to user problems, and assisting users in problem solving with or without the input of research-based knowledge.

In the other two agencies, SRS and Manpower, there simply is no capability under current budget limitations to move in the OE direction on anything like the same scale. Manpower operates its own document storage and dissemination center exclusively for those products which have come out of its own R&D program. SRS has funded an outside center to perform a similar clearinghouse function. SRS also has a mininetwork of extension agents called Research Utilization Specialists in each of nine states; these specialists are supposed to enter into dialogue with potential users on needs and to provide relevant information as appropriate.

5. Microsystem Building

A sophisticated knowledge flow system will include some activities in which many elements of the problem-solving dialogue are simultaneously present and are allowed to interact on a small scale. We use the term "microsystem building" as a general heading to cover these activities.

The most elementary form of microsystem building involves bringing together researchers (or developers) with representative users for purposes of dialogue about needs and solutions. These interchanges should produce two-way influence to make researchers more attuned to user needs and more concerned about generating useful products, while at the same time users are becoming more aware of the research process and the value of research findings. For example, researchers from IBM's Advanced Systems Development Division, seeking to develop an airline reservation system, set up a joint project together with American Airlines which sent not only engineers, but users of the terminals as well, to the workshops at which human factor studies were conducted. System designers have made too many errors that could have been avoided with earlier and greater participation of the intended users. For this reason, most system designers are tending increasingly to bring their researchers together with the users in early experimental tests, in participation sessions, and by surveys.

We found little formal recognition of the interchange function among our four agencies; although it is clear that such activities do transpire sporadically, there is no regular way in which they can be budgeted and planned for as part of the overall utilization strategy.

A somewhat more elaborate and organized form of microsystem building puts researchers and users together in the same projects (some times called "experiments" or "demonstration projects"), where both research and use are supposed to take place concurrently. In such "user collaborative R&D," practitioners are supposed to learn to be "researchers" while researchers "get their hands dirty" by serious involvement in user problem situations; there is a strong pressure to deliver meaningful help to the user from the activity, regardless of the research objectives of the enterprise. We sense from our interviews that this sort of action research has fallen out of favor somewhat in recent years.

The most elaborate and extended types of activity which fall within this category could be called "integrated R&D&U programs." Such programs are planned and coordinated very explicitly around some specific and limited goals related to user needs and are expected to be accomplished within a given time frame.

6. Macrosystem Building

The role of the federal government in the United States is to regulate the complex of institutional forms that provide service and perform social problem solving. It aims to serve and represent the general public and the general good by coordinating separate efforts and by supporting them financially where necessary. If that is so, the government should see to it that R&D communities and service professions work together with users so that they collectively function as a problem-solving system to the benefit of the society.

The agencies of government can work to shape and reshape the macrosystem by applying legal sanctions, rules and regulations; through protection of other individuals and subsystems; through financial support and subsidy for various subsystems; and through creation of new roles, institutions, and other facilitating mechanisms to fill recognized gaps and help the total system function more effectively and beneficially.

One important macrosystem function involves filling recognized gaps with new roles or organizational forms. Three of the units studied have done a great deal of gap filling and institution building. We have mentioned the ERIC system, with its nineteen subject area clearinghouses. Both OE and SRS have also established a network of specialized linking agents based in state agencies. SRS and the Manpower Administration have also supported utilization laboratories where research, dissemination, and research on utilization can go on simultaneously with longer-term planning and funding. All of these developments are relatively recent. They deserve close watching, because they represent potential models for future national problem-solving systems and system elements. The National Institute of Education, if it proceeds according to its plans, may soon commit itself to a kind of agricultural model. This emphasizes information dissemination to local practitioners through resource centers and extension agents. If their system is successful, it should be adopted for other problem areas. There is a need for comprehensive one-stop information centers which are easily available and usable by all the people, not just the experts.

In our interviews we have also asked respondents to tell us of their philosophy or overall theory of how change comes about and how knowledge gets used. There appear to be major differences among our agencies on these matters, as well as on the specifics. In education, which has the largest and most systematically structured utilization unit, there is a dominant philosophy that major progressive change can be brought about through heavy investment in a highly planned research, development, and diffusion sequence with objectives specified in advance and each function budgeted and programmed in linear fashion from start to finish. It is clearly the "moon shot" model translated into the social problem sphere.[1] At the other extreme is NIMH, relying heavily on individual initiative and creativity in the academic community, minimizing centralized planning and policy making, and allowing the existing "natural" networks of communication within the mental health professions to carry the major dissemination load. SRS and Manpower are somewhere in between. The Manpower unit relies heavily on informal networks and dialogue between users and researchers. In SRS, there is some network building with an emphasis on locally initiated problem solving.

Our society is moving simultaneously in three directions: first, toward more structure and accountability; second, toward larger and

---

1. The "moon shot" model had several centuries of celestial mechanics, including the Newtonian triumphs and other major advances in science, to *use*, while unfortunately, the level of science underlying the more complex problems of education is far below the minimum necessary for applicability. (Ed.)

more intricate informal networks; and third, toward more local initiative in problem solving. They are partly contradictory trends, but each may be positive for a more responsive and healthy society. In the long run, I think that the most effective utilization programs will be able to make a creative compromise or synthesis among them.

The Linkage Process

Linkage starts with the user as responsible for recognizing and meeting his need, for solving his problems, even if it is with the help of others. We must first consider the internal problem-solving cycle within the client-user. The client (community) experiences an initial "felt need" which leads him to make a "diagnosis" and a "problem statement"; he then works through "search" and "retrieval" phases to a "solution," and finally to the "application" of that solution. The linkage model stresses that the user must be meaningfully related to outside resources.

The user must contact the linker and interact with him so that he will get help to meet his need or solve his problem. He may enter into a *reciprocal relationship* with the linker; this means that something must be going on inside the linker that corresponds to what is happening in the client group. In effect, linkers and other resource persons must *simulate* or recapitulate the need-reduction cycle of the user; they should be able to (1) simulate the user's need; (2) simulate the search activity that the user has gone through; and (3) simulate the solution-application procedure that the user has gone through or will go through. It is only in this way that the resource person can come to have a meaningful exchange with the user.

Linkage is not simply a two-person interaction process, however; the linker, in turn, must have access to more remote and more expert resources than himself. In his efforts to help the user, the linker must be able to draw on specialists, too. Therefore, he must have a way of communicating his need for knowledge (which, of course, is a counterpart of the user's need) to other resource persons and these, in turn, must have the capacity to recapitulate this same problem-solving cycle at least to a degree. Only in this way will they be able to develop a functional relationship with each other.

Therefore, an effective change process requires linkage to more and more remote resource persons, and ultimately these overlapping linkages form an extended series which can be described as a "chain of knowledge utilization" (*see* Havelock et al., 1969, chapter 3, for an analysis of this idea) connecting the most remote sources of expert knowledge with the most remote consumers of knowledge.

How does resource linking work? Consider the simplest case of a person, the client, who needs some sort of help, and another person we will call the "resourcer," who has knowledge, skill, products, or materials which could be useful to the "client." As we noted earlier, every client will have his own customary processes of problem solving. Without help from any outsider he will find some sort of solution, however inadequate. On the other hand, there may be someone somewhere who has a better solution (or can make a better diagnosis or can adapt and apply solutions more effectively). If this person exists and if he can intervene in the right way at the right time, the client will be "helped."

We sometimes forget, however, that the resourcer has his own way of formulating the problem and defining appropriate solutions. Can he, in his effort to be helpful, successfully match the client's need and provide the right kind of resource at the right time in the right way? Unless he is either a mind-reading expert or an extremely lucky gambler, the resourcer will not be able to provide meaningful help without first listening to what the client has to say about his problem and what he has done so far in trying to solve it. In other words, some sort of two-way communication between resourcers and clients has to take place before helping can really be relevant and effective. At the beginning, two-way communications are clumsy and difficult, but over time, with the experience of repeated contacts, trial expressions of need, and trial efforts at helping, a truly effective helping relationship is built up.

Because these human resource linkages are difficult to build, there is a special need for the linker, someone who knows about resources, knows about people's needs, and knows how to bring clients and resourcers together. The primary mission of the linker is to put himself out of a job by helping clients to become effective resource linkers for themselves. Resource linkers should also be able to show clients the resources they have within themselves and among their own group. Linking, therefore, is important not only for client-to-resourcer but also for client-to-client. Ultimately the client is best served by a network of two-way contacts with other clients and with a variety of resource persons, groups, and institutions. Effective problem solving and self-renewal over time require multiple exchanges with inside and outside resourcers, each representing a special knowledge, skill, or service relevant to different needs at different times. The linker, therefore, is not simply a one-time joiner, but a network builder. His efforts at one point in time on one problem may seem trivial, but each link established adds to a growing client capacity for reaching out and pulling in relevant helpers to work collaboratively on his problems.

We can hope that within the next generation we will develop an improved resource linking capacity locally and nationally. Comprehensive and locally dispersed one-step information and referral services may well be a part of a national network to achieve this. Such centers will need to be staffed by persons with the linkage skills outlined here.

References

Arthur D. Little, Inc. *Technology Transfer and the Technology Utilization Program.* Report to the National Aeronautics and Space Administration. 1965.

Denver Research Institute. *The Channels of Technology Acquisition to Commercial Firms, and the NASA Dissemination Program.* Springfield, Va.: COSATI, 1967.

Fairweather, G. *Methods for Changing Mental Hospital Programs.* NIMH Grant #MH09251–03, Progress Report. East Lansing, Mich.: Michigan State University, 1971.

Glaser, E. M. *Increasing the Utilization of Applied Research Results.* Los Angeles, Calif.: Human Interaction Research Institute, 1971.

_____. et al. *Utilization of Applicable Research and Demonstration Results.* Los Angeles, Calif.: Human Interaction Research Institute, 1966.

*Havelock, R. G. *The Change Agent's Guide to Innovation in Education.* Englewood Cliffs, N.J.: Educational Technology Publications, 1973.

Havelock, R. G., with Guskin, A. G., et al. *Planning for Innovation.* Ann Arbor. Mich.: Institute for Social Research, University of Michigan, 1969.

Mackie, R. R., and Christensen, P. R. *Translation and Application of Psychological Research.* Goleta, Calif.: Human Factors Research, Inc. Technical Report 716-1, 1967.

*Muthard, J. E.; Rogers, K. B.; and Crocker, L. M. *Guide to Information Centers for Workers in the Social Sciences.* Gainesville, Fla.: Regional Rehabilitation Research Institute, University of Florida, 1971.

National Institute of Mental Health. *Planning for Creative Change in Mental Health Services: A Distillation of Principles on Research Utilization.* Prepared by Edward Glaser and Goodwin Watson. Washington, D.C.: U.S. Government Printing Office, Stock #1724–0146, 1972.

*_____. *Planning for Creative Change in Mental Health Services: A Manual on Research Utilization.* Washington, D.C.: U.S. Government Printing Office, Stock #1724–0149, 1972.

Richardson, E. L. *Responsibility and Responsiveness: The HEW Potential for the Seventies.* Washington, D.C.: Department of Health, Education, and Welfare, #OS 72–19, 1972.

Richland, M. *Final Report: Traveling Seminar and Conference for the Implementation of Educational Innovations.* Santa Monica, Calif.: System Development Corp., TM–2691, 1965.

Rogers, E. M., with Shoemaker, F. F. *Communication of Innovations: A Cross-Cultural Approach.* New York: Free Press, 1971.

Sieber, S. D.; Louis, K. S.; and Metzger, L. *The Use of Educational Knowledge.* New York: Bureau of Applied Social Research, Columbia University, 1972.

*Starred items represent different attempts to create handbooks on the process of change and on the art of knowledge linking.

Part IV

Concluding Comments and Directions for Further Study

To complete the picture of community self-help through information and referral, Part IV will bring together some of the more significant findings and insights that have emerged so far. They originate from discussions of basic issues, as well as from the distillation of experiences with problems, solutions, and analyses reported in the first three parts. The next five chapters, taken together, present grounds for hope and a basis for sound recommendations.

The first chapter in Part IV is the transcript of a discussion by a panel comprised of people who have thought deeply about various aspects of information for the community. The panel was originally planned as a discussion of problems in the pooling of resource files, which is the theme of the chapter by BenDor, but it was later broadened to deal with the role of I&R in the mental health field. As such, it should be read in conjunction with the chapters by Long and Forsman. One of the panelists represented the views of many mental health planners, whose primary concern is the collection of high-quality data about existing facilities and how they operate. Other panelists represented the needs of individuals and communities, weaving a kind of contrapuntal theme throughout the discussion. Particular suggestions for worthwhile pilot projects emerged from the panel discussion, especially in relation to alcoholism and the use of "problem-oriented medical records."

The two following chapters suggest research and report on ideas and experimentation in progress. Crickman discusses research on communication patterns in the community and the information sources newcomers to a community turn to in seeking help. This is related to the chapters on the evaluation of I&R centers and the development of a more scientific rationale for planning them. By connecting diffusion studies with research into the information needs of community organizations, Crickman contributes to the first of the three lines of inquiry suggested by Kidd in his chapter.

The study of "who speaks to whom" has long been of interest to political scientists and sociologists. Everyone is familiar with the "small world phenomenon": the surprise of a person who, on first meeting a stranger, discovers that they have a common acquaintance. It should not be so surprising. Suppose the average person in a community of one million has 100 acquaintances, and assume that the chances of a randomly chosen person falling into the circles of acquaintances of two people is independent. Consider person A. Each of A's acquaintances has 100 acquaintances of his own, and there are 10,000 out of the one million people in the community whom A could meet who have an acquaintance in common with A. This is a one percent chance. But falling into the circles of acquaintance of two people who are likely to meet is not independent, and raises that one percent considerably. If stratification of people into groups whose members are likely to meet is taken into account, then the chances of two such people having a common acquaintance is surprisingly high, rather than low. The chances of A knowing someone who has a common acquaintance with someone he meets, even in the independent case, is already $100 \times 100 \times 100$, or a million out of a million.

The importance of a common acquaintance, or a chain of these, demonstrates the usefulness of such chains in the gossip grapevine. That is how hard-to-codify data about the quality of professionals, for example, is distributed. The informal network defies formalized quality control, and rumor, libel, and slander can go through as easily as valuable information. It is clear, however, that effective I&R centers should be coupled intimately with these informal networks.

It was Kenneth Boulding (Boulding, 1972) who stressed the importance of the gossip grapevine for communication in a community. He pointed out that it serves several functions that could be performed by computer-based information systems only with great difficulty, if at all. It is most fascinating, as well as practically important to ask why.

BenDor describes the first steps towards pooling of resource files in chapter 16, reporting an experiment in pooling the resource files used by underground agencies that were mostly staffed by volunteers in a medium-sized college community. The heart of the research problem is how to get agencies with multiple, and perhaps conflicting, funding sources to cooperate, to share information. It is essentially an organizational problem. Investigating it leads to difficult questions of control in a community, and to some ideas for newer forms of community organization.

The Women's Crisis Center that BenDor describes is a good example of the kind of I&R center that serves a real community need. In the summer of 1973, the Ann Arbor, Michigan, City Council awarded the center more money than it requested because of an increase in the number of reported rapes and the center's effectiveness in counseling victims. The increase in the reporting of rape cases is probably due to the center's existence, because victims are less likely to fear disclosing their experience to women—sometimes victims themselves—than to the police, attorneys, or courts. Not many viable alternatives to such centers have been tried.

The CRIS[1] system described by BenDor for pooling resource files is interesting because it deals with several problems. One of the most difficult is how to provide a service for several related agencies having multiple funding sources. The actual steps towards this system were initiated when a half-dozen of the I&R services in Ann Arbor got together and formed two committees. The events that triggered this were two spectacular suicides, two girls who burned themselves. It appears that they had tried to reach someone through these telephone services, but were not referred to appropriate community resources quickly enough. The representives of I&R services felt that inadequacies in their referral system, particularly such defects in the resource files as incompleteness, inaccuracy, and imperfections in vocabulary and cross-referencing might have caused the system to respond inadequately.

One committee was dedicated entirely to the pooling and improvement of resource files. It was a highly motivated, energetic, and competent group in which representatives of the establishment (e.g., the American Red Cross) and the underground (mentioned by BenDor) communicated easily and agreed on general goals. Manfred Kochen, whose interest in these questions was known to some of the people from a course he had taught, was invited as a consultant and observer. He offered the use of some of the resources of the Mental Health Research Institute of the University of Michigan.

The natural leader of the group was a representative of the county's

1. Not to be confused with the Columbus Regional Information Service (CRIS), referred to earlier by Donohue.

mental health center, which was charged by law to set up such a service. Despite her interest in a project to pool resource files using computers, the group proved remarkably resistant to initiating any action, even to meeting again to discuss or plan it. Subtle conflicts of interest were a constant undercurrent. Various organizations assigned different priorities for this effort. Only the effort by BenDor, independent of this committee and on his own, led to CRIS. He was helped and encouraged by Kochen, who obtained a small grant from the American Society for Information Science to help BenDor develop the project. CRIS thus is an enterprise launched entirely by one individual. It should, in time, be self-supporting if it delivers the services needed by I&R centers.

CRIS raises another important problem. The CRIS files contain "private information." Some is only a pointer, e.g., "negative comment available." That in itself may already deprive a community agent, such as a doctor, of income, reputation, or clients. Perhaps he could even sue CRIS for damages. There is a legal problem involved with who is responsible, whom to sue. The University of Michigan, the ASIS, WCC, and others are not responsible, and those who made the comments are anonymous. The law must protect clients as well as servers. There must be enough checks and balances in CRIS to minimize the likelihood of errors of commission, of unjustly damaging a doctor or an agency that occasionally errs but usually provides a valuable service. They must also minimize the likelihood of omission errors. The professional who consistently harms rather than helps clients—perhaps inadvertently, perhaps merely by depriving clients of the opportunity to obtain more competent help, perhaps out of malice or fraud—should be detected and rendered harmless. Private comments supplied spontaneously and independently by enough clients could be used to at least alert others and initiate an investigation. BenDor has not yet probed deeply enough into this central question, and CRIS's viability, as well as its value as an example, will depend on how this is handled.

Providing evaluative information on the performance of professionals, and especially of medical doctors, is a daring and important development, and sure to be resisted by those affected. Doctors and dentists, at least in the United States, will seldom "blow the whistle" on even the most incompetent or dishonest of their peers. Furthermore, they usually prevent a patient from even having access to his own records, although they will release them at the patient's request to another doctor, a lawyer, or an insurance company. Thus, the person who pays the bill is treated as if he were mentally incompetent. The CRIS system, containing evaluative data, is a step in the direction of open access to important information.

Concluding Comments

Prior to assessing the need of a community for better information systems, there should be a way of assessing the community's need for better need-arousal *systems,* for systems that increase its awareness of problems. A community may have a serious potential water pollution problem but fail to be aware of it, sufficiently concerned about it, or both, and this despite an excellent community information system. It is important to understand the boundaries or limitations of what can be expected of the ideal community information system.

In the last chapter an overview of what has been said throughout the book is presented. This provides a reasonably coherent picture of how information for the community is being supplied, distributed, and used. It provides some insights into the nature of the needs, and gives our assessment of how well they are being met. It attempts to synthesize the various opinions, views, and conclusions expressed throughout this book into a judgment on how to do it better. It provides recommendations to various groups of readers, and suggests, to those who want to try, some of the practical steps in setting up an I&R center that we think likely to succeed.

The final section of the book is a bibliography. It is not a cumulation of the bibliographies of the respective chapters, but one specially prepared as a guide to literature and organizational sources of information on the I&R movement. We believe it will be especially useful to researchers and those who are attempting to develop new services, or to expand or improve existing ones.

References

Kochen, M. (chairman). "On the Economics of Information." Summary of proceedings of SIG/BSS, ASIS meeting, Denver, 11 November, 1971. *Journal of the ASIS,* 1972, *23,* 281–83.

Milgram, S. "The Small World Problem." *Psychology Today,* 1967, *1,* 60–67.

Pool, I. de S., and Kochen, M. *Contact Nets.* Unpublished manuscript, MIT and University of Michigan, 1960.

White, H. C. "Search Parameters for the Small World Problem." *Social Forces,* 1970, *49,* 259–64.

Chapter 14
Information Systems for Mental Health

by Joseph Caponio, Joseph Donohue, Belver Griffith,
Manfred Kochen, Morton Kramer, Howard Lewis,
and Kjell Samuelson

Introduction

This chapter is the report of a discussion of how information scientists can help improve health services. Community needs for mental health services are now quite extensive. The Midtown-Manhattan Study (Srole, 1962), for example, showed that only 20 percent of a random sample of people in that area were judged by a team of psychiatrically trained interviewers to be in complete mental health; another 20 percent were judged to be sufficiently disturbed as to require hospitalization or therapy.

Marital conflict, alcoholism, and depression are obvious examples of widespread problems. Community resources aimed at coping with these and other problems such as drug abuse, problem pregnancies, and runaways, abound. However, there is a need to match community *resources* with community *needs* in order to better services in the mental health area. Perhaps information scientists can make a positive contribution to health services by helping to solve the matching problem.

To explore the role of the information scientist in mental health delivery systems, the Special Interest Group on Behavioral and Social Sciences of the American Society for Information Science conducted a panel discussion at the ASIS's Annual Meeting on October 23, 1972,

Dr. Caponio is Director, Environmental Sciences Information Center; Dr. Donohue, Library and Information Management Scientist, Bureau of Foods, Food and Drug Administration; Dr. Griffith, Professor of Information Science, Drexel University; Dr. Kramer, Head, Biometrics Division, National Institutes of Health; Mr. Lewis, Systems Analyst, Atomic Energy Commission; Dr. Samuelson, Professor, Stockholm University and the Royal Institute of Technology of Sweden.

in Washington, D.C. The panel meeting was arranged and chaired by Manfred Kochen. Members of the panel are information scientists who are concerned with information problems that relate to mental health and community welfare. What follows is an edited transcript of that session. To start, each panelist presented his position on the central issue of how to match community mental health resources with needs. This was followed by a discussion best characterized as "groping for focus" (third section). The last section reports specific ideas for what can be done next.

Opening Statements

BELVER GRIFFITH

For the past eight years as an experimental psychologist, I have studied the information needs of users of information systems. Prior to that, I worked on mental retardation and observed the practices of clinical psychologists. These experiences led me to question whether a unified information system in mental health can seriously affect mental health, and whether the likely benefits are worth the cost.

The practitioner has numerous information needs, many of them different from those of the researcher. There is an immense amount of interaction between the practitioner and nurses, sheriffs, mayors, and other action-oriented people, and the practitioner is particularly concerned with community relations. On the other hand, he is likely to be disheartened by the complexity of the literature produced by researchers. There seems to be only a small role for the information specialist in helping with mental healing, except for chemotherapy. There is now, however, some evidence of greater community concern for mental hygiene in the emerging support of information and referral (I&R) centers; these constitute an area where the information scientist may likely make a contribution.

MORTON KRAMER

The general aim of the National Institute of Mental Health's Biometrics Division, which I head, is to promote mental health by reducing morbidity. To this end, we systematize data about the mentally ill to be used for clarifying issues. We are also interested in the development of community programs. The quality of information and the purpose for which it is to be used are our primary concern in this discussion.

By a community mental health program I mean a series of activities by governmental and voluntary organizations that apply public health principles to (1) improve mental health and (2) reduce disability.

Also included are consulting services intended to direct people to agencies working to improve interpersonal relations, communication, and rehabilitation. We conceptualize these community mental health programs as located in up to 100,000 catchment areas that provide (1) inpatient and outpatient care, (2) emergency help, (3) halfway houses, and (4) consultation services to community agencies.

To improve the programs, we need reliable information about characteristics of the population, such as age, sex, family structure, and incidence of various problems, as well as information about the agencies dealing with the problems. Prerequisite to the specification of a needed information service is knowing (1) what the various problems are, (2) what knowledge we need to solve them, and (3) what reliable and relevant knowledge we already possess.

KJELL SAMUELSON

Let us consider simple, understandable, useful directories, such as the Yellow Pages, to mediate between people with mental health problems and helping service agencies, since the task is to distribute and communicate information at the time it is needed.

Are the problems faced by clients for mental health services worse in smaller, less developed communities? Are there universal needs? Is the structure of information services that now prevails in communities the right structure to meet the needs?

JOSEPH CAPONIO

Information science has witnessed the growth of information systems that are the result of what I call the "literature disorder syndrome" caused principally by federal funding of research. We have too much literature and we don't know what to do with it. We need to know much more both about user needs and criteria for the development of information systems. We need to identify problem areas such as, "What information is needed in the mental health area?"

Most systems developed in the last decade arose not in response to the demonstrated needs of users, but from beliefs held by professionals and managers about what would sell, what would be good for clients. There was virtually no consideration for the mass of users, and little improvement in terms of literature utilization. Breakthroughs in science or development of services were *not* due to improved literature searches, or computer-based systems.

Communication and information systems should be anticipating needs. But that has not been the case. Consider, for example, the historical background which led to the use of L-DOPA in the treatment of Parkinson's disease. The definitive chemistry of Parkinson's disease was discovered, and the first trials of L-DOPA were made in the late 1950s, with results published in the early 1960s. A physician in Europe was using L-DOPA on an experimental basis in 1961. A review of papers presented at the Parkinson's Disease Symposium, Washington, D.C., in 1963 shows that the European work relating to L-DOPA was only casually mentioned in one of the discussions, never in the context of possible therapeutic effects.

A symposium on the chemistry of basal ganglia held in New York in 1965 at the Parkinson's Information Center brought together, apparently for the first time, scientists from all over the world who were working on chemical aspects of Parkinson's disease. At this meeting, the European workers who had done the original work reviewed L-DOPA and its use as a therapeutic agent. Not only was the presentation important, but even more productive was the informal interaction of the scientists at the meeting. For example, the work of the European physician was mentioned during session breaks. Such informally given information led the present director of the Neurological Research Institute at Columbia University and a neurologist at Brookhaven National Laboratories to experiment with L-DOPA in their own laboratories.

In two short years, the investigations and clinical trials stimulated by this meeting produced results that were presented at meetings late in 1967 and the spring of 1968, convincing results of the therapeutic effect of L-DOPA on Parkinson's disease. These findings led to a snowballing demand for L-DOPA and a demand for crash work to allow it to be released on prescription for the treatment of Parkinsonism.

As with other drugs, it will be years before its long term effects are known, but some experts have referred to L-DOPA as the neurological drug discovery of the twentieth century. In any case, researchers were able, through information related by word of mouth, to find a new method for the control of a disease. Thus direct, informal communication must be credited with this breakthrough, rather than a literature search or a formal information system.

I have the feeling that in the mental health area we are confronted with a number of dilemmas. First, we simply have no way to identify specific problem areas or specific needs. We tend to generalize. We have seen the development of many clearinghouses, many information systems in mental health, such as those concerned with drug abuse or with mental retardation. But we have little sense of the overall picture. My particular premise here is that we are prone to confuse the information problem with the literature problem. Until we are able to identify the needs of various user groups more precisely, all of the information systems developed on the basis of the past two decades' experience are going to be, in my estimation, for naught. The view that I want to express is rather a negative one: only when we are able to ascertain precisely what is needed can we begin to develop information systems that will be responsive to those needs.

JOSEPH C. DONOHUE

The public Information Center Project tried to help the Baltimore Public Library provide its clientele with *information* as distinguished from *publications* in the area of health and welfare problems. In doing so, we cooperated closely with the Health and Welfare Council of Central Maryland, which operates an Information and Referral Service. In this kind of effort, social workers have left librarians at the starting gate. Of course, some librarians feel that this is not the proper function for public libraries. The question of respective roles points up an issue that needs some consideration: to what extent should information services be operated by information types, as distinguished from those people who are concerned with a discipline or substantive mission?

A decade ago, some scientists who set up scientific information centers insisted that these centers be run by scientists, rather than by librarians or other information professionals. Some centers started that way, but later found that a mix of talents and training was needed. I think attention should be given to delineating the roles of the various kinds of people working in the information field, whether they serve the needs of science or public welfare.

HOWARD LEWIS

Why do we have such a multitude of data bases? As soon as we can define the scope of a problem, we build another data base. We are constantly building systems, yet we never satisfy needs. I appeal to you as users to clearly define your requirements. As a system designer, I try to develop something that will be broad enough and relevant enough to solve your problems. Designers conduct "feasibility studies," in which we try to determine user requirements. Much more time and patience should be put into this aspect before creating an information system. Also, designers should be concerned with community systems, not with systems that satisfy the requirements of the individual researcher only.

We can start on the problem before us by defining the present mental health service system. What are the different components? How are they tied together? What are we trying to put together? By answering such questions, we can define an information system that is related to the mental health system and show how data processing might help solve problems of this larger system.

Discussion: Groping for Focus and Orientation

Kochen: Can any of you suggest specific problems for which help might be given by a community information service for mental health, taking into account uses, users, and priorities? Where would we start if we had to design or suggest a project now?

Kramer: Different people will approach the problem in different ways, depending on how they define the population for whom they plan to provide information services. In the mental health field, the sources of data are limited. We do have systematic data on the frequency of occurrence of mental disorders, broadly defined as all those disorders in Section 5 of the *International Classification of Diseases,* which includes the functional psychoses: schizophrenia, affective disorders, paranoia. Then there are the psychophysiologic disorders: neuroses, the personality disorders, mental retardation, and the like.

The only available sources of information concerning the frequency of these disorders in a population are the state and county mental hospitals. We developed data from outpatient clinics, psychiatric services, and general hospitals, in addition to a limited amount of information from vital statistics. We know something about the distributions of the patterns of care of the mentally ill in a catchment area, and the frequency of the occurrence of disorders related to a particular problem.

In order to get at aspects of the target population, one of the things we have done recently is to set up a series of programs based on the demographic characteristics of populations within catchment areas, using United States census tapes. We have a series of programs that can spell out for any catchment area in the country the whole series of economic indicators; for example, socioeconomic status, ethnic composition, household composition, family structure, style of life, condition of housing, community, etc. We have taken existing data and organized it in a way that seems to be relevant to the definition of a target population in a community.

Another problem with these data is that questions about the patterns of patient usage of facilities in a catchment area cannot be answered simply because state departments of mental hygiene, by and large, have not tabulated data by census tracts and then taken the census tracts and put them into the appropriate catchment area. This is a problem in which the data are available, but unable to be tabulated in a way that is relevant to a program. So a tremendous amount of effort has to go into convincing state departments of mental hygiene to put a simple piece of relevant information onto routinely tabulated data.

It is important to know something about the organization of the health and welfare organizations within a community. We put out a directory of all the community services in the United States by state, location, etc. These data are available. We update the directory through various procedures.

What we lack is something that a data system probably cannot provide, a political organization or governmental organization at a local level that has the power and authority to coordinate services in a meaningful way. Such an organization can set up a data system at the local level that will provide the people running the programs with the data needed to determine who is getting services, where, when, and how much. We need to follow up patients to learn something about the subsequent course of disability of those patients who have received certain clinical services. We need an appropriate organization at the local level to clearly define goals and objectives, in order to obtain data that are relevant to these particular programs. Some of these are available, some are not.

To get the data not yet available would require a type of organizational structure that is fairly complicated, because we need to develop data collection instruments, procedures, and measures to use systematically on patients who have gone through various kinds of experiences. Controlled clinical trials might be an answer, but this is another issue which doesn't get into ongoing programs. In ongoing programs one usually needs historical data, before, during, and after, in order to get at these issues.

Another problem involves the manner in which programs have been developed by the federal government, which tends to fragment services. For example, we now have alcoholic centers that may or may not be related to the mental health centers. We have narcotic drug centers that may or may not be linked to these other services. We also have the systems of medical care and social services for the aged that are set up under still another system, Medicare or Medicaid. If you want to learn something about the fate of the mentally ill now in nursing homes, or something about the extent to which nursing homes are being used to care for the mentally ill, or about how these programs are related to others, you will find that you simply do not have the data. It is not just a question of data systems—we have more techniques and technology than we need at this point to systematize data once it is collected. One of the basic problems is persuading the appropriate political organization, whether governmental or community, to develop integrated programs through which you can get integrated data. You need people who know how to ask questions about what kind of data they need in order to run programs. We have sophisticated data systems that just sit around; nobody knows how to ask a question that the system can answer because they cannot think in the proper terms. This is true of administrators who are running clinical systems; they have beautifully stored automated clinical records, but no one knows how to ask the appropriate questions.

We are all looking for the button to push that will give us the answer that has been stored in the computer. There are certain programs that can get these answers, but many of the needed answers are not contained in the system. We need to set up other kinds of data collecting mechanisms to get the data relevant to the question being asked.

Some of the constraints on data collection in the past are catching up with us now. For example, there have been constraints on collecting data on race in the United States. With the current emphasis on providing services to minority groups, it is difficult to find data by race that defines the problem more precisely with respect to the various population groups. This is a real problem and one that requires a lot of discussion: to what extent do the contraints we put on data collection in the name of social justice actually retard our obtaining data that would help promote social justice?

There is also the problem of confidentiality and leakage. People are asking questions about the relationship of mental disorders to crime and delinquency. We can pursue these questions in a variety of ways; one way is to link records across data systems, if possible. In certain conditions it is impossible. If you want to link data on people who have gone through a series of services, be they public, private, church, or whatever, you need to link the records on these people. You have to have some way of identifying patients in order to link records in order to get the information needed to answer the questions. The administrators then will tell you that they have to maintain the confidentiality of data. So you are caught in the system. But I hope that some of you can resolve these problems so that those of us who need data can get them in a meaningful way. I hope you can help us use the knowledge we have so that we can measure the extent to which we are moving toward tangible goals in the programs that we establish.

Person in Audience: Most of the information systems developed during the last twenty years have been information systems representing literature, particularly published literature in a certain field. But what you envision is a sort of management information system—hard data rather than bibliographic data.

Kramer: I use both, but I am speaking from my point of view. We use MEDLARS, which will provide all the literature on schizophrenia that was published, for example, in the USSR or in iron curtain countries. We can look at this and see who the author is. What is lacking is information about the reliability and validity of the observations. From a general point of view, it is invaluable for us to be able to obtain this information.

Griffith: There is considerable variation in the handling of such terms as schizophrenia, even in individual cases.

Kramer: Yes, that is true. We supported a study on psychiatric diagnoses in New York and London, where we looked into the problem of the extent to which the same diagnostic methods were being used in the same or different manners. We now have a nine-country study going on under the World Health Organization on a similar kind of problem. We detected huge differences in certain systematically collected data in the United States and the United Kingdom. It showed that there was a preponderance of affective disorders in the United Kingdom mental hospital population as compared to the United States population, but more schizophrenia in the United States. When you use standardized diagnostic criteria on both populations, the differences disappear. This is an important consideration for those who are summarizing data on a diagnostic quantity from the United States and the same diagnostic quantity from the United Kingdom. You don't know if you're reporting on the same thing; you find differences in the results of treatments; you don't know whether the differences are related to the different patient populations or to other factors.

Caponio (to Dr. Kramer) : Let us raise the question with respect to the rationale that is presently being used for the development of information banks. In the area of mental health, let us use mental retardation as our example. We have had a clearinghouse for the past ten years that is still operational. Have there been critical analyses of these systems or of a typical prototype? Is this a sufficiently successful model to use as a prototype in the mental health area?

Kramer: We used an information system, in a limited way, to obtain runs of information from systems. For example, we got information on Soviet studies on schizophrenia. But utilizing such systems for the evaluation of community mental health programs is useless, because they weren't set up for this purpose. Another problem concerns the validity, reliability, adequacy, and completeness of stored data in systems for various uses and users.

Griffith: So far we seem to be discussing management information systems. How can we get data that we can use to manage a national mental health service? Like any other management information system, the one we are discussing is based on management assumptions. A treatment model is implicit and is used to decide what data to collect and how to collect it. We are not concerned that the number of therapeutic techniques is limited and that, with the exception of chemotherapy, they are of limited efficacy. I would like to see an interaction between this system and the intellectual system that is wrestling with the content of psychiatry and psychology. Most of the intellectual models we now use in mental healing are unlikely to work, not only in alleviating mental illnesses but in other areas in which behavior must be modified and in which we identify social ills.

Kramer: I tend to deal with these global issues as follows. Some of the models and data we use, such as mortality statistics, started with such questions as the causes of death by age six. Then we looked at a model for morbidity data. This model is something other than a national scheme for the systematic collection of death or birth certificates. Rather, it is a sample survey design.

In the mental health field, nobody has developed a successful model for collecting morbidity data locally, much less nationally. There have been national studies on the prevalence of mental disorders, but these studies have not come up with any systematic case-finding techniques that can be used appropriately. As a substitute, we have a system of data collection on a broad group of psychiatric services. This system provides some indicators, particularly the model on the fate of the state mental hospital, where there has been a tremendous population drop since about 1955.

When we consider a model of the community mental health center, nothing we have nationally applies, because we are dealing with local areas that involve interaction between suppliers of service, clinicians, social agencies, universities, and the National Institute of Mental Health.

About 1960, a committee of the American Public Health Association reviewed existing knowledge on the prevention of mental disorders. They published a little-known report, *The Mental Disorders: A Guide to Control Methods.* This was an attempt to summarize knowledge that could be utilized in an applied way.

Person in Audience: It would help if we brought the individual into the discussion. We have discussed a variety of systems for government, for funding, for political units and finally for the community. Consider a person in need of help. He has to be referred by someone. He has to be acquainted with the fact that there is help. He has to be diagnosed, a process that is far from error-free. If I were so unfortunate that I had to rely on this kind of service, would you trace for me what I would have to do and encounter, and how people in the clinic would utilize information in assisting me to recovery?

Kramer: If you felt you needed help, what would you do first?

Person in Audience: I would go to my own doctor. Then he would refer me, or perhaps prescribe a tranquilizer.

Kramer: You are at the mercy of a practitioner with his own limited knowledge of the organization and his own limited sophistication in diagnosis and treatment. Some studies, for example those of Shepard and others in Britain, have demonstrated that at least 14 percent of the patients in need of mental health services were under the care of general practitioners.

Person in Audience: I would then be sent to a diagnostic clinic which would decide if I were a danger or in danger.

Kramer: This depends on where you live, your socioeconomic status, your race, etc. You may be referred to a variety of places, depending on your condition. Insurance is an important factor.

Person in Audience: Where do you think data bases and information systems fit in?

Kramer: The information system in this instance is the general practitioner. Where does he get his information? One of the problems is to organize a community so that GPs can be instructed and given appropriate information about resources for the care of people with emotional ills. What directories are available to do this?

Person in Audience: There seems to be a great chasm between the ultimate user, the intermediary, and the system, depending on geography, status, etc.

Samuelson: The essence of our discussion may be a matter of distribution and communication channels. How do we upgrade the information that practitioners need and that they have the time to cope with? Unless we create a utility, we are still running pilot studies. We are building on existing institutions, which is just another big size intercom. We have not yet learned to reach out to the service stations. We've not learned to live with the existing "nonsystem."

Let me turn to another problem. How can underground and establishment systems be helped to communicate and collaborate with one another? One way is to spend money and assistance on items other than equipment and buildings.

Yet another problem: we need confidentiality in the doctor-patient relationship, which is threatened by the linkage of data bases that facilitate the creation of dossiers. We also need to spend money for reaching out.

Person in Audience: I belong to a volunteer organization, the American Schizophrenia Association. Could the panel indicate with a "Yes" or "No" whether in the foreseeable future we want or are likely to have an information system for mental health services? It is the patient and his family that are the real users.

Lewis: There will never be one system. Identifying the user is the biggest problem. Every time the user changes, so does the information he needs. One system will not contain all the data needed by every possible user.

Kramer: I don't believe that we will have a unified system either. In the past, the development of data banks was intended primarily for the professional user: the clinician or the researcher. We have never developed data banks for the person with a problem. If we had them, we would certainly not have the chaotic conditions that we now experience at the community level with respect to where an individual goes for help. This is where the community as a whole has failed miserably.

I think that the possibility of developing a single system is remote for a variety of reasons. If a system is designed for a certain class of users, a vocabulary for that class must be developed. People from different socioeconomic groups use different vocabularies. For instance, we have just completed a series of studies in which we showed videotapes of presumed schizophrenics or affective disorders to a sample of psychiatrists in Britain and in the United States. The vocabulary used to describe these patients is quite different for the two groups.

Only after good systems have been developed for several specified target populations, e.g., for parents of disturbed children, for researchers, for administrators, etc., will it be possible to link them together into a worldwide system. The World Health Organization now has a glossary of mental disorders that will presumably gain international acceptance. This is one step toward a unified vocabulary for use among clinicians.

Griffith: I find that there is either one system or no system. There is one system if you are wealthy. You can get into the knowledge system by committing yourself to the psychiatric ward of a teaching hospital. However, going to an individual practitioner is not sufficient. If you are an ambulatory schizophrenic, have just gone through four jobs, and used your last money to call an agency or two, you very likely will have access to no system.

Ideas for Next Steps

The discussion then focused on particular projects in which information scientists might contribute assistance to the person with a mental health problem.

Person in Audience: Can information scientists, who have no special training in social work, really occupy the role of intermediaries for matching the needs in a community for mental health services and the numerous helping resources of the community?

Kochen: There is no reason why information scientists should not know something about social services, or at least be able to collaborate with people who do know. Information scientists are not simply clerical workers or professionals who know how to index. Descriptor-based information services in mental health are probably inappropriate, creating a challenge to information scientists to do the basic research for more appropriate methods.

Donohue: We have defined information science too narrowly in one sense and too broadly in another. We have made it too narrow in our overweening concern with formal information retrieval and dissemination of verbal information. There is a whole world of research services to be delved into by information people; for example, nonverbal communication. We have not even begun to scratch the surface of communication patterns, including patterns that relate to health and welfare services.

Samuelson: In our search for a specific idea, I was fascinated by the idea of a "psychological mirror" which our chairman mentioned in preparatory correspondence. Could he expand on this?

Kochen: Behavior modification techniques have been successfully used with a number of community mental health problems. These are systematic methods based on a sharply defined goal, the attainment of which can be ascertained unambiguously; precisely specified reinforcement contingencies; and systematic collection of data, aimed at achieving that well-defined target behavior. A good place to start attacking problems of community mental health is the study of child-rearing patterns and family disorders. Advances in developing such techniques for family counseling have been reported in the literature (Stuart, 1969). Recent findings have shown that the extent to which parents can be positive toward each other and toward their children is an important determinant of mentally "healthy" behavior. Many people are unaware of how much of their behavior is viewed as negative in interpersonal relations.

If a person wishes to move toward a certain goal, there are systematic training and conditioning devices he can use to increase the frequency of occurrence of specific behaviors. The devices encompass simple monitoring, coding, and counting of positive acts by two or more people. The judgment of what is positive is made by the person toward whom it is intended to show positive affect. The process of record-keeping, tallying, and displaying trends in positive behavior is a small personal information system, a mirror of changing behavior. A computer-based system can keep track of behavior and even analyze affect, reflecting the image back to the client so that he can see how his behavior is seen by others. Outside help by a therapist comes from occasional meetings, plus detailed instruction on how to monitor, record, observed, and change behavior toward the agreed-upon target.

Such techniques provide an opportunity to amplify the effectiveness of one therapist. They might help a community cope with the discrepancy between supply and demand of qualified therapists which, in turn, might lead to a significant amplification of community resources to deal with important overt and latent mental health problems.

Person in Audience: After twenty years as a psychiatrist in a Swiss hospital, I don't see clearly the value of computers and extensive funding for information systems in mental hospitals.

Caponio: Information systems now need to emphasize those areas where there is considerable knowledge that is useful for helping patients. I do not know of any proven models in this regard that are worthy of emulation. What we might do is bring to the community knowledge about available services in order to raise the level of the patient's expectations. The patient has a right to know what he can expect from the present state-of-the-art. One reason behind ineffectual services is that not enough of the total community is engaged and interested.

Person in Audience: There are experiments aimed at matching a patient's profile with the literature to determine how physicians reported the care and management of other patients with the same profile. This kind of work should be stressed.

Person in Audience: It would be useful if an inventory were compiled of services at various levels.

Donohue: On the local level numerous health and welfare councils have compiled up-to-date directories of mental health services. At the national level there are also some inventories.

Caponio: Welfare councils do have directories, but they include only very broad subjects. Also, health and welfare services are so fragmented that it is difficult for a client or patient to get oriented. A good approach might be to pick a problem, like alcoholism. Information science could then contribute any available existing knowledge for direct use.

Kochen: Suppose we picked alcoholism as the subject for a pilot project. Soon we would need data on individuals to study changes over several years. We would quickly face a fundamental information science problem: how to ensure the confidentiality of personal records.

Lewis: There are technological devices and techniques for protection of records in an information retrieval system against unauthorized use. There are algorithms and transformations to bury information so that no one can interpret it. Once this is done, a link or key to the system must be maintained to allow access to the information. Some organizational entity at the user level is needed to disseminate and control access to the keys. The confidentiality issue can be solved.

Caponio: In relation to alcoholism, a center at Rutgers[1] has existed for the past ten years for the accumulation and dissemination of information. Also, the Services Administration of the National Institute of Mental Health has sponsored the development of a similar type of information activity. Despite the existence of these information systems, we have yet to demonstrate how they have helped ameliorate the problem to any degree.

Lewis: What is needed to make an information system useful is proper organization and management support to coordinate the various people involved.

Person in Audience: I suggest a possible project based on the problem-oriented medical record. This is a new technique for medical audit teaching. It is spreading slowly. It assumes that the doctor is not an oracle. We could study the impact of the problem-oriented medical record as an information base on health care.

Person in Audience: There are, however, many medical schools that do not consider the problem-oriented record useful or a step in a sound direction.

Kochen: We might make a comparison to see if there is a significant difference in workdays lost between a community with institutions using the problem-oriented medical record and those which don't use it.

Person in Audience: We could propose that the American Society for Information Science sponsor a project to study the problem-oriented medical record as an information system and to evaluate its importance in the delivery of health care.

Samuelson: I would modify that to say "some construct like the problem-oriented medical record" where evaluation is built into the design.

Donohue: Perhaps we should make inquiry of the Medical Library Association and the Special Libraries Association to see if we might elicit sufficient interest among their members to initiate a cooperative project.

Person in Audience: The Joint Association on Hospital Accreditation is another possible organization to approach.

Person in Audience: A relatively new organization, the Association for Health Records, is concerned with this issue.

Samuelson: Such a study should be institution-independent.

---

1. Center of Alcohol Studies, Rutgers University, found recently that more than one million Americans over age 50 suffer from alcoholism, but that obtaining accurate figures on the dimensions of the problem is difficult.

Conclusions and Recommendations

Kochen: Many information scientists have stated that research and development on information systems is progressing vigorously in a fruitful direction. That direction has been primarily to maintain and improve communication among scientists. Progress has been primarily along lines of computer-related studies of indexing by descriptors, of content analysis, and of bibliographic control stressing improved access to the primary literature.

Matching the needs of people for services in a community and making the services more responsive to the needs is an important area in which information scientists can contribute. But it seems to have been overlooked or given very low priority. I recommend that these priorities now be reversed.

A good approach would be to pick a specific community mental health problem, such as alcoholism, and to work toward creating a useful pilot information system. Its users would be (1) the afflicted, (2) their healers, (3) administrators, and (4) researchers. All such available, up-to-date knowledge that exists at any time, and that has been shown to help or is likely to actually help reduce the social and personal cost of alcoholism, would be brought together for these users. An exceptionally clever design may result in a general-purpose system capable of serving the various users. Problems such as shifting from one vocabulary to another, merging and quality control of very diverse data bases, and a management structure to ensure that clients are actually served and their privacy protected must be solved, however. Alternatively, several more modest systems could be planned, each specialized to a particular data base for a narrower class of users and uses. Perhaps the system can later be tied together. In either case, evaluation and improvement procedures must be incorporated in the design.

A novel version of the problem-oriented medical record, adapted to match alcoholics with community services, might be a concrete starting point. The panelists seemed to agree that qualified and interested intellectual entrepreneurs should approach some of the potential sponsors mentioned and assemble a competent team to work toward a meaningful information system to improve one aspect of mental health in a community.

Bibliography

This bibliography was distributed to panelists in preparation for the discussion.

Baldwin, J., and Evans, J. "The Psychiatric Case Register." *International Psychiatry Clinics,* 1971, *8,* 17–38.

Berlin, D. "Evaluation of a Mental Health Information and Referral Service." *Community Mental Health Journal*, 1970, *6*, 144–54.

Brodsky, S. L., ed. *Psychologists in the Criminal System*. American Association of Correctional Psychologists, 1972.

Caponio, J. "Information Networks in Biomedical Area." *American Documentation Institute* (30th Annual Convention, New York City, 22–27 October 1967).

Clay, M. "Monitoring Alcoholism Control Programs for Planning and Evaluation." San Antonio, Tex.: Twenty-First Annual Meeting of the North American Association of Alcoholism Programs, 27 September 1970.

Donohue, J. "Planning for a Community Information Center." *Library Journal*, 1972, *92*, 3284–88.

Eaton, M.; Altman, H.; Schuff, S.; and Sletten, I. "Missouri Automated Psychiatric History for Relatives and Other Informants." *Diseases of the Nervous System*, 1970, *31*, 198–202.

Griffith, B., and Mullins, N. "Coherent Social Groups in Scientific Change." *Science*, 1972, *177*. 959–64.

Gross, S. P. "Psychiatric Information Network." *Comprehensive Psychiatry*, 1970, *XI*, 559.

Hayes, J. E. "The Medical Information System of 1975." *Computers and Biomedical Research*, 1970, *3*, 555–60.

Holder, H. "Mental Health and the Search for New Organizational Strategies: A Systems Proposal." *Archives of General Psychiatry*, 1969, *20*, 709–17.

Horvath, W. "The Systems Approach to the National Health Problem." *Management Science*, 1966, *12* (10).

————. *Evaluating the Effect of System Inertia on Forecasting Future Trends in the Health Service*. Mental Health Research Institute Communication #296, University of Michigan, Ann Arbor, July 1972.

Kiselev, A. "Centralized System for Collection and Analysis of Data on Patients in the USSR." *American Journal of Psychiatry*, 1972, *128*, 1019–22.

Kochen, M. "Directory Design for Networks of Information and Referral Centers." *Library Quarterly*, 1972, *42*.

————. "Information Systems for Urban Problem-Solvers." In *Proceedings of COINS-72 Symposium on Information Systems*, edited by J. Tou. New York: Academic Press, 1973.

————. "WISE: A World Information Synthesis and Encyclopaedia." *Journal of Documentation*, 1972, *28*, 322–43.

Kramer, M. *An Introduction to the International Classification of Diseases*. Seminar on Diagnosis, Classification, and Statistics of Mental Disorders, Tokyo, Japan, 8–14 December 1971.

————, and Taube, C. A. *The Role of a National Statistics Program in the Planning of a Community Psychiatric Service in the United States*. Presented at the Second World Psychiatric Association—Deutsche Gesellschaft fur Psychiatrie und Nervenheilkunde, Symposium on Psychiatric Epidemiology, Mannheim, German Federal Republic (West), July 1972.

————, Taube, C. A.; and Redick, R. W. "Patterns of Use of Psychiatric Facilities by the Aged: Past, Present and Future." American Psychological Association, *Task Force Report on Aging*, Spring-Summer 1972.

————; Rosen, B. M.; and Willis, E. M. "Definitions and Distribution of Mental Disorders in a Racist Society." In *Racism and Mental Health*, edited by C. V. Willie, B. M. Kramer, and B. S. Brown. Pittsburgh, Penna.: University of Pittsburgh Press, 1973.

_____; Taube, C. A.; and Starr, S. "Patterns of Use of Psychiatric Facilities by the Aged: Current Status, Trends, and Implications." *Psychiatric Research Reports,* 1968, *23,* 89–150.

Kreiger, G. "Issues Facing Federal Mental Hospitals in the Seventies." *Hospital and Community Psychiatry,* 1972, *23,* 255–57.

Laska, E., and Logeman, G. W. "The Multi-State Information System for Psychiatric Patients." *New York Academy of Sciences Transactions,* 1971, *33* (8) .

Mather, B. "Suggestions Concerning the Requirements for Successful Design of Automated Clinical Information Systems." *Medical Journal of Australia,* 1970, *1,* 278–80.

Maultsby, M., Jr., and Slack, W. "A Computer-Based Psychiatry History System." *Archives of General Psychiatry,* 1971, *25,* 570–72.

National Institute of Mental Health. *1970 Census Data Used to Indicate Areas with Different Potentials for Mental Health and Related Problems.* Rev. ed. Rockville, Md.: NIMH, October 1971.

Neufeldt, A. "Electronic Information Programs: A Multiple-Facility System." *Hospital and Community Psychiatry,* 1970, *21,* 1–6.

Pederson, A., and Babigian, H. "Providing Mental Health Information Through a Twenty-Four-Hour Telephone Service." *Hospital and Community Psychiatry,* 1972, *23,* 139–41.

Srole, L. *The Midtown-Manhattan Study.* New York: McGraw-Hill, 1962.

Stuart, R. "Operant-Interpersonal Treatment for Marital Discord." *Journal of Consulting and Clinical Psychology,* 1969, *33,* 675–82.

Szewczyk, H. "Prerequisites of Cooperative Research in Psychiatry." *Zutschrift fur Aertzliche Fortbildung* (Jena) , 15 October 1969, 1113–20.

Whittington, H., and Steenbarger, C. "Preliminary Evaluation of a Decentralized Community Mental Health Clinic." *American Journal of Public Health,* 1970, *60,* 64–77.

Chapter 15
Community Communication Patterns

by Robin D. Crickman

Studies of "who speaks to whom," and under what circumstances, in a community are valuable to information scientists trying to understand how knowledge is transferred from one mind to another. Research into communication patterns has posed and studied such questions as: Do some groups of people know more about their community than others? Do people who communicate frequently know more about the community than those who don't? What is the nature of barriers to communication? The answers to these and many other questions can help information scientists design better systems to facilitate the spread of knowledge about community services.

To see how community communication patterns are relevant to the design of community information systems, let us consider two hypothetical communities. Imagine that a new community has been established in Alaska to accommodate workers maintaining the oil pipeline, and their families. No other settlement is nearby. All the employees and their families have moved in during the last six months and hardly know one another. Now suppose that the teen-age son of one family is very unhappy in his new surroundings. He has become difficult to manage at home and in school. He has few friends and no hobbies. Finally the boy steals a car and gets caught by the police. Where will the family seek help? Assume they want a lawyer and a family counselor, and that they want to see their son become involved in several productive activity groups for youth. Whom will they ask in order to find the needed professionals and activity groups? The family hardly knows its neighbors, and such friends as they have at work don't know any more about community services than they do,

Dr. Crickman is a recent graduate of the Ph.D. Program in Urban and Regional Planning at the University of Michigan, Ann Arbor.

assuming that such services are already available. Such a community needs a community information system to help residents with problems obtain aid. Such a system should also act as an advocate, to see that needed services are established. Because no one has as yet provided other channels to inform residents of needed services, such an information system must be the major source of information.

Now let us consider the opposite extreme. Imagine a small midwestern town which was founded over 100 years ago. It is about eighty miles from a large city and surrounded by farms. Most residents have lived in the community all their lives and know almost everybody else in town. Now let us imagine the teen-age son of one family has become alienated, as in the previous example, and is in trouble for car theft. How does this family find the desired aid? The husband might ask a trusted co-worker for the name of a lawyer. The co-worker remembers that Mr. *A* had a similar problem with his son, contacts Mr. *A* and relays to the distraught father the name of the lawyer, and probably some reasurring information that everything finally came out right for Mr. *A*'s boy. The wife calls a friend of hers, Mrs. *Y*, who does volunteer work for the Red Cross. Can Mrs. *Y* suggest a good family counselor? Mrs. *Y* doesn't know of one so she calls her friend, the director of the Red Cross, who remembers that last week at the United Fund meeting she was talking with Miss *Z*, the head of the local social services agency. Miss *Z* met a young psychologist a few weeks ago who has a real gift for working with troubled teen-agers. The information on how to contact the psychologist is relayed back to Mrs. *Y* by the Red Cross director, and finally to the family in need. In this instance, the residents of this midwestern community have almost no need for a formal information system at all. As long as each resident has a large number of contacts within the community, and some of the residents have contacts outside the community, the function of a community information system can be fulfilled by interpersonal communication for most needs.

These two examples illustrate the extremes of interpersonal communication within a community. Very few communities ever fall at either extreme. By understanding the processes that affect the spread of information throughout a community, we can learn a great deal about the need for and use of a community information system. How communication spreads information, and the kind of communication that takes place, has an important bearing on the kind of system the community needs and the level of support that system should receive.

Communications Research

Studying the transfer of information has been relevant to many disciplines but central to none, at least not until information science began to develop as a study area in its own right. Because information transfer has been peripheral to several disciplines, it has resulted in studies being done in many different subjects with distinct methodologies and diverse focuses. Two particular areas have turned up rather interesting contributions to information transfer: diffusion theory and the sociology of communication. What follows is a summary of the more interesting findings and some further research that they suggest.

It is important to realize the significance of private channels of communictaion, since they play a greater role in the dissemination and use of information than the more public channels. Public channels include newspapers, radio, and television. Private channels are largely conversations and, to a slight extent, personal letters. People find information from private channels to be more significant to them than what is spread in the public channels. There are several possible reasons for this. For one thing, people judge the validity of the information by using their evaluation of the speaker providing the information. If the speaker is credible, so is what he is saying. Another reason that private channels may be favored is that they are specific. If one asks a question of a friend, he does not have to wade through a great deal of extraneous information to obtain the answer. Public channels do not allow for immediate feedback on the value or appropriateness of the information, while private channels do. Finally, private channels may be valued for the affective support they give, as well as for the information they provide. When a person has a serious problem, he may value support and sympathy as much as information in resolving the difficulty. One of the research findings on information channels comes from the work of Katz and Lazarsfeld (1955). They found that, while public channels may be more important in providing the initial information about an innovation, the private channels of information are far more important in helping a person decide whether he wants to try the innovation or not. This would suggest that formal information systems may not be able to meet some of the needs of citizens nearly as well as private communication channels, and that private channels should be used whenever they can be counted on to function well.

Unfortunately, private communication channels do not always function well. The most obvious barriers to communication are the physical ones. The effect of natural barriers such as lakes on the spread of ideas was studied extensively by the geographer Hagerstrand (1968). Physical barriers effectively cut off a group of people from the rest of their peers and isolate them from the informal communication channels. While it is true that modern communications can easily overcome physical obstacles to communication, the visual presence of one's peers seems to be necessary to maintain a viable private communication channel. If a superhighway is suddenly run through a neighborhood, a good many communicaton channels may very well get destroyed. It would be most interesting to know at what rate the channels deteriorate when a new barrier is constructed and how replacements are found, or indeed if they are ever found. This would help planners make a more accurate reckoning of social costs of such a highway when doing a cost-benefit analysis. It would also tell community social workers where and when to expend the most energy in helping to reestablish communication channels.

Social barriers to effective private communication may not be quite as obvious as physical barriers, but they are just as important. Rogers and Shoemaker (1971) report that "the most effective communication occurs when source and receiver are homophilous." Homophily is defined here as the condition in which two people share similar beliefs, values, educational level, and social status. It is easy to see that an effective private communication channel is not likely to develop between a Chicano who speaks no English and a WASP who speaks nothing else, even if the two live side by side. What is not so obvious is that communication will also not take place very effectively between two citizens who have no language difficulties but are substantially heterophilous in some dimension. Perhaps another way to view the generation gap is to consider that youth today are substantially heterophilous to their parents, i.e., they hold different beliefs, values, and educational level. The result of this heterophily is a difficulty in communication, which is what is often meant by the term generation gap.

Another way that private communication channels may malfunction is in the provision of quality information. It is perfectly possible that the information which one individual provides another will be false. It seems unlikely, however, that the channel will continue to be used if information is consistently false. If the wrong information is always received from a source, the seeker will stop asking him. Even more serious, the help offered may be a hindrance, as, for instance, when a person who wants to borrow money gets directed to a loan shark. Effective mitigation of this problem lies in society's enforcement of legal and social pressures to prevent abuses in situations of personal need.

Against the occasional misinformation that a person could receive through private channels must be balanced the information available through information and referral centers. The helper in the private channel may grasp the problem more quickly because of shared experience and communication habits between himself and the person asking for help. The advice given by the helper is probably perceived as credible and therefore followed if possible, where information from some counselor at an I&R center may be sought and then ignored. Moreover, the private channel will not give out counterproductive advice if it is recognized as such. To tell a disadvantaged youth to apply for a job he cannot possibly hope to be hired for may be a necessary coping mechanism of an overburdened unemployment office, but it is devastating for the youth to be turned down time and again. If one of his friends suggests a job, chances are it is one he will at least have some chance of being hired for. Granted, often friends may not know about any available jobs, but at least their information is valid when provided. The problem of not knowing, or knowing that no help is available, may make life difficult for the troubled person, but at least it does not present the frustrating experience of being offered help that is no help at all.

An area that has received very little study to date is the topic of change in communication channels over time. Rogers and Shoemaker (1971) found that an innovation will diffuse through a population following an S-shaped curve over time. Unfortunately, the effect of blocking a social channel or slowly increasing the heterophily of a group has not been explored, any more than the effect of erecting new physical barriers. It would be most valuable to know how the private channels of communication change as the members of the community age or as the racial or ethnic composition of the community changes. Communication patterns for communities in flux deserve much more attention than they have been hitherto given, especially since such a large portion of our country's communities are in flux. This knowledge would allow for the establishment of information systems far more responsive to the needs of the changing community than are present systems.

The number of contacts needed to provide adequate information by any one member of the community when using only private channels is also of great interest. On the one hand, it is possible for a person to have so few contacts that there are not enough others to talk with in order to gain the information. On the other hand, if a person has a great number of contacts, much effort must be expended in maintaining the communication channels, and very little energy remains for other purposes. In addition, the person is in danger of an information overload if he contacts too many people and receives a number of disparate responses.

An adequate number of contacts within a community has at least two results. First, as was previously pointed out, it brings about an adequate probability of hitting the sought information through private channels. But an adequately diverse communication net for a person also produces another result. Fanelli (1956) found that people who communicated with many others had a more accurate picture of their community than those who had only a few contacts. It would seem likely that people with numerous contacts would also be more able to tolerate changes within the community, since they have enough redundancy in their communications net to insure that total disruption will not result from slight change.

It is equally important that adequate communication is received from sources outside the community. If there is not enough information flowing in the private channels because there are not enough contacts outside the community, the residents will not be informed about new developments or ideas that might be of value to them. If there is *too much* contact outside the community, the residents will not have enough communication energy left over to form strong communication contacts among themselves. In fact, Sykes (1951) found that residents with outside orientation knew less about their community than those oriented to the community, even though the outside-oriented residents had higher economic and educational attainment. He defined outside orientation as being born, educated, working or having many friends outside the community of residence. Therefore it becomes very important for the well-being of the residents to ascertain how many contacts will be enough to provide information about the doings of the outside world, without so distracting the residents from their own community that they do not know enough people in the community to utilize interpersonal communication channels effectively. The designer of an information system would know that a community with a dangerously low level of outside contacts would need an information system to supplement these, while a community full of outside contacts would need help in establishing and maintaining intracommunity communication channels.

Theoretically, the ideal community information system would not be one that received more calls each month, but one that received fewer. The goal of the perfect community information system, like the goal of the perfect teacher or doctor, would be to "work itself out of a job." The best way to help the residents of the community would be to give them enough skill at locating contacts to allow them to depend on their own resources and those of their private contacts to solve problems that arise. In these days of rising public sector costs and severe spending cutbacks, an institution dedicated to working itself out of a job might be very attractive to government bureaucrats. Working itself out of a job is only an ideal, of course. Unless residency in the community is very stable, there will always be some new citizens who need the guidance of an organized system to help them find information and establish productive channels for obtaining aid.

Moreover, some citizens will find themselves in circumstances so changed from previous ones, that they no longer have knowledge of appropriate channels.

Community workers and community information system agents should encourage, whenever possible, the development of private channels of communication in the community. One important activity to overcome social barriers would be to heighten the interpersonal contact of residents with one another. While it is probably neither possible nor desirable to raise the level of homophily in most communities, it is desirable to raise levels of communication between heterophilous groups if they are to live together peacefully and productively. It seems that one way to enhance communication would be to make members of each separate group more aware of the beliefs and values of the other groups. Contrary to the truism, familiarity breeds acceptance and trust, not contempt.

Another important area to consider in order to enhance interpersonal communication is the physical design of the community. With so much emphasis on new towns and planned residential communities today, it is most important that we consider how to design the community physically so that it will encourage the development of rich and productive interpersonal channels for communication. That way we can insure that the residents will be able to help one another in providing necessary information on services and aid.

Measuring Levels of Communication

In order to help a community develop richer interpersonal communication channels and to arrange for rational allocation of resources for doing so, it is first necessary to have some idea of the present condition of the community in this respect. Those communities with the poorest private communication channels are the ones that should be considered first when resources are available to fund public communication projects such as a community information system. How is it possible to decide whether a community is closer to the Alaskan pipeline town or the midwest farm community described earlier? What would the most useful evaluation method suggest?

A few methods have been devised to study private communication patterns. The most well-known is the sociogram. This technique requires surveying a large sample of the population by questionnaire. Such questions as "Whom would you ask about ...?" are presented to each person surveyed, and the communication patterns are then charted. This technique suffers from two serious drawbacks. It is time-consuming and hence expensive to produce and analyze the questionnaire. Moreover, if one key resident leaves the area of the analysis after the sociogram has been finished, the communication patterns are likely to change radically. Because of these drawbacks, it seems valuable to devise a better method to measure communication levels in a community.

What is recommended in place of the sociogram is an index to measure the viability of private communication channels in a community. The index would be based on such readily available information as socioeconomic status, zoning types, and number of natural barriers. The purpose in constructing the index is to use easily obtained information to indicate the probable information transfer effected through the private communication channels, a factor almost impossible to determine directly. The index would make it possible to rank communities according to the amount of needed information supplied through private channels. It would, for the first time, make it possible to determine just how badly a publicly supported community information system is needed.

The form of the index could be a linear combination or some other function of directly observed variables. Each variable would be weighted according to its influence and importance. In order to decide which variables to use in our index, we must first consider the situation of private communication channels.

For communication channels to develop it is necessary that certain physical and psychological conditions both be met. Of the physical characteristics, proximity is one of the most important. It is also desirable to have collective areas of neutral activity, such as central garbage disposal bins, central mail pickup, laundromats and parks. Areas where small children can play under their parents' observation, such as in "tot lots," are especially valuable since children often initiate communication among their parents.

It is simply not enough that there be places in the environment where space is provided for people to gather and casually interact. A whole set of psychological factors must also be met if private communication channels are to be established. Examination of many communication situations suggest the following four as being most important.

1. People need another reason for being present at a site to interact comfortably. They must have some ulterior reason for attending a place, such as emptying garbage, walking the dog, or watching the children, before it is acceptable to initiate or respond to casual conversation.

2. People need to feel that entry and exit are unrestricted. They will more readily enter a conversation if they feel they may do so or walk away as they wish. Forced presence stifles conversation.

3. People converse more readily when they have time on their

hands. In situations such as laundromats, where a person must wait a fixed time, it is far easier to initiate communication.

4. People communicate more readily if they perceive that the strangers around them are neighbors. They feel assured if they think the surrounding people are like themselves, or at least live in the same area. People also communicate more often if they believe some shared interest is present.

By giving careful attention to the psychological aspects of settings, we can identify those settings most likely to indicate viable private communication channels and can begin to correlate setting with the functioning of channels.

There are two major considerations to take into account when initially selecting the variables to be included in the index. First, the variables chosen must be those that cause significant difference in communication level. Perhaps the number of park benches per 1,000 people in the community provides a measure of how much time citizens spend outdoors and might indicate the time they have for interacting with passersby, but this measure is not likely to explain the difference in communication between one community and another in the temperate zone. The second important consideration in selecting the variables is that they be readily observable and quantifiable. Clearly, the larger the percentage of sociable, well-informed people who live in a community, the better the private communication channels will function. But how are we to identify these wonderful people? And even if we could come up with an unequivocal definition of the sort of people we are looking for, where can we find the number tallied, or how could we go about obtaining a head count, even an appropriate one?

In part we will need to depend on studies that have been done in the past to give some indications of the variables that can be successfully used. Previous research has shown that the presence of a large number of commuters in a community adversely affects communication and levels of knowledge about the community. Physical barriers such as lakes, rivers, mountains, and superhighways also cut off communication. Homophily should also be included in the index and would probably take several variables to adequately represent it. Some possibilities are socioeconomic status, educational level, and racial and ethnic diversity. Others include family size, job mobility, number of community meeting places for adults, climate, and number of shopping centers.

The index format could, most simply, be a linear combination of the variables in the form:

$$N = a_1X_1 + a_2X_2 + \ldots + a_jX_j$$

where N is the numerical value of the index for a given community,

$X_1, X_2, \ldots X_j$ are the real-valued variables selected and $a_1, a_2, \ldots a_j$ are the scalar weights.

This involves a set of strong assumptions. For one thing, all the variables are assumed to form a ratio scale. The attractiveness of expressing the index as a linear combination is that some of the more powerful analytic and statistical techniques can be brought to bear upon the problem. Determination of whether this gain offsets the penalty of imposing a possibly unrealistic assumption awaits empirical and analytical research.

We have already discussed the selection of some likely variable to be included in the index. Equally important to the design of the index are the weights. There are at least two separate considerations that should go into determining each weight. The first is the impact that any variable contributes to the total of the index. The variables will not be equal in either the direction or the magnitude to which they reflect communication problems or assets. To correct for this it is desirable to put into the weight a factor to reflect the direction and the importance of this variable relative to all the others. The second component of weighting is the cost involved in not knowing. This component would be applicable only for variables that apply to portions of the population. The reason for this component is to help in rational allocation of resources. We do not wish to weight as heavily variables denoting those who are merely inconvenienced by not knowing as those who will suffer severely for lack of knowledge. So it becomes very important to consider just how much not knowing about a program will cost someone who is seeking information about it.

Consider a simple example of an index with just two variables. The first variable, X_1, would be the number of residents per hundred in the community who use the local laundromat. The weight assigned to it, a_1, would be the value for the importance (empirically determined) that these persons attach to using the laundromat, in terms of maintaining private communication channels. Another variable, X_2, might be the number of commuters per hundred in the population of the community. Its weight, a_2, would show the importance of this variable. Its sign would be negative since the commuters contribute adversely to the maintenance of private communication channels. The summation of the two weights would give us a number for the community telling us something about its communication channels. Like the index of unemployment, this index would not tell us a great deal by having only one value. It is necessary to compare the score of one community with that of another to get some perspective on whether a given value is high or low. Further, we would also do well to determine how the index changes over time to see if the trend is toward improvement or deterioration.

Building the Index

To actually obtain values for the index would take considerable time and refinement. No doubt the values initially obtained would be crude and show only gross differences between communities. Several years of application and ongoing research directed at refining the idea would undoubtedly improve results if the project could be carried on for a sufficiently long period. Nevertheless, it seems valuable at least to suggest at this time how one might go about obtaining index values for communities. Aside from the problem of selecting the variables, we must find some appropriate method to assign the weights. The major difficulty in this enterprise is that of selecting a normative basis for developing applicable weights. One way to do this would be to take a sample of the population and administer a questionnaire, composed of two parts. One part would attempt to classify the variable categories applicable to the person (e.g., How old are you?). The other portion would simply ask him to tell the survey researcher about problems he has encountered recently. By analyzing the number of different informational needs presented by each person in his response to this open-ended question, it would be possible to begin to develop weights. Because it is highly unlikely that the weighting will be obtained with sufficient accuracy on the first attempt, it is desirable to ensure that the index be formulated and collected on a national scale by a reputable and respected organization in order to allow for ongoing redevelopment and reformulation. Let us now turn our attention to the consideration of the organization to be charged with maintaining the index.

On a national scale the logical organization to monitor and develop such an index would be the Department of Health, Education and Welfare. In a very real sense the index would measure a large part of what affects the welfare of the community. HEW has the resources, prestige, and continuity necessary to support the research needed to find the most significant variables and appropriate weights, to publish widely the results of applying the index to communities all over the nation, and to keep track of changes in the values over many years. It is not enough, however, to simply leave the development and publication of results of the index to a national organization. True, national policy makers should find the index valuable in deciding which communities should have highest priority in receiving the limited funds available to support information centers. But local workers are the ones who will be trying to develop more efficient communication patterns and head off difficulties arising from the disruption of existing communication systems already functional. Ideally, the local workers involved with the index would be a coalition of country and/or city social planners, public librarians, and social workers (especially if they can be freed by a guaranteed annual income from the burdensome duties of administering welfare). The librarians possess a large amount of knowledge about the information-seeking behavior of the community that is too rarely tapped. The mission of the local branch offices working on the index of community communication would be twofold. First, they would collect the statisics necessary to obtain a value for the index, much as the Labor Department collects values for the consumer price index. Second, they would take charge of formulating programs to improve their local community's communication patterns. Without the second activity, the first is of little value. The combination of a nationally recognized and respected organization and a committed corps of local researchers should go a long way toward developing a truly meaningful index.

Benefits of producing an index would accrue to a wider constituency than first seems the case. Not only is the index of value to national or regional managers trying to allocate funds in a rational manner, but it is also of importance to local decision makers who want to compare their situation with that of other communities to see if they are doing as well (or as poorly) as they believe they are. Equally important, the index would help researchers identify communities which possess exceptionally well-developed private communication channels. The workings of these channels could then be studied in depth in an effort to discover what factors help to establish and maintain rich private communication channels. This knowledge could then be used to upgrade the channels in other communities.

We cannot know all the uses of such an index until we develop it. It is clear at this time that a vacuum exists with respect to a rational procedure for deciding whether or not to implement a community information system. The more we learn about the needs of communities for information and the manner in which they meet these needs, the better will be our abilities to create responsive information systems that will support a full satisfying life for every member of the community.

References

Fanelli, A. "Extensiveness of Communication Contacts and Perceptions of the Community." *American Sociological Review*, 1956, *21*, 439.

Hagerstrand, T. *Innovation Diffusion as a Spatial Process.* Chcigao: University of Chicago Press, 1968.

Katz, E., and Lazarsfeld, P. F. *Personal Influence: The Part Played by People in the Flow of Mass Communication.* Glencoe, Ill.: Free Press, 1955.

Rogers, E., and Shoemaker, F. F. *Communication of Innovation.* New York: Free Press, 1971.

Sykes, G. "The Differential Distribution of Community Knowledge." *Social Forces,* 1951, *29*, 376.

Chapter 16
CRIS: A Community Resource-Sharing Information System

by Michael D. BenDor

The experiment reported in this chapter is one of a series of experiments designed to develop a new type of community organization. The purpose of this particular project, the Community Resource Information Sharing (CRIS) System, is to develop and test the feasibility of a technology for facilitating and motivating the sharing of resource information by individuals and agencies. This project is an application of some of the latest inventions in information technology to the task of reducing human suffering.

For purposes of this discussion, a community is defined as a group of people who are interdependent in some way. An organization is defined as a structure in a group of people such that interactions between members and the organization are governed by their relation to the whole of the organization. Thus, a community organization refers to a group of people who interact within a structure and are interdependent in some way.

Human organizations are based in part on the available information technologies. Usually an individual is designated as an authority by some mechanism. This mechanism might be based on traditions such as heredity (kings and queens), on individual characteristics (size, intelligence, wealth, age, sex) or on some type of communal procedure such as a rite of passage, a payment, or an election. By designating authoritative sources of information, the community frees itself from the tasks of searching for information sources and making

This project has been partially supported by funds from the American Society for Information Sciences, Washington, D.C.

Mr. BenDor is Director of the Gestalt Institute of Ann Arbor and is in private practice as an organization consultant and Gestalt counselor.

judgments about their quality. In addition, the community preempts information coming from accepted authority, and therefore frees itself from having to sort through potentially conflicting messages.

Each invention in information technology has increased the potential for people to share information with one another. The sharing of information leads to a shared perception of reality, which in turn makes it possible for people to function interdependently. The sharing of information about resources makes it possible to match resources to needs, which includes people mutually helping each other instead of struggling alone.

The invention that has possibly the greatest potential influence on authoritative provision of information is the computer. The computer makes it possible to manipulate symbols automatically and with an accuracy and speed not otherwise possible. The consequences of this new tool are very broad. Problems can be solved that otherwise are not solvable, and large data files can be maintained and manipulated in ways that would not be economically feasible using other methods. In concert with the other new tools and techniques, the computer makes possible the development of new ways of sharing information, and hence some new forms of community organization.

The existence of a technology does not necessarily imply its use. The application of a technology to real problems requires an understanding of both the technology and the problems to which it is to be applied. The experiment described here is an example of an attempt to deal with the problems a large number of people share: the problems of finding appropriate goods and services within a limited geographic area. The experiment focuses on existing organizations and is based on the idea that if resource information can be more efficiently and effectively shared, then everyone involved will benefit.

The pilot experiment, to test the technology, has been conducted with the Ann Arbor Women's Crisis Center.

The Ann Arbor Women's Crisis Center

In Ann Arbor, there are approximately eleven different telephone services that deal with crisis situations and offer some combination of information, counseling, and referral. The Crisis Walk-In Center (CWIC) and SOS operate under the auspices of the Washtenaw County Community Mental Health Center. 76-Guide, a service operated by the University of Michigan, primarily handles student problems. Drug Help, Inc., can send out "on call" teams to help individuals with drug related problems, in addition to their telephone and walk-in services. The Gay Hotline provides telephone counseling to homosexuals. Ozone House provides services to young runaways. The

250

Community Switchboard provides general information and arranges rides. The Council on Aging and the Social Security Administration, in a joint effort, provide information oriented toward the needs of older people. In addition, such agencies as Catholic Social Services, The American Red Cross, University Hospital, The American Cancer Society, and The Free People's Clinic provide some information and referral services as part of their functions. Finally, the Women's Crisis Center attempts to meet the particular needs of women.

Each of these organizations is oriented towards different needs in Ann Arbor. Various combinations of private donations, county, state, and federal moneys fund these organizations. Drug Help, Inc., for example, is funded mostly by donations and a small grant from the city council. The differing sources of funds often means that the organizations must fulfill different requirements. The Washtenaw County Community Mental Health Center must comply with federal and state regulations, as well as meeting certain professional standards. Drug Help, Inc., however, must focus its attention on maintaining its reputation in Ann Arbor, providing reliable service to its clients, and providing rewarding and satisfying experiences to its volunteer workers.

Each organization responds to a different set of forces within its environment, depending on what that organization needs in order to survive. However, all of these organizations have some needs in common. These needs relate to the sharing of information about resources within Ann Arbor which would be helpful to their clients. The needs include the sharing of information *within* the organization, between workers, and sharing information *between* organizations so that information gathering will not have to be duplicated.

The Ann Arbor Women's Crisis Center (WCC) will be used as an example of the problems which I&R organizations face. The WCC was started by a group of women who felt that their special problems (e.g., rape) were either being ignored or inadequately handled by the traditional organizations. The women saw themselves as organizing to help each other, and they saw their group as potentially including all of the women in the county.

The telephone has provided the basic structure of the WCC. Any woman can call the center and obtain help. Men call also; almost six percent of the calls have been from men. Although the WCC was originally conceived as a means of dealing with only one problem, the growing problem of rape, it became evident that women had many other needs that could be served by the WCC, and the concept of the WCC was expanded to that of a general "crisis intervention" center.

The WCC is an entirely volunteer organization. It is located in a small donated room in a church. The WCC describes itself, in its March, 1973, *Activities Report*:

> We are an all-volunteer organization running on our collective energy. We have no bosses, no red tape to cut through before we can do a job. We use our own judgment in helping others, guided by the empathy training which we all receive initially. We make our own decisions as to how far we want to get involved and in which activities. Major decisions affecting the center are made at council meetings every other Sunday at 7:30 p.m. at the Center.
>
> We are a mutual help organization. We both give and receive help during the course of our relationship to the Center. Our membership is fluid.

All of the WCC counselors go through training. It consists of a weekend-long session of learning empathy skills and a four-hour session devoted to problem-solving. Additional sessions are available for women interested in problem pregnancy counseling. The empathy training is conducted in groups made up of six trainees and two trainers. The training is designed to help the trainees get in touch with their own feelings and impart specific skills in listening, in hearing the expression of feelings, and in responding. Upon completion of the empathy training, the trainees ready for actual counseling work are selected by mutual discussion and agreement.

There are several important factors that have enabled this volunteer organization to function. First, there is a core group of very committed women who have provided an organizational thrust, defining tasks that need to be done and eliciting help in getting them done. Second, there is the opportunity to do work that is intrinsically important and satisfying—work that is well-defined and can be kept within time limits. Third, there is the fact that the organizational structure is flat. There is no hierarchy. There are no bosses. Work is self-defined by those[1] doing it. Finally, the WCC is constantly redefining itself and restructuring itself to deal with the changing needs of the community and those working in the center.

The WCC has difficulties in two major areas aside from the areas it deals with as an organization. These are its internal, intraorganizational communication, and its external, interorganizational (interagency) communication. The internal communication difficulties stem from the fact that most of the women who participate in WCC

---

1. Except for those who were recruited and motivated by the core of very committed women who define the tasks. (Ed.)

activities do so at different times. Each of the WCC's committees meets separately, and counseling is done in shifts of two counselors working for four hours. Consequently, the members of the WCC have no occasion to interact with more than a few of the other members. There is normally no time when all of the members can meet together.

Several experiments are being tried to deal with these difficulties in addition to the one described in the next section. These include a "telephone chain" to provide for rapid communication, and informal get-togethers to alleviate feelings of isolation that volunteers experience because they do not know very many members. After the initial training program, the entire group of members rarely get together except for informal events.

The WCC not only provides peer counseling but also serves as a broker or clearinghouse for information about community services. Thus it must communicate constantly with other agencies and individuals. External communications are also complicated by the internal communication problems. Some individuals have contact with and even work for other organizations, but their knowledge is not easily shared with other volunteer counselors at the center. The collective memory of the WCC consists of a thick, tattered loose-leaf notebook. However, it is never completely up-to-date, for after a counselor gathers information in the course of helping a client, she rarely has time to record her findings.

The next section of this chapter describes an experiment in pooling resource information, both on an internal basis and on an external basis with other I&R agencies.

The Community Resource Information Sharing System

In order to function effectively, the WCC needs to have an accurate and up-to-date system to provide information about all potentially useful resources, both public and private. The information should be organized so that it is accessible to each of the counselors, indexed in a readily usable manner, and accurately presents the services which resources can actually provide. Accuracy is necessary to avoid the experience of making unsatisfactory referrals, an experience that decreases the client's trust in the WCC, and injures the WCC's reputation as a good source of referrals.

There are two principal sources of resource information. First, there is the knowledge that individual counselors have about various resources, based directly on their own personal experiences with these resources. Second, there is knowledge gained through the experience of making referrals, which involve two techniques: the *follow-up call,* and the *conference call.*

Since the WCC has three telephone lines, it is possible to install a

SynchroCom® Conference Phone[2] device which enables the counselor to be a party to the telephone referral. This device combines the conversations taking place on two or more telephone lines. The counselor calls the referral agency or other resource on another telephone line and puts the lines together, enabling her, her client, and the referral agency to talk together. This makes it possible for the counselor to act as an advocate for her client, and also gives her firsthand information about the actual services being offered to her client. Consequently, the *conference call* method of making referrals is an effective means of collecting accurate and up-to-date information.

The *follow-up call* enables the counselor to find out what services her client actually received. This method allows her to consider her client's problem solved, or allows her to try again to help her client. A system for recording the information gathered in these calls and the conference calls would develop files about each referral agency utilized.

Another source of referral information is potentially in the experience of other I&R agencies. Since their focuses are likely to be different from that of the WCC, they would be likely to have information about resources the WCC has not utilized. Although the WCC may not have immediate use for most of the information, it could be of potential value in particular circumstances.

Until August 1974 there was no adequate method or system for meeting these information needs. Although the WCC had probably the most complete and up-to-date I&R notebooks in Ann Arbor, they were inadequate for the task. The difficulty in using notebooks is the burden of unrewarding clerical work on the counselor.

Since each counselor works a four-hour shift, she has a very limited amount of time. While she is on shift, she necessarily spends most of her time and energy talking with clients. Since the writing of information and indexing is time-consuming and offers few immediate rewards (as compared to telephone counseling), the counselors are not likely to put much information into the notebook. The difficulties with indexing a notebook causes additional frustration.

The Community Resource Information Sharing System (CRIS) is a system designed to meet the needs of organizations such as the WCC, using modern information technology. CRIS is a communication and information system that enables organizations with I&R functions to easily maintain and share their data on resources, both internally (intraorganizationally) and externally (interorganizationally).

2. Available from Lafayette Radio Company for approximately $50. In some areas, the telephone company provides Custom Calling Service® which includes three-way calling using the same telephone line.

The CRIS system is made up of several parts: (1) a data base of community resources; (2) a system for training members of subscriber organizations to use the CRIS system, and (3) working software for updating the data base, producing appropriate indexes, etc.

The CRIS technology has been pilot tested at the WCC for four months, and is (at the time of this writing) going to be pilot tested in several other I&R agencies early in 1975. The present CRIS data base has taken over three years to develop, has involved the labor of more than twenty volunteers, and approximately two person years of paid time or the time of students working for course credit. The problems involved in building a new data base using volunteers center around the issue of coordination. A coordinated approach means that efforts will not be duplicated (finding out information about the same resource more than once), and that efforts will be complete (all the necessary information gathered the first time).

The CRIS data base is made up of several parts: (1) an inclusive *data bank* listing every known resource, with extensive objective information (including where appropriate: services offered, procedure for use, fees, hours, eligibility for services, transportation, a description of the resource, etc.) ; (2) an *index,* developed with the requirements specified by each subscriber to the system (presently only the WCC), which enables the subscriber to find the resources that the subscriber feels deal with the particular problem areas in which he is interested; and (3) *private* information or communications about resources. (Presently no information is included in this category.)

The data bank will include any existing resource that any subscriber feels ought to be included. An analogy can be made to a utopian library, designed to include any published book that any user might conceivably want. The data bank will be maintained by an organization (CRIS)[3] independent of the subscriber agencies, which will be responsible for checking information put into the data bank. Any entry that is found to be incorrect by any user will be correctly updated, automatically, for everyone using CRIS. Initial plans call for updates on a monthly basis, subject to funding constraints. This will make CRIS an effective communication system for updating every subscriber's information, and for automatically sharing the updated information. Since the information will be checked by the CRIS staff, it will be "objective" in the sense that at least two people found the same information. Information in the data bank is generally to be of a noncontroversial nature.

---

3. The Community Resource Information Sharing System of Washtenaw County is being incorporated as a nonprofit corporation.

The *index* is analogous to the card catalog[4] of a library. Just as some libraries have more than one card catalog (e.g., a subject catalog and a separate author and title catalog), CRIS will have more than one index to the data bank. There will be an alphabetical listing that will include the name of each resource and cross listings for resources known in the community by several different names. In addition, there will be a subject listing developed by each subscriber. Since each subscriber agency has to recommend services that in its judgment will meet its clients' needs, subscribers will not necessarily list the same resources as offering a particular service. Subscribers may also choose their own categories for listing resources.

The index will appear in two places in the printout. Under each resource in the data bank, there will be a list of all the key words under which the subscriber lists that resource in the index. In the index, the resource will be listed under each key word category in the data bank entry. A change can be made in the indexing each time the system is updated, by changing the key words associated with a resource.

It will also be possible for subscribers to share their indexes with other subscribers. This can be done automatically; the list of key words which subscriber *A* is using will be expanded to include the key words of subscriber *B*, indicating which subscriber has included each particular key word. Words that both subscribers use will be indicated by the codes of both subscribers following those key words. An example of this is shown below.

The *private information* is a controversial part of the CRIS system. This part of the system will be developed slowly and with much experimentation. There is the capacity, technically, to share any comments about any resource with any subscriber or set of subscribers. In a sense this is an automated grapevine.

In our present system, private information is limited to whatever subscriber organizations want to put together in their own files. The use of the CRIS system is limited to identifying their file numbers, using their CRIS index. Private comments can be placed in other subscribers' files in a limited way: Negative Comment Available, Positive Comment Available, Comment Available. This will allow subscribers to contact each other directly for information concerning a specific resource.

---

4. There is a real question whether such an index is appropriate for what has been called an "explorable field," for which directories, rather than indexes, are indicated (Manfred Kochen, *Principles of Information Retrieval*, Los Angeles: Melville/Wiley, 1974, p. 114). (Ed.)

As an automated grapevine, comments would not be monitored. The results could lead to possibly libelous statements being made, without any means of sorting or filtering such statements. This is an area in which CRIS will be making experiments.

It is true that the information now given out over the telephone by various hotlines and crisis centers can be the basis for a libel suit. Untrue statements that cause material harm can be made both with and without the aid of an information system. I&R services can protect themselves from such suits by confining their external statements about resources to their recommendations. This can be done without sharing the comments upon which those recommendations are based: "You can't be sued for not recommending somebody." The reputation of the referral source—its authority—will be determined by the experiences of its clients, whether or not referrals turn out to provide the services that the referral source said they would provide.

An example of an entry in the data bank which appears in the WCC's current (1974) version of CRIS is:

Legal Aid Society
209 E. Washington, Ann Arbor
665–6181

Description: Free legal aid. Does not handle felonies, unless it is a juvenile case (under 17). The Public Defender takes felonies for people who can't pay. They also do not handle civil cases which are fee generating, i.e. where the attorney receives a percentage of the settlement.

Staff includes 3 full-time lawyers, plus a VISTA attorney, 10–15 law students, and 2 part-time social workers. In addition, 2 attorneys and 30 law students are part of the UM Clinical Law Program and are associated with the society.

Eligibility: To qualify a person must be a resident of Washtenaw County and have an income of $3,000 or less. If there is 1 dependent, the income must be no more than $3,800; 2 dependents, $4,450; 3 dependents, $5,100; 5 dependents, $6,250; 6 dependents, $6,800; 7 dependents, $7,400. Outstanding debts are sometimes a factor.

Hours: Monday-Friday, 9:00–5:00 P.M. Call for an appointment.

Keywords:	Problems	Services	
	Legal	1. Information/Referral	(WCC,CWIC)
		2. Public Services	(WCC,CWIC)
	Rape	1. Legal Counseling	(WCC)

Private Comments:
1. Expires: 8 Mar 1975
   Positive Comment Available (Contact Sue Sweet 999–0000)
   (WCC)
2. Expires: 10 June 1975
   Negative Comment Available (Contact Mr. Loser 222–0000)
   (CWIC)
3. Expires: 11 July 1975
   Comment Available (WCC)

The private information is bogus. At this point only one subscriber agency, WCC, is using CRIS, so the initial references to the origin of keywords are bogus for CWIC. However, this illustrates how two (or more) subscribers could share their key words/indexes.

The system has been implemented by keypunching all of the information. A computer compiles the data bank, using this information, and produces a printout. Presently, the printout is held on magnetic tape and is used, with updated cards, to produce an updated data bank. On-line updating is also under way. From the data bank, the computer compiles the indexes and private information, creating a unique printout for each subscriber. Through the new Computer Output Microfilm (COM) technology, the information is directly printed onto microfiche. Due to the large amount of information involved, some form of miniaturization is necessary. One microfiche can contain up to 200 pages of computer printout. The use of microfiche printouts enables the CRIS system to be both flexible and financially feasible.

The data base is available to the individual telephone counselor, through the use of a microfiche reader. In addition, a notebook is an integral part of the present CRIS system, since CRIS is now updated relatively infrequently. Day-to-day updates are contained in the notebook, providing an "instant" update capability, and also a simple means of capturing new updates. Through the notebook, updating work is shared among all the counselors, rather than having that burden be the sole responsibility of a few individuals. The *data base,* which consists of the information in the computer printout which is read with a microfiche reader, and the continually updated notebook, is the visible part of the CRIS System. The second part of the system, training in its use, is much less visible, but no less necessary.

Training to Use the CRIS System

The success or failure of all information systems is dependent on the participation and cooperation of those who make up that system. The human implementation depends on gaining the support and cooperation of those people who are to use the system. People generally act in their own self-interest, as they themselves see it. Consequently, training must include enough information so that the people who are to use CRIS can see that using it is, in fact, in their own self interest.

Specific examples, using CRIS to solve problems in finding information, help to show the members of subscriber organizations that using CRIS is in their own interest. In addition, it is necessary to know some specific skills and procedures: (1) how to use the microfiche reader; (2) how to use the index to find resources; (3) the format of resources listed, including keywords, in order to quickly find the relevant information within a listing; (4) how to fill out the forms for recording information; and (5) how to make a referral using a telephone conference, or arranging for follow-up.

Without this training, we have found that the system will not be utilized. The system was placed in an agency other than the WCC for two months. We were not permitted to train the telephone counselors directly. Even though the system was carefully demonstrated at a regular meeting, it was not used.

Our experiences at the WCC is that training is directly related to use. Experimental learning—"hands on" experience—is necessary for individual workers to feel comfortable in using the "machines" (the readers) and for them to be reasonably efficient in finding information when they are faced with a direct request. The training part of the CRIS system consists of a series of structured experiences, making actual use of the system.

The only organization we have as yet trained to use CRIS is the WCC. We have modified our training as we have found out the problems counselors have had in actually using CRIS, and we are currently planning to revise our training program. Our current plans include a three- to four-hour training module which will include some training in telephone advocacy as well as training in the technical steps necessary to use the microfiche reader and correctly fill out forms.

CRIS Software

The computer program which CRIS presently uses was developed by a professional computer programmer, Sheldon Laube, and by a method best described as successive approximation. As I worked out a clearer conceptualization of what features a CRIS-type program should include, Mr. Laube fed back his interpretation of what that would look like as input-output from a program.

The computer program provides the constraints of the system, but within these constraints, a wide variety of methods can be used to "capture" relevant information. We have developed forms which are easy to use for the purposes of changing, deleting, and adding information. In addition, we are experimenting with forms for collecting subjective reports of individual experiences with resources.

The CRIS software, and even the CRIS hardware will change over time as we develop. Indeed, an on-line version is operational on the Michigan Time-Sharing System under SPIRES (Stanford Public Information Retrieval System). The important focus is that the CRIS system is a means for people to interact in an interdependent way. If CRIS or some other system is able to provide a means for people to interact in such a way as to make them all better off, the effect will be to reduce human misery.

Example of CRIS in Action

A caller had a husband who was dying of cancer. Her husband was quite depressed, and she wanted to know if there was anyone who could help. In the present CRIS printout, two agencies are listed in the WCC index as providing bereavement counseling. In addition, the American Cancer Society was found to offer services to cancer patients. The caller was referred to several telephone counseling services and was offered telephone counseling at the WCC as well. The particular counselor who took this call only knew, initially, of one service—which was no longer in existence. In just this one case the system was able to provide the caller with a list of five resources, although the counselor was not personally familiar with any one of them.

The Future

Financing such an experiment remains a major problem. At this time, we do not have adequate financing. We have received some aid from the American Society for Information Sciences, Special Interest Group on Behavioral and Social Science, in the form of seed money. In addition, the University of Michigan's Mental Health Research Institute has provided some facilities.

Ideally, CRIS will become self-financing by charging subscribers for the computer services and for the information provided. Just as various agencies pay for telephone services to make themselves more effective, they will probably pay for computer services that allow them to communicate internally and externally and to obtain information they would otherwise not have practical access to.

CRIS is one of a series of experiments utilizing modern information technology to form new types of organization. Just as our legal system is based on the printed word, the organizations of the future will be based on computer-telecommunication technology. The CRIS type of system makes the communication of many people to one person possible and, for the first time in recorded history, practical. The only other forms of the many-to-one type of communication have been voting, petitions, and surveys—none of which allows the originator to fully define his or her message. In the future, systems of computerized communication may solve the age-old information problems of overload, distribution, and democratic control in even better ways.

The CRIS system is designed to be decentralized, to make use of a network of microcomputers which will allow people to interact in their common interest. It is important, I believe, that we develop the human organizational capabilities to utilize the machines—computers —to help us deal humanely with one another. Without these organizational capabilities, the use of these tools will be confined to the few who can afford them and the training necessary to use them. And in that case, we will not be living in a democratic community. We will be living in a society where a few have the advantage.

It will be possible, within a few years, to develop large-scale networks to share information on a democratic basis. In fact, some of these networks already exist; they handle credit and criminal information. If we can work out the organizational problems, we can develop large-scale communities which will ensure that all of us will be better off. Perhaps that is the revolution which is taking place in the 1970s.

The development of large-scale communities, based on modern information technologies, is an ongoing project which will take many years and the cooperative efforts of many people. We would like to solicit the interest and invite the participation of other people who are either working in this area, or who would like to collaborate with us in our experiments. Our technology is available for others.[5]

5. Contact: Michael David BenDor, 506–508 Packard, Ann Arbor, Michigan 48104, (313) 994–5777.

Chapter 17
Planning to Meet Information Needs
of Communities

by Joseph C. Donohue and Manfred Kochen

A central message emerges from the preceding pages. Members of large modern communities are increasingly disoriented about how to obtain and use human services to meet their various needs. I&R centers have the potential for providing such orientation. To realize that potential requires creative and energetic development of ideas, methods, and. experiments. That in turn requires the active support of many different people.

In this chapter we will try to bring together, in the form of recommendations to various groups of people, the conclusions that may be drawn from what has been said. In the first part of the chapter, we state suggested next steps. In the second part, we sketch how to plan and develop an I&R service.

It is perhaps not an exaggeration to view survival—as individual humans and as civilized societies—as the key task of our time. Information can be, to a greater degree than ever before, a vital determinant in survival. Information controlled by official institutions helps survival if those in power are sufficiently concerned, competent, and wise to ensure a decent level of existence for all people. Can we afford to assume that those employed by an official institution—the federal government, for example—because of their credentials, are more competent, better motivated and more responsive to needs than those who are not in power?

Coping with survival-related problems makes great demands on information services for accurate and timely information. There is competion among agencies that supply information. Some are seeking to influence and control. Others appear to offer information freely in the interest of free choice. Existing, established agencies, health and welfare councils and public libraries among them, represent large capital investments. Can they do the job adequately, or will it be necessary for their supporters to cut their losses and run? If these agencies survive, they need the continual stimulation and irritant of grass roots and underground services to keep them lively.

We may hope to see in the next decade the rise of public forums and information services that can openly alert us to problems and help us find acceptable solutions. If not, the alternative may be information grapevines that are forced to convey their messages in cryptic forms, like those of the Christians in the catacombs, adapting pagan symbols to new meanings, or those of the medieval cabalists, conveying messages both sacred and profane in a script known only to the elect.

Issues

Funding. How should I&R services be paid for? Sole reliance on self-support would only perpetuate social inequity. It the poor were given tokens, or money were earmarked for the use of I&R services, would they use these to advantage? Hungry people need food more than information, but information could help them obtain food. Does it make sense to give them tokens to buy such information rather than only tokens to buy food? Probably yes, because they will learn.

What should be the roles of various levels of government, foundations, philanthropic groups, churches, civic groups, commercial establishments, and others in funding I&R services as a contribution towards improving the quality of life? A guiding policy and possibly legislation are needed.

The budget category for I&R services overlaps those of welfare, education, libraries, health, and many others. Perhaps it should have a category of its own. Proposals for a fourth branch of government should perhaps be taken seriously. This would be an estate responsible for an enlightened public and wise decision making that would exist in parallel with the legislative, executive, and judiciary branches, and financially independent of them. It would be directly accountable to the people.

Organization. What lines of authority and responsibility should exist? Decentralized systems are most responsive to client needs, but may not fully utilize all the professional competence and quality to which clients are entitled. Sometimes clients prefer "quick and dirty" responses to a full, detailed scholarly report weeks after the need has ceased to be urgent. Perhaps a spectrum of services, from highly responsive, general-purpose, decentralized neighborhood centers to highly specialized, centralized systems, should be available as options. But how much is such freedom of choice worth? What are good ways of allocating resources over this spectrum?

The question of decentralization has been explored in a series of papers by Kochen and Deutsch. An application of the kind of thinking suggested by Kidd at the end of his chapter has been made by Deutsch and Meier. The issues, however, are far from settled. Considerably more research, basic and applied, is required.

Privacy. The issue of how to protect an individual's right to privacy and the confidentiality of data concerning him is one of increasing and paramount importance for I&R centers. How this issue is dealt with determines how much faith people will have in their information services, and in each other. That is one of the vital factors in community problem solving.

The proposed role of secrecy, if any, in the affairs of a community must be clarified. The growth and dissemination of scientific knowledge, as well as its utilization, have depended largely on its openness. Everyone theoretically is free to use, challenge, or verify it. This is not the case for feelings, opinions, and values, around which conflicts and confrontations occur. In a military confrontation, the elements of surprise and deception are of primary importance, and secrecy is vital. In situations structured to meliorate human suffering, those elements seem bizarre and out of place, and are counterproductive, just as they are counterproductive to the progress of science, as distinguished from the solely technological applications of science.

Most of the real interpersonal problems, many of which lead people to use I&R centers, lie somewhere between the ideal of pure science and the baseness of a contest of pure force.

Recommendations

Various groups working together can have a tremendous effect on the future of I&R centers in any community. Our recommendations to several of these interested groups are listed below.

I&R center workers should attempt a reexamination of their motivations, qualifications, and performance in the light of what has been said here, which may lead to efforts at continuing education, continuing examination of their services, and consequent improvement thereof.

Educators in the community should become aware of the needs of I&R center workers for continuing education. The new master's degree program for a "Community Information Specialist" at the University of Toledo and the Urban Library Institute Program at Case Western Reserve University may provide lessons after an initial trial period. Educational programs for novices entering this field may also be expanded. Knowledge about the existence and use of I&R services, as well as other community agencies, should also be taught in elementary schools to develop greater enlightenment and motivation in their use by the general public.

Workers in the communications industry, including reporters, commentators, advertisers, and their sponsors, should all be made aware of the I&R services and share this awareness with their audiences through the mass media. They should also channel feedback from their audiences to the I&R services in order to help improve the quality and responsiveness of the services.

Potential developers of community information services should seek out local investors and present them with a plan to set up an I&R service for their community that will, in a specified time, become self-supporting or profitable. This will not be a service only to the disadvantaged; middle-class members of the community are also disoriented. Even long-term residents of a community may at times need help in finding a *good* professional or in locating particular goods or services.

To meet the need for support, local philanthropists, foundations, or city or county government should be sought out. If none of these provide it, an attempt to piggyback on a profitable or nonprofit but self-supporting enterprise could be made.

Potential investors and members of local government should seek out local entrepreneurs with the dedication, managerial-organization skill, vision, and technical competence to initiate the needed I&R centers and provide for the necessary support. Potential talent in the underground and counterculture communities should not be overlooked. To minimize errors of omission and commission in engaging the key people, local educators should be consulted.

Voters must make sure that the I&R service personnel do not directly report to or depend on the local administration. They must be free and independent, yet accountable to the citizens. An ombudsman who reports to the mayor does not inspire the same trust as one whose primary loyalty is to his profession. A professional without commitment to his clientele is not as useful as one whose primary loyalty is directly to his community, and who interprets the community's needs in a statesmanlike and professional way.

Information scientists should investigate, by high-level pure and applied research, at least the problems raised in this book. They should engage in dialogue with information workers of many fields and disciplines, execute sound and bold experiments, and develop a sound theoretical basis. More progress may be inspired by the sense of wonder aroused in first-rate minds about how communities help themselves than by uninformed, though zealous, determination to solve society's problems. Zeal, like love, is not enough.

Technologists and planners in information technologies should specify the requirements for microfilm, computer hardware and software, user protocols, vocabularies, and other technical facets of information systems, based on a thorough analysis of needs and likely use patterns. They should provide a spectrum of products of a variety of I&R services, and specify standards likely to be adhered to, publicize them, and encourage compatibility in formats, codes, and, where feasible, procedures. They should also provide considerable education and consultation for I&R system personnel, possibly setting up joint projects.

Lawyers and legal researchers should draft legislation to ensure the protection of privacy and regulate the updating, maintenance, and use of I&R centers.

Opinion leaders in all areas should give thoughtful attention to the emergence of I&R centers. What this phenomenon betokens and portends is worthy of deep analysis. There is considerable power in the movement, and it must be continually appraised and redirected. Its potential for improving the quality of life must be realized by an enlightened public.

Planning and Developing an I&R Service

There is a story told about the Scottish historian Thomas Carlyle. He often sat with his aging mother, and as she rocked silently in her chair, Carlyle discoursed at length about the woes, sins, and follies of mankind. Once he insisted to her that "it's not that people don't know what they should do—they know and they won't do it." After a moment's silence, the old lady resumed her rocking, and replied simply, "Ay, Tammas, and will ye kindly tell them how?"

Several people who knew that this book was in progress said as much—"kindly tell them how!" The book is not intended as a "how-to" book, but rather seeks to provide an overview of both theoretical and practical aspects. But, as a matter of fact, a great deal has been presented in these chapters that can be used to guide the planning and development of information services. A review of the biographies of the contributors will reveal their significant practical experience in making information systems work. In a field of endeavor so vast and complex as is the one presented here, it would perhaps be presumptuous for us to attempt to lay out a set of formal instruction to guide the building of any and all community information services. Nevertheless, we present here some general guidelines that we think will be useful in designing new services and in improving old ones. They are given in an order that seems to correlate roughly with the chronology found in the building of a new system.

1. *Review existing needs and resources.* This may be done formally or informally, and in varying degrees of depth. Ideally, before services are created, both needs and resources need to be carefully assessed, and projections made.

2. *Determine what needs to be done* by way of innovation in the

structure for information delivery. This step involves important judgments about the viability of new services within existing agencies versus the placing of these services in new agencies. The caveats given in our Preface, and the chapters by Long and Childers, are especially relevant to this determination.

3. *Ascertain the resources needed.* These include, as a beginning: (*a*) financial resources; (*b*) facilities; (*c*) personnel of several types; (*d*) training; (*e*) effective contacts; and (*f*) a system for information functions, including data gathering, processing, storage, retrieval, and dissemination.

4. *Build the support base.* The degree of emphasis that will be devoted to this step will depend on assumptions about the degree to which the need is acknowledged by potential supporters, their motivation for or against the provision of the service, the competition for funding, and the expected permanence of the service. The chapter by Wilson and Barth on cost-benefit analysis is an especially provocative treatment of the problems involved in gathering and allocating resources.

5. *Obtain and equip facilities.* The experience of the systems reported in Part II contains much that will suggest considerations in facility selection and preparation.

6. *Staffing and training.* It cannot be emphasized often enough that the people who operate a system are its most important resource. Again, the existing models reported in Part II contain especially relevant data and suggestions on selection and training of staff. There are by now some very relevant and useful publications not included in this book. For example, Ruth Mednick mentions in chapter 7 that the Baltimore I&R group compiled a handbook for the Social Security Administration, Bureau of District Office Operations (Social Security Administration Publication, BDOO–PUB–23–72, June 1972), to be used in the training of the administration's staff. It is a succinct, logical statement of things that need to be learned by anyone who intends to offer I&R service. Other useful publications include those of the Citizens' Advice Bureaux. The development of a satisfactory—and satisfying—career ladder for people who staff information services should be discussed with more regard to personnel selection and training. The kinds of people who are needed—alert, intelligent, sensitive, humane—may often be attracted to public information work because of its psychic satisfaction, only to be used so poorly that they eventually lose their motivation and turn to other work.

Public service agencies expect a great deal from their employees, including their willingness to work at whatever task is at hand, even if the task is repetitive, boring, or below the employee's skill level. That expectation is reasonable to a certain extent. It is also reasonable for hard-working staff members to expect that the administration will make every effort to use them at the highest level of their skills as much as is feasible, and will provide an orderly progression in a career ladder. Even in an occupation that assumes a large measure of altruism, "the laborer is worthy of his hire."

7. *Develop contacts.* The formal information system must always be looked upon as the tool of the informal information system. *Contacts*—lively contacts, kept lively by constant tending—constitute the basis of the informal information system, a network of people of many kinds.

Social snobbery, whether upward, downward, or sideways, can cripple an information agent's effectiveness. For example, personal prejudices, whether against elements of the establishment or elements of alternative cultures, can prevent a person in an information role from being a communicating link. The ideal attitude contains a good measure of both humane concern for people as individuals and a pragmatic opportunism that recognizes that everybody has something good and useful to offer, at least potentially.

8. *Devise and set up the technical system* for collecting, processing, storing, retrieving, and disseminating information. This is not the place to describe the varieties of systems that are already available. The field of library science and the broader field of information science is rich in methods, proven and experimental, from simple alphabetic filing systems using manual equipment, to systems that involve complexities of both logic and equipment. One thing we might mention, for those readers who are not themselves expert in information systems: keep the distinction between principles of operation (conceptual), techniques (operational), and tools or equipment (physical entities) clearly in mind. Too often, confusion reigns in the organization of new information services, because people who may be highly sophisticated in other areas attempt to develop systems without benefit of system expertise, confusing ideological, conceptual, operational, and physical entities. Expensive equipment, like a computer, will be a poor investment if the job does not call for it, or if the data is poorly organized. Even the investment in a relatively inexpensive card file may be unwarranted until the task and its needs have been defined.

9. *Plan for evaluation,* and evaluate in order to plan. Information needs change quickly, and so do resources. No matter how well designed and implemented the service or system, it is in some respect obsolete from the beginning. Plan for evaluation on a regular basis, and use the data found in evaluation in order to plan gradual changes. Violent upheavals are disruptive and wasteful, whether in the natural or the social order. They can be avoided or mitigated if there is a

continual feedback that identifies the strengths and weaknesses of the system, and if that feedback is converted into corrective action.

This last principle—that of corrective feedback—is, in a sense, what all of this book is about. For community information services are intended to register the strains in individual human lives, and to provide feedback to the individual about how he may correct the conditions causing the strain. Conversely, they can provide social systems with the knowledge of these strain conditions and their magnitude, allowing for planned corrective group action. Community information systems may thus help us to improve the human condition and to develop a more stable and humane society.

References

Deutsch, K. W., and Meier, R. L. "Confederation and Decentralization of Urban Governments: How Self-Controls for the American Megalopolis Can Evolve." Working Paper No. 77. University of California, Berkeley, October 1968.

Kochen, M., and Deutsch, K. W. "Decentralization and Uneven Service Loads." *Journal of Regional Science*, 1970, *10*, 153–73.

_____. "Decentralization by Function and Location." *Management Science: Application*, 1973, *19*, 322–43.

_____. "A Note on Hierarchy and Coordination: An Aspect on Decentralization." *Management Science*, 1974, *21* 106–14.

_____. "Pluralization: A Mathematical Model." *Operations Research*, 1972, *20*, 276–92.

_____. "Toward a Rational Theory of Decentralization: Some Implications of a Mathematical Approach." *The American Political Science Review*, 1969, *63*, 743–49.

A Resource Guide to Information and Referral Centers

by Carolyn Forsman

What follows is a highly selective, annotated list, updated in late 1975, of organizations and available documents to help persons interested in delving further into special aspects of what is covered in this book. It is divided into organizations, bibliographies, directories, training manuals and organizing guides, general books, reports and a selected list of books, and articles useful for research and practice. The compilation and collection of these documents was partially supported by the American Society of Information Sciences' Special Interest Group on Behavioral and Social Science with a view toward providing a continually updated version to its membership, on demand or periodically. The Alliance of Information and Referral Services is planning to disseminate copies of future editions of this guide.

Organizations

Alliance of Information and Referral Services. 1515 East Osborn Rd., Phoenix, Ariz. 85014.

Formed in 1972 as an outgrowth of the Information and Referral Workshops, held annually at the National Conference on Social Welfare. Publishes AIRS *Newsletter,* a directory, has prepared National Standards, plans to sponsor regional workshops. Annual meeting held in conjunction with the NCSW.

Call for Action, 1785 Massachusetts Ave., N.W., Washington, D.C. 20036 (202) 797-7800.

A nationwide I&R and advocacy service operating in over forty cities through agreements with local radio or television stations. Call for Action guarantees exclusive rights within a 50-mile radius of each city, and, in return, each broadcaster assures its nonpolitical, noncommercial character. Established in 1963 by Ellen Straus, it became a national project in 1969 in cooperation with the Urban Coalition. Briefly associated with the National Center for Voluntary Action in 1973 and 1974, it is now independent. Monthly newsletter, *Call for Action.*

Ms. Forsman is Chief, Telephone Reference, District of Columbia Public Library as well as a Ph.D. candidate in Library Science at the University of Maryland.

Citizens' Advice Bureaux, 26 Bedford Sq., London WC1, England.

A national system of local I&R centers offering information and advice on any subject to any person, confidentially and independently. Publishes a classification scheme for internal use, in-service training manuals, centralized information-updating service, annual reports, etc.

Clearinghouse on Information and Referral, National Clearinghouse on Aging, 330 C St., S.W., Washington, D.C. 20201.

Contact Teleministries USA, Inc. 900 South Arlington Ave., Rm. 125, Harrisburg, Penna. 17109. (717) 652-3410.

A national network of 24-hour telephone counseling providing crisis counseling and community I&R. Affiliated with the Life Line International (see below). Publishes *Contact, News and Views, Directory of Contact Centers*, handbooks, audiovisual materials. Holds annual conventions. Sixth convention to be held in Oklahoma City, 1977.

Federal Information Centers, 18th and F St., N.W., Rm. 5108, Washington, D.C., 20405. (202) 343-7761.

Under the General Services Administration coordinates a national system of local information centers in the United States, providing aid to local residents on the services of the federal government.

IFOTS (International Federation for Services). 20, rue du Marché, Ch-1204, Geneva, Switzerland.

Affiliated in seventeen countries, but none in the United States. English affiliate: The Samaritans. Annual conference.

InterStudy. 123 East Grant St., Minneapolis, Minn. 55403. (612) 338-8761.

Formerly the Institute for Interdisciplinary Studies, American Rehabilitation Foundation. Under a Title IV grant from the Administration on Aging, it developed and refined a method of providing I&R services. As consultant to the Wisconsin Information Network demonstration project, it published the project's newsletter, as well as manuals, a bibliography, and other publications. Nicholas Long, Project Director, was author of many of the publications.

Life Line International. 210 Pitt St., Sydney, NSW 2000, Australia.

Founded in 1966, has affiliates in eleven countries. Holds Triennial Conventions; the fourth convention is to be held in May 1976 at the Disneyland Hotel, Anaheim, Calif.

National Easter Seal Society for Crippled Children and Adults. 2023 West Ogden Ave., Chicago, Ill. 60612. (312) 243-8400.

The establishment of I&R services is part of the Easter Seal program. It has prepared a *Guide* to organizing one, and other publications. Its annual convention includes a session on I&R.

National Free Clinic Council. 1304 Haight St., San Francisco, Calif. 94117. (415) 864-6232.

Established 1968, it publishes a *Newsletter*, a directory of free clinics, and distributes other publications. It sponsors annual meetings and is the primary source of information on free clinics.

National Hotline Exchange, Minneapolis, Minn. 55404.

Established in 1970 as a clearinghouse for information on hotlines and other youth-oriented crisis services. It published *The Exchange* newsletter, the *National Directory of Hotlines*, bibliographies, and distributes other material. Coordinated the Third International Hotline Conference. It dissolved in 1975. *The Exchange*, a newsletter, will continue under the editorship of the Center for Youth Development and Research, 325 Haecker Hall, University of Minnesota, St. Paul, 55101.

United Way of America. 801 North Fairfax St., Alexandria, Va. 22314. (703) 836-7100.

I&R services are part of United Way's program. It has developed standards, prepares a *Directory* of centers, sponsors seminars and workshops on the management and establishment of I&R centers. The UWASIS (United Way of America Services Identification System) instrument for classifying services is widely used. Its "loan folders" on I&R services contain sample proposals, annual reports, forms, brochures, etc.

Bibliographies

Adams, E., and Cope, S. *Volunteers: An Annotated Bibliography*. Alexandria, Va.: United Way, n.d. 26p.

Includes recruitment, training, placement, and supervision of volunteers.

Bolch, E., Long, N., et al. *Information and Referral Services, an Annotated Bibliography*. Minneapolis, Minn.: Institute for Interdisciplinary Studies (now Inter-Study), 1972. 264p.

Consists primarily of agency reports, conference papers, and other primary source materials. No citations to library literature. Indicates source where document may be obtained.

Childers, T. *The Information-Poor in America*. Metuchen, N.J.: Scarecrow, 1975. 182 p.

A state-of-the-art review; the final report of a study entitled "Knowledge/ Information Needs of the Disadvantaged," funded by the Bureau of Libraries and Learning Resources, Office of Education.

ERIC. *Research in Education*. 1969. Monthly.

Use search term "Referral" to locate documents on I&R indexed and abstracted by ERIC.

Forsman, C. *Crisis Information Centers: A Resource Guide*. Rev. ed. Minneapolis, Minn.: National Exchange, 1973. 21p.

Periodically revised. Its scope includes hotlines, free clinics, switchboards, and I&R centers, as well as specialized crisis centers, e.g., rape, runaways, suicide. Describes organizations, periodicals, directories, bibliographies, research, organizing guides, training manuals, funding sources, courses, conferences, as well as background reading. Former title, *Sources of Information on Crisis Information Services*, originally appended to author's article in *Library Journal*, March 1972, *92*, 1127-34.

————. "Resource Guide to Libraries as Neighborhood Information Centers." *RQ*, 1973, *12*, 350–54.

Annotated guide includes directory of Neighborhood Information Center (NIC) projects in public libraries as of March 1973, and a bibliography of the library's role as a NIC.

Kiefl, B., comp. *Community Information Centres: A Bibliography; Selected Materials Written About and By Community Information Centres*. Mimeographed. Ottawa: Secretary of State, Citizenship Branch, Dept. of Communications, 1972. 38p. (130 Slater St., Rm 919, Ottawa, Canada. (613) 996-2716.)

Alphabetical, unannotated bibliography covering activities in the United States, Canada and England. Scope of subjects includes suicide, social planning, and citizenship participation as well as I&R, and libraries as NICs. Type of material identified includes books, articles, reports, papers, theses.

Machlowitz, M. "Bibliography on Hotlines." *Crisis Intervention*, 1974, *5*, 47–55.

Alphabetical, unannotated.

National Center for Voluntary Action. *Clearinghouse Green Sheets.* 7th ed. Washington, D.C.: NCVA, 1974. (1785 Massachusetts Ave., N.W., Washington, D.C. 20036. (202) 797-7800).

A set of twenty-three annotated guides to organizations and publications. I&R is included in the section "I&R/Hotlines/Crisis Intervention." Revised annually, single copy free.

Directories

Alliance of Information and Referral Services. *Directory of Information and Referral Services in the United States and Canada.* Phoenix, Ariz.: The Alliance, 1975.

Becker, C. A. *Community Information Service: A Directory of Public Library Involvement.* College Park, Md.: University of Maryland, College of Library and Information Services, 1974. 92 p.

Based on a questionnaire sent first to state library agencies and then to sixty-two individual libraries. Geographically arranged; includes information on funding, type of activity, date opened, staffing, and citations in the literature about the service.

Contact Teleministries USA. *Directory of Contact Centers.* Mimeographed. Harrisburg, Penna.: Contact Teleministries. Frequently revised.

National Exchange. *National Directory of Hotlines and Youth Crisis Centers.* Minneapolis, Minn.: National Exchange, 1974. 78p.

Former title *National Directory of Hotlines, Switchboards, and Related Services.* Geographically arranged, including Canada. Type of services included are I&R centers, switchboards, free clinics, runaway programs, and contact teleministries. For each service gives address, telephone number, hours, and type of services provided.

National Free Clinic Council. *Free Clinic List.* San Francisco: NFCC, 1973.

National Youth Alternatives Project. *National Directory of Runaway Centers.* 2nd ed. Washington, D.C.: NYAP, 1974. 64p. (1830 Connecticut Ave., NW, Washington, D.C., 20009.)

Based on a questionnaire regarding clients served, services, staff, funding, management, advocacy work. First part summarizes findings in each area. Second part lists centers, geographically arranged. Questionnaire is included.

United Way of America. *Directory of I&R Centers.* Mimeographed. Alexandria, Va.: United Way, 1974. 18p.

Frequently revised. Geographically arranged, including Canada. Gives name of director, address, telephone.

Training Manuals and Organizing Guides

Croneberger, R., Kapecky, M., and Luck, C. *The Library as a Community Information and Referral Center* (Library Service Guide 8). Morehead, Ky.: Appalachian Adult Education Center, April 1975 (Morehead State University, Morehead, Ky. 40351.)

Delworth, U., et al. *Crisis Center/Hotline: A Guidebook to Beginning and Operating.* Springfield, Ill.: C. C. Thomas, 1972. 144p.

Includes chapters on financing tips, legal considerations, and evaluation.

InterStudy. *I&R Services: A Training Syllabus.* Working draft. Washington, D.C.: Administration on Aging, DHEW, 1971. 39p.

Includes course outline. Bibliography pp. 35–38.

_____. *I&R Services: Notes for Managers.* Working Draft. Washington, D.C.: Administration on Aging, DHEW, 1974. 28p.

Long, N., et al. *I&R Services: The Resource File.* 3rd ed. Washington, D.C.: Administration on Aging, DHEW, 1973. 115p. (OHD/AoA 73–20111)

Detailed instructions on building and updating a nonautomated file that is compatible to future computerization. Includes sample forms, questionnaires, flow chart of steps to update file, glossary, bibliography.

National Easter Seal Society. *Easter Seal Guide to the Organization and Operation of an Information, Referral and Follow-Up Program.* Chicago: NESSCCA, 1967. 38p.

Social Security Administration. *Information and Referral Service: District Office Training.* Baltimore, Md.: SSA, Bureau of District Office Operations, 1972. 49p. (BDOO–PUB–23–72)

Fourteen-unit syllabus covers the resource file and interviewing skills as applied to the specific problems of income, housing, health, child and family, drug abuse, and alcoholism. Each unit covers objective, background materials, presentation, participation, and review. Hypothetical inquires for each problem area are listed in the unit "Diagnosing Specific Needs."

Tessian, D., et al. *I&R Services: Information Giving and Referral.* Rev. ed. Washington, D.C.: Administration on Aging, DHEW, 1974.

Another InterStudy guide, the merger of two earlier working drafts on *Interviewing and Information Giving,* and *Referral Procedures.*

Books, Journals, Reports, Articles, etc.

Adelphi University, School of Social Work, Garden City, N.Y. 11530.

Established an I&R training program. Contact Risha Levinson.

Alliance of Information and Referral Services. *National Standards for Information and Referral Services.* Phoenix, Ariz.: The Alliance, 1973. 12p.

Based on United Way's Standards, it covers organization: auspices, staff, facilities, financing, and access to service; program components: resource file, methods utilized for provision of service, data collection.

Alliance of Information and Referral Services. *Newsletter,* 1972.

News of publications, conferences, legislation, etc.

Bay Area Reference Center. *The Library as the Community Switchboard.* Mimeographed. San Francisco, Calif.: San Francisco Public Library, BARC, 1973, 91p. Proceedings of a workshop held 14–15 February 1973.

Bloksberg, L., and Caso, E. *Survey of I&R Services Existing Within the U.S.: Final Report to the Public Health Service.* Waltham, Mass.: Brandeis University, Florence Heller Research Center, 1967. 92p.

Data on 269 agencies based on a questionnaire in two national mailings. Characteristics of agencies and services compared in twenty-eight tables. Sample questionnaires included.

Brasnett, M. E. *Story of the Citizens Advice Bureaux.* London: National Council of Social Service, 1965. 78p. (26 Bedford Sq., London, WC1B 3HA.)

The history and development of the once all-volunteer community I&R system in England, upon which Kahn based his NIC. Chapters on volunteers, services, organization, and relationship to the British government out of print. Superseded by brochure and annual reports of the National Association of Citizens' Advice Bureaux.

Brooks, R., and Eastman, D. J. *Project IRMA:* Development and Demonstration of a Computer-assisted Citizen Information Resource System to Enable Urban Residents to Make Use of Available Public Services. Final Report. Washington, D.C.: Bureau of Libraries, Office of Education, DHEW, July 1974. Available from ERIC.

Canadian Council on Social Development. *Issues for Citizen Information Services.* Ottawa: Canadian Council on Social Development, 1972. 142p. (55 Parkdale Ave., Ottawa, K1Y 1E5.)

Report of a National Consultation on Community I&R Services, convened in 1971. Includes papers, as well as edited transcripts of floor discussion and reports from interest groups. List of participants appended.

_____. *Projection Information Exchange; An Inventory of Studies, Briefs, and Social Action Projects.* 3rd ed. Ottawa: Canadian Council on Social Development, 1973. 76p.

An annual directory that includes a section on I&R projects in Canada. For each project, description, dates, funding source, availability of reports, are given. Above edition described twelve projects.

_____. *The Neighborhood Information Centre.* Ottawa: Canadian Council on Social Development, 1970. 38p.

A study on the need for and effectiveness of NICs and the issue of private versus public auspices; recommends their establishment.

Cauffman, J. *Search: Inventory of Health Services.* 3rd ed. Los Angeles, Calif.: University of Southern California, School of Medicine, 1973. (2025 Zonal Ave., Los Angeles, Calif. 90033.)

Encompasses law, education, consumer services, as well as health. A computer applicable instrument for surveying community resources, originally designed for Los Angeles County, and now also used by the Wisconsin Information Service. For each topic, the design is a matrix of problems/services provided.

Consumers Association of Canada. *Community Information Network.* Ottawa: Consumers Association of Canada, 1971. 51p. (100 Gloucester St., Ottawa, 4, Ontario.)

A proposal, available from ERIC (ED 054 834).

Cushing, M., and Long, N. *I&R Services: Reaching Out.* Rev. ed. Washington, D.C.: Administration on Aging, DHEW, 1973. (SRS 73–20110)

Another InterStudy guide.

A General Survey of Free Clinics as Alternatives to Existing Health Care Institutions. Mimeographed. Washington, D.C.: Office of Youth Development, DHEW, 1972. 49p.

A general overview of free clinics, including theory and development, summary of facilities, services, staff, clients, funding, decision making; based on visits to thirteen clinics. Separate chapters on the National Free Clinic Council and the Southern California Council of Free Clinics. Appendix of primary source material.

Hamburg, J. *Where It's At: A Research Guide for Community Organizing.* Somerville, Mass.: New England Free Press, 1967. 95p. (60 Union Sq., Somerville, Mass. 02143.)

A classic social action outline that could serve as a blueprint for a community directory.

Head, W. A. *Partners in Information: A Study of Community Information Centres In Ontario.* Toronto: Ontario Dept. of the Provincial Secretary and Citizenship, 1971. 68p.

Based on a survey, its data are still valuable when transferred to an American context. Sample questionnaire included. Available from ERIC (ED 059 735) .

Herron, K. A., and Jordon, R. "Info-U." In *Communications for Decision-Makers.* ASIS Proceedings, 34th annual meeting, Denver, 7–11 November 1971. Westport, Conn.: Greenwood Pub. Co., 1971. *8,* 327–29.

Hohenstein, C. L., and Banks, J. *I&R Program Configuration: A Guide for State-wide Planning.* Athens, Ga.: Hohenstein and Assoc., Dec. 1974. Available from the Administration on Aging (OHD 75-20114) .
Data based on a survey of nineteen I&R facilities.

Howard, E. N., guest ed. "Community Information and the Public Library," RQ 1975, *14,* 5–38.

Indianapolis Service Identification System. Indianapolis, Ind.: Community Service Council, 1973. (615 North Alabama St., Indianapolis, Ind. 46204.)
An instrument for classifying community services, ISIS is adapted from UWASIS, *United Way of America Service Identification System.*

InterStudy. *I&R Services: Follow-Up.* Working draft. Washington, D.C.: Administration on Aging, DHEW, 1971. 7p.
_____. *I&R eSrvices: The Role of Advocacy.* Working draft. Washington, D.C.: Administration on Aging, DHEW, 1971. 12p.
_____. *I&R Services: Volunteer Escort Service.* Working draft. Washington, D.C.: Administration on Aging, DHEW, 1971. 9p.

Kahn, A. J. *Neighborhood Information Centers: A Study and Some Proposals.* New York: Columbia University, School of Social Work, 1966; Reprint ed., Brooklyn, N.Y.: University Book Service, 1971. 150p.
Excellent for its historical overview, its description of the British Citizens' Advice Bureaux (CAB) , and its definitions for the range of services provided: from simple fact giving to advocacy. Considers institutions in the United State which might be hospitable to NIC.

Kochen, M. "Directory Design for Networks of Information and Referral Centers." *Library Quarterly,* 1972, *42,* 59–83, and in *Operations Research: Implications for Libraries,* pp. 59–83, edited by Chicago University, Graduate Library School. Chicago: University of Chicago Press, 1972.
_____. "Referential Consulting Networks." In *Toward a Theory of Librarianship* (papers in honor of Jesse Hauk Shera) , pp. 187–220, edited by C. H. Rawski. Metuchen, N.J.: Scarecrow Press, 1973. Available from ERIC (ED 027 923) .
_____. "Switching Centers for Inquiry Referral." In *Interlibrary Communications and Information Networks,* pp. 132–39, edited by J. Becker. Chicago: American Library Association, 1972. Available from ERIC (ED 057 858) .

Kronus, C. L., and Crowe, L., eds. *Libraries and Neighborhood Information Centers.* Allerton Park Institute Series No. 17. Urbana, Ill.: University of Illinois, Graduate School of Library Science, 1972. 142p. (Order from Illini Union Bookstore, 715 South Wright St., Champaign, Ill. 61820.)
Papers presented at an institute 24–27 October 1971 explore the concept and implications of library-based community I&R centers, drawing on the experiences of both library and nonlibrary projects.

Lester, D., and Brockopp, G. W., eds. *Crisis Intervention and Counseling by Tele-phone.* Springfield, Ill.: C. C. Thomas, 1973. 322p.

Long, N., et al. *Information and Referral Centers, a Functional Analysis.* Minneapolis, Minn.: Institute for Interdisciplinary Studies (now InterStudy) , 1971. 47p. (OHD–72–20235) . (Available from the Administration on Aging, Office of

Human Development, 330 C St., SW, Washington, D.C. 20201.)

Seminal work in this area; combines theory with data. Includes a historical overview, analysis of services and the planning function, and the integration of findings into a model.

_____, and Yonce, L. *Information and Referral Services: Evaluation Design for a Network Demonstration*. Minneapolis, Minn.: InterStudy, 1974. 111p.

The network in the title is the Wisconsin Information System demonstration project. Chapters on goals, objectives, criteria, research strategy and methodology, and reporting results. Appendix of forms and reports.

Meyer, F. H. "Concepts for a Community Information System." In *Urban Regional Information Systems; Paper from the 7th Annual Conference of the Urban and Regional Information Systems Association, Sept. 4–6, 1969*, pp. 265–81, edited by J. E. Rickett. Kent, Ohio: Kent State University, 1969.

Moore, J. R. "Information and the Urban Dweller: A Study of an Information Delivery System." Dissertation, Case Western Reserve University, 1974.

Motto, J. A., et al. *Standards for Suicide Prevention and Crisis Centers*. New York: Behavioral Publications, 1974. 114p.

National Easter Seal Society. *Information, Referral and Follow-Up Programs in the Easter Seal Society*. Chicago: NESSCCA, 1972, 16p. (Care and Treatment Publication T–23.)

Defines three current levels of program structure, based on a 1972 survey, and four future models: metropolitan, urbanized, rural, and small self-contained.

Ogg, E. *Tell Me Where to Turn: The Growth of Information and Referral Services*. New York: Public Affairs Comm., Inc., 1969. 28p. (No 428).

Widely distributed booklet is a good introduction to I&R services for the layperson. Can be used in conjunction with the film of the same title.

Public Policy Concern. *Community Information Centres—A Proposal for Canada in the '70s*. Ottawa: Information Canada, 1971, 67p. (171 Slater St., Ottawa).

Purvine, M. *The Human Relations Advisor—Identification of an Emerging Social Work Role and an Educational Plan for Its Development*. Mimeographed. New Brunswick: Rutgers University, Graduate School of Social Work, 1969. 37p.; supplement, 1970, 10p.

Pyper, T. "What Is the Role of the Neighborhood Information Center?" *Canadian Welfare*, 1973, *60* (5), 13–14.

Critical look at the compatibility of the functions of community development and advocacy within a general community information center.

Smith, D. "Role of the Free Clinic in America's Changing Health Care Delivery System." *Journal of Psychedelic Drugs*. 1975, 7, (1).

Turick, D. A., guest ed. "The Neighborhood Information Center" *RQ* 1973, *12*, 341-63.

Entire issue of the journal of the Reference and Adult Services Division of the American Library Association, edited by the National Project Director of the Five Cities Neighborhood Information Center Project, Cleveland Public Library. Available as a reprint.

United Way of America. *National Standards for Information and Referral Services*. Alexandria, Va.: United Way, 1973, 16p.

Standards and criteria for staff, facilities, financing, access to service, program components that are recommended as minimum goals for general as well as specialized services application, where I&R service is either a major task or a total system and not merely a by-product of the agency's total social service.

_____. National Study Committee on I&R Services. *Final Report and Recommendations.* Alexandria, Va.: United Way, 1972.

United Way's long-range objectives and the most effective means of offering I&R services; its responsibility for I&R both as an enhancement of all agencies work with clients and as a service in and of itself.

University of Toledo. Community Information Specialist Program, Dept. of Library and Information Services (Toledo, Ohio 43606.) (419) 537-2803.

Describes a one-year program leading to a Master of Library Science, with emphasis on I&R activities.

Vocations for Social Change. *Getting Together A People's Yellow Pages.* Cambridge, Mass.: VSC, 1972. 19p. (353 Broadway, Cambridge, Mass. 02139.)

Details the compilation, printing, pricing and distribution, based on their experience. A list of PYPs, directories of community resources serving the alternative culture, is appended.

Warner, E. S.; Murray, A. D.; and Palmour, V. E. *Information Needs of Urban Residents.* Washington, D.C.: Division of Library Programs, Office of Education, DHEW, December 1973. 283p. (OEC–O–71–4555) .

Final phase of a study performed by the Regional Planning Council of Baltimore and Westat, Inc., of Rockville, Md. A methodology for assessing the capability of both library and I&R agencies was tested, using the "most important" problems identified earlier in the survey.

Whitehouse, J. E. "Compiling a Police Social Service Referral Directory." *Law and Order,* 1972, *21,* 48–51 + .

Part II is an annotated guide to sources of information useful in compiling a community directory in any context.

Wisconsin Information Service. *Data,* 1973, monthly. (Minneapolis: InterStudy) .

Statistical reports from the Wisconsin project.

_____. *Newsletter,* 1972, monthly. (55 N. Dickinson St., Rm. 166, Madison, Wisc. 53703.)

Reports on the progress of the Wisconsin I&R Network project as well as other news of interest to I&R centers. Formerly published by InterStudy.

YMCA. *Call for Action: A Survival Kit for New Yorkers.* Rev. ed. New York: Quadrangle, 1975. 291p.

A comprehensive subject arranged directory of over 2,000 references that can serve as a model for other urban communities.

Yin, R. K., Kenney, B. L., and Possner, K. B. *Neighborhood Communications Centers: Planning Information and Referral Services in the Urban Library.* Santa Monica, Calif.: Rand Corp., Nov. 1974. 62p. (R–1564–Mf) .

Examines five cases, chosen to represent the variety of relationships found within library systems.

Index

Index

Index